# IN DEFENCE OF EUROPE

# PRAISE FOR *IN DEFENCE OF EUROPE*

'A deeply insightful book that illuminates how only a combination of skill and passion can save Europe.'

*Enrico Letta*, former Prime Minister of Italy, Dean of Paris School of International Affairs, Sciences-Po

'The European project has traditionally been driven by the region's political, business, and technocratic elites, with ordinary people indifferent and often hostile to it, even as beneficiaries. This clear-sighted, non-ideological book shows how this has to change for the project to survive. Tsoukalis argues Europe needs a wide range of reforms that deepens integration in some areas, while allowing for greater differentiation and democratic decision-making in others. He eschews simple solutions and magic pills. It is the book's great virtue that it clarifies both the scale of the problem and some of the ways forward.'

*Dani Rodrik*, Ford Foundation Professor of International Political Economy, Harvard Kennedy School

'An inexorable analysis. An eye opener, a heart cry from a true European.'

*Herman Van Rompuy*, former President of the European Council, Minister of State, Belgium

'This is an important and enlightening book in which one of the most knowledgeable scholars of European integration takes a hard look at what has gone wrong over the last quarter century. Though deeply committed to the success of the European project, the author's account of present European crises is characterized not only by an unflinching realism but also by the masterly integration of economic and political analyses – and by the perceptive reconstruction of the conflicting interests and (mis-) perceptions that explain German, British and Greek contributions to present policy failures. Remarkably, nevertheless, the book ends neither in a counsel of despair nor in idealistic precepts but in a series of pragmatic proposals whose usefulness is not obviously in conflict with political feasibility.'

*Fritz W. Scharpf*, Emeritus Director of the Max Planck Institute for the Study of Societies, Cologne

'As ever thoughtful and thought-provoking, Loukas Tsoukalis prompts us to re-examine the fundamentals of contemporary European integration. His deep analysis is timely, nuanced and challenging.'

*Professor Dame Helen Wallace FBA*, British Academy

# IN DEFENCE OF EUROPE

*Can the European Project Be Saved?*

LOUKAS TSOUKALIS

OXFORD
UNIVERSITY PRESS

# OXFORD

UNIVERSITY PRESS

Great Clarendon Street, Oxford, OX2 6DP,
United Kingdom

Oxford University Press is a department of the University of Oxford.
It furthers the University's objective of excellence in research, scholarship,
and education by publishing worldwide. Oxford is a registered trade mark of
Oxford University Press in the UK and in certain other countries

© Loukas Tsoukalis 2016

The moral rights of the author have been asserted

First Edition published in 2016

Impression: 1

Published in the United States of America by Oxford University Press
198 Madison Avenue, New York, NY 10016, United States of America

British Library Cataloguing in Publication Data
Data available

Library of Congress Control Number: 2016940755

ISBN 978–0–19–875531–9

Printed in Great Britain by
Clays Ltd, St Ives plc

*In memory of my parents who lived many years of their life on the dark side of European history and hoped we would never have to live through such times again*

# CONTENTS

# PREFACE

This book has travelled a great deal before reaching publication. The ideas contained in it have been tried out with many people from the world of policy and politics, business, journalism, and academia, and with different audiences across Europe and beyond. They were enriched and further developed as a result. The decision to write the book goes back to the Cyril Foster Lecture I was honoured to give in November 2014 at the University of Oxford. In my young and not so young days in Oxford, I attended several of these annual lectures and learned a great deal. But it had never crossed my mind that one day I would be asked to rise to the challenge. Some people, including notably my editors at Oxford University Press, suggested that I should try to turn the lecture into a book. It has been some journey, but here it is. Although most of the work is new, I have also drawn from previous writings, especially from a long essay that was published earlier in 2014 by Policy Network in London and was very quickly translated and circulated in French, German, Greek, Polish, and Spanish by leading European think tanks: a small proof that the European public space is slowly but surely taking shape.

I belong to the privileged minority of Europeans that has been steadily growing in numbers for years for whom open borders and regional integration have literally shaped their lives. I have lived and worked in different countries and have been travelling constantly. It has felt as if Europe was becoming small in many ways, although still highly diverse. Europeanization for this privileged minority has been the regional version of globalization, only much more so since Europe has gone far beyond than any other region of the world not only in breaking down national barriers but also in searching for ways to manage jointly the interdependence that came as the result. Yet, I have always been acutely aware of the fact that my way of life was not at all typical of most of my fellow Europeans. Now, I fear that some of the things we have come to consider as given not only for the privileged minority but for Europe as a whole may no longer be so.

Athens has been my home base for several years. And it has felt like being in a state of siege during the various peaks of the economic crisis and more recently the refugee crisis that came one on top of the other. But again, I escaped regularly and in various directions. Oddly enough, the two countries I know best, Greece and the UK, are nowhere near the European mainstream and each one for very different reasons. Does this make me an untypical observer of the European scene? It is not for me to judge. Perhaps, I have been sufficiently Europeanized although, hopefully, not in the bland manner the term is usually meant to imply. The last part of the book was written on the other side of the Atlantic in Cambridge, Massachusetts, where I came as visiting professor to teach a graduate course at the Harvard Kennedy School on Europe in crisis: so much to talk about. Distance offers a certain perspective on things, and I was fortunate enough to enjoy that luxury from a very special observation post.

In my long European journey, professional and otherwise, I have made many debts which I shall never be able to pay back in their entirety. After all, I come from a country that has become notorious for its debts. Let me at least acknowledge some of my own. I was privileged to have mentors who were intellectual powerhouses, people who guided me in the early stages of my academic career and taught me a great deal: Hedley Bull, (Lord) Ralf Dahrendorf, and Susan Strange. I have had trusted friends with whom I have been exchanging views on Europe for decades: (Lord) William Wallace and (Dame) Helen Wallace. And I have had the privilege of engaging in numerous enlightening conversations with people at the centre stage of European politics, José-Manuel Barroso, (Vicomte) Étienne Davignon, Enrico Letta, Mario Monti, and Herman Van Rompuy among others.

The list of people who have contributed in various ways to the shaping of ideas contained in this book is very long indeed. It includes Othon Anastassakis, Tony Barber, Jens Bastian, Iain Begg, Declan Costello, Olaf Cramme, Nikiforos Diamandouros, Thanos Dokos, Janis Emmanouilidis, Sylvie Goulard, Elena Flores, Peter Hall, Anton Hemerijck, Christopher Hill, François Heisbourg, Liesbet Hooghe, Dimitris Katsikas, Brigid Laffan, Zaki Laïdi, Michael Landesmann, José Leandro, (Lord) Roger Liddle, Gary Marks, Anand Menon, Ashoka Mody, Kalypso Nicolaïdis, George Pagoulatos, Eleni Panagiotarea, Jean Pisani-Ferry, Xavier Prats, Jacques Rupnik, André Sapir, Daniela Schwarzer, Pawel Swieboda, Helen Thompson, Nathalie Tocci, Panos Tsakloglou, Shahin Vallée, George Zanias, and Jan Zielonka. I apologize to those whose names have been omitted.

I owe special thanks to my close friend and collaborator Nikos Koutsiaras who has had the patience to read virtually everything I have written in the last twenty years and more and comment on it. He also managed to be ahead of me with much of the literature. Most of all, I am grateful for his friendship. I should also like to thank Ruby Gropas for her invaluable help and support over many years; Clemens Domnick, David Schäfer, and Giannis Vintzileos for their help in collecting data and preparing the graphs; Matina Meintani for her assistance with some of the background material and with references, but most of all for helping me to keep things under control.

I have had a new editor for this book with Oxford University Press. Matthew Cotton has been extremely supportive and understanding, very careful with editing, constructive in his comments, and remarkably efficient. He promises to beat any previous record in terms of speed of publication. What else can one hope for from an editor? I should also like to thank Rowena Anketell for her extremely meticulous copy-editing, Carolyn McAndrew for proofreading, and Michael Tombs for preparing the index.

For Maria, Christos, and Panos, there is no need for words. I owe them more than they can imagine.

*March 2016*

LOUKAS TSOUKALIS

xi

# 1

# High Stakes

## Then and now

Europe went through a remarkable transformation during the second half of the twentieth century. Peace within and beyond national borders, the spreading and strengthening of democracy, ever growing prosperity, the breaking down of barriers, and the closer unity of a still disparate continent were the main components of this transformation. Sure there were exceptions, but the general trend was clear and strong.

From the dark continent,[1] in the words of one of its best contemporary historians, Europe turned into a model for many people in other parts of the world: a social model stemming from an unprecedentedly ambitious attempt to reconcile democracy and markets with the aim of creating inclusive societies, and a model of open borders and shared sovereignty as a way of collectively managing interdependence. Europe as a model was indeed an attractive proposition for an old continent trying to reinvent itself in a world where it no longer called the shots. Some people went even further, claiming that Europe offered a new model of behaviour in international relations relying on the 'soft' power of example and persuasion, as opposed to the more traditional 'hard' power represented by military and/or economic coercion, although this particular argument has never been terribly convincing.[2]

European integration—the initiated often prefer to call it the European project—was part and parcel of this transformation. The European

Union (EU) in its different incarnations and with ever widening membership was the embodiment of this project. It helped to reconcile old foes, established common institutions and rules, created multiple networks across national borders, provided an anchor and benchmark for new democracies as well as a vehicle for modernization, and projected— even if only partially—the unity of the old continent vis-à-vis the rest of the world. And most importantly, it helped to create a large internal market, a single market if you prefer, still the biggest in the world. The steadily rising standard of living enjoyed by most Europeans became inextricably linked with this integration project. So were peace and democracy, although more indirectly. Those living in less stable parts of Europe recognized this link more than others. The contrast with a not too distant past was stark: material deprivation, deep divisions, and bloody wars have been recurring themes in European history.

Europe served as a live laboratory for a major political experiment merging sovereignties and jointly managing interdependence with a blend of consensus and democracy. This is precisely what differentiated European integration from empires in the past and from traditional forms of interstate relations in which the strong habitually impose their will on the weak. It was a peaceful revolution that could provide useful lessons about how to begin managing interdependence in a rapidly globalizing world which now lacks an obvious global hegemon to impose the rules. For sure, there was opposition to European integration from diehard nationalists, while many more people disagreed about particular aspects of it: too much liberalization or too much regulation, depending on either ideological preferences or self-interest or both; too much or too little money in the hands of European institutions and those (faceless?) bureaucrats conversing in foreign tongues; too much or too little effort invested in manufacturing unity out of a still very diverse continent; and so on. But real doubters remained for a long time a relatively small, albeit vocal, minority in some countries. True, even in the good times, regional integration did not necessarily create Europeans out of proud citizens of old nation states, but it did help to create a large majority of pro-Europeans who were apparently happy with an integration project widely seen as delivering the goods.

In academic jargon, it was 'output legitimacy'[3] that European institutions and the European project relied upon, since loyalties remained mostly national and local. In simple words, this means that the legitimacy of European institutions and the European project in general depends on their capacity to deliver. Unlike nation states, Europe has very few shared myths and symbols and little common identity either to draw from. As long as this remains true—for a long time, I suspect—the European project will be fragile. Its fragility becomes most obvious in times of crisis.

Around the turn of the new century, regional integration was continuing at an accelerated pace and many of Europe's political leaders apparently believed at the time that it would continue to be more of the same. If anything, they became much bolder in their ambitions: a European constitution, a common currency, and the extension of Pax Europaea to a large part of the former Soviet empire that had collapsed with a mere whimper back in 1989. It was about building a new political and economic order in Europe, no less. But in trying to do so, those leaders failed to notice the underground tremors in their societies, misjudged the economy, and naïvely believed that political will would be enough to shape events. Alas, events have an unforgiving logic of their own. As for political will, when it came to the test it was found wanting.

There have been many crises in European integration, both big and small. How could it have been otherwise? High stakes, a weak centre, and a wide diversity of interests to reconcile: hardly an easy task and with no precedent to learn from. However, the crises experienced during the last ten years or so go much deeper than this. Some of the fundamentals on which European integration had been premised for decades have changed. The European order has also changed as a result, and not in the way that had been intended. Furthermore, the external environment has rapidly deteriorated.

First, it was the political crisis created by the failure of the constitutional project, which left big scars. Europe was apparently not ready for the big political leap forward and this came as a shock to true believers. Before the EU had the time to recover from this crisis, it was the turn of the new common currency, the euro, to go through a very difficult stress test. It all began in the United States in 2007–8 after the bursting of the biggest financial bubble since 1929. The crisis that ensued soon turned viral and reached European shores. But it took Europe's political leaders quite some time to recognize that a US-born crisis had been transformed into an existential crisis for the euro and European integration in general—and to act accordingly.

The early state of denial was followed by measures that would have belonged to the category of 'unthinkables' only a short time ago. But these measures never proved to be enough. Admittedly, Europe's political leaders, especially in the core countries, showed (as ever) a strong instinct of survival every time they came close to a disaster. But their collective capacity for strategic vision left much to be desired and so did European solidarity. The gap was conveniently filled by complacency: 'We have turned a very difficult corner and we are now on the right track', they kept on repeating until the next corner appeared. Was it the triumph of hope over experience, or just buying time? To be fair, the task facing them was of gigantic proportions.

The creation of the euro had been undoubtedly the most important and ambitious act of European integration. A few countries decided to abstain in the early years of its creation. With the benefit of hindsight, they may have acted wisely. But those who went ahead have consti-tuted de facto the core group of European integration and this has in turn created new tensions between the 'ins' and the 'outs'. Those 'in'—the numbers have been steadily increasing despite the crisis—are still experimenting with ways and means of turning a heterogeneous group of national economies, with different political systems, different policy priorities and interests, into a workable currency area: a close-to-impossible task, the sceptic will contend. Trying to save the euro, national political leaders have repeatedly stretched the limits of poli-tical feasibility at home. As for the 'outs', protecting their interests as members of the EU and the internal market while not being marginalized or simply outvoted by the majority of 'ins', has not always proved to be an easy task.

Most political leaders and close observers of the European scene know (suspect?) that the costs of a break-up of the euro would be very high for the countries directly concerned. It would also constitute a huge political and economic setback for the European project from which it would be very difficult to recover. Furthermore, given the economic weight of the eurozone, an eventual break-up would have a major impact beyond its borders. This is clearly understood by British, Americans, and Chinese alike. In other words, it is the kind of existential risk that nobody wants to take, at least not before having tried all other alternatives. Most of Europe's political leaders may still be reluctant to admit in public that the euro, at least in its original design, was a terrible mistake. They remain, however, convinced that it would be a much bigger mistake to undo it by trying to return to national currencies.

Europe has paid a huge price in political, economic, and social terms for the crisis that followed the bursting of the international financial bubble—much more so than any other part of the world. It has been Europe's crisis in many ways. The catalogue of ills is long and depressing: a long and deep recession, what we now call the Great Recession; unemployment rates in double-digit figures and youth unemployment reaching the stratosphere in parts of Europe; economic fragmentation between and within countries; welfare systems under attack and inequalities further on the rise; democracy under stress in times when the political system is distributing pain rather than gain; the strengthening of anti-systemic protest parties across Europe; last but not least, public support for the European project reaching a record low.

Europe is no longer seen as delivering the goods. In the years since the crisis, widening economic divergence, combined with rising populism and nationalism, has produced a divided Europe. Recriminations have flown across borders and old stereotypes returned with a vengeance. Trust has been low and European politics often turned toxic.

Common institutions and the so-called Community method of reaching decisions have given way to interstate relations in which the strong have often imposed their will on the weak. The balance of power inside Europe has also shifted in a big way: Germany is now the leader. It used to be politically incorrect to talk about the balance of power in Europe, since regional integration was always meant to act as a substitute for power politics. It is no longer. The European political landscape has been transformed.

And if Europe's economic crisis were not enough, large numbers of refugees and economic immigrants began to arrive in 2015 from different parts of its distressed neighbourhood and further afield. The numbers shot up dramatically and the reaction in many parts of Europe was *sauve qui peut*: closing the borders was the best that some political leaders could think of under strong domestic pressure. The link with the rising threat of imported terrorism hardly made things any easier. Europe was buffeted by a succession of crises, each more difficult than the last, and the effect has been cumulative.

## The fault, dear Brutus

There can be two very different readings of the way Europe has so far tried to handle this succession of crises, especially the economic crisis that has been around for much longer and is not completely over yet. If you prefer to look on the bright side, you will stress the capacity of the European project to survive through the worst economic crisis since the end of the Second World War, much against the predictions (or hopes) of all kinds of doomsayers. No doubt, this is no small achievement. If anything, the economic crisis has so far led to *more* integration not less.

Traditionally, the doomsayers are to be found more on the English side of the Channel and across the Atlantic than on the European continent. Once again, they seem to have underestimated the reflex of cooperation strengthened over the years—perhaps more correctly, the survival instinct of a critical number of Europe's political leaders each time they reached the edge of the precipice. They know only too well that the stakes are high. Hence their readiness, when it comes to the crunch, to do whatever it takes (or almost) in order to prevent the undoing of the European project. The same may in the end also happen with the refugee crisis, but is this extra crisis stretching Europe's luck a bit too far?

Indeed, a costly break-up has so far been avoided, but Europe has been painfully slow in responding to crises, in learning from past mistakes, and also in adjusting to a rapidly changing political and economic environment. Perhaps, muddling through comes naturally given Europe's slow and cumbersome way of reaching decisions, the weakness of its common institutions, the diversity of interests within, and the weak political base on which the whole thing rests. Indeed, Europe has so far survived a very difficult test, but it is hardly in good shape and the prospects are not good.

The crisis is not just economic nor is it confined to European integration. In fact, the crisis goes much deeper. In exactly the same way that the European project had been part and parcel of the early European success story, it is now inextricably linked with many of the big issues that form part of a difficult and divisive political agenda in individual countries. It could not have been otherwise. Those issues relate (among others) to the unequal effects of globalization and technological change contributing to a general trend of growing inequalities within countries, financial instability in markets where the genie has been let out of the bottle, the intergenerational gap, and the (unsustainably?) high levels of public and private indebtedness.

And there is a much broader issue, notably the growing disconnect between politics and economics, democracy and markets. In a world of rapidly globalizing markets, this is not just a European problem,[4] although it is felt more strongly in European countries not only because of the openness of their economies but also because of popular expectations of what political power is meant to deliver. This disconnect has become much more pronounced because of a crisis that has very clearly exposed the limitations of political power in relation to a borderless economy that sets the pace and often dictates the rules. Europe has not succeeded so far in providing an adequate answer to the dilemma posed by the coexistence of national democracies and increasingly global markets.

The attitude of young people is characteristic of the key problems and challenges facing the European project today. The postnational narrative goes down more easily with the young (many of them at least), because they are the generation that has taken real advantage of Europe without borders—precisely that Europe without borders that is now under mortal threat. They tend to take the achievements of European integration for granted. They are also not attracted by Europe's bureaucratic face. In their eyes, the European project looks stale—and they certainly do not feel they 'own' it.

At the same time, an increasing number see themselves as the biggest losers in highly indebted and rapidly ageing societies with dual labour markets in which the young are expected to fill the second tier, if at all. This is, of course, truer for some countries than others. The intergenerational divide has been accentuated because of the crisis. Some of the young people already vote with their feet, while others have begun to throw stones. For those young people in protest, 'Europe' is part of the system they have come to resent.

'The fault, dear Brutus, is not in our stars, | But in ourselves' (we might say *European* stars).[5] The centre of the problem may indeed lie within our own countries and the way they interact with global markets and the world at large. But this is difficult to recognize politically, hence Brussels often serves as a convenient scapegoat. In the eyes of many Europeans, regional integration and common institutions are now seen as part of the problem and not part of the solution. The prevailing mood has radically changed since the turn of the century: Euro-euphoria has been replaced by Euro-pessimism, plans for further integration and more members by fears of a break-up or individual country exits.

Grexit has been on the radar for some years, referring to a possible exit of Greece from the eurozone: an inordinate amount of time and money has been spent to prevent it with virtually none of the parties involved being happy with the outcome. On the other hand, the threat of Brexit looms large: the referendum to decide whether Britain stays in or leaves the EU will take place in June 2016. The British prime minister has taken a huge gamble hoping that, when faced with a clear choice between in and out, his fellow citizens will vote for the devil they know instead of the unknown. In the meantime, he will have to resort to dangerous acrobatics in order to impress his domestic audience. The outcome of the referendum may also largely determine whether Scotland remains part of the UK. Meanwhile, the independence movement in Catalonia is gathering strength. And in a strange way, the very existence of Europe as a collective entity may make secessionism politically and economically more palatable. That was certainly not the intention of the architects of the European construction.

## The world around us

Meanwhile, the world has been changing and so has Europe's immediate neighbourhood. Regional integration had grown for years under the protection of the US security umbrella in the peaks and troughs of the Cold War. The threat from the East had in fact been one of the driving forces for integration. It had also played an important role in shaping domestic social contracts in Western Europe, since the threat of communism had been perceived as coming from both within and without. The end of the Cold War was therefore a big turning point, opening the way for the reunification of Germany—and the European continent as a whole in a much looser form. At the same time, it was also the triumph of the European project since all countries of the continent wanted to be part of it, with very few exceptions that could afford to stay out. There was no other game left in town after 1989.

The end of communism in the former Soviet Union and the countries under its control did not, however, signal the end of history,[6] nor was the unipolar phase destined to last for long. After centuries of Western dominance and only a few decades of virtually undisputed US hegemony following the collapse of the Soviet Union, the centre of gravity of the global system has been moving eastwards. There is much talk of the twenty-first century being the century of Asia,[7] with China, perhaps also India, at the forefront. Even when we make allowance for the exaggerations of fashion, often based on easy extrapolations of trends observed during the last two or three decades, there is little doubt that the global balance of power is shifting rather fast and not in the direction of Europe and the West as a whole. Size continues to matter a great deal and, already today, there are no big European powers by international standards. It will be even truer tomorrow. Economics and demographics will take care of it.

The economic crisis has been a shock and an eye-opener. While Europeans were trying to deal with the big crisis at home, they had to ask for help from outside. Asking for American help was something that Europeans had long been used to, mostly in the security field, but having the International Monetary Fund (IMF) as an arbiter and provider of record amounts of financial assistance for an internal European crisis, was something they were not prepared for. Nor were the others, especially in emerging economies, now being asked to fork out substantial amounts through the IMF in order to save countries much richer than themselves.

Divided, declining, and increasingly irrelevant is how Europe is nowadays being perceived by many people in Beijing, New Delhi, and Pretoria, although less so in Brasilia or Buenos Aires. American frustration with European dithering during the crisis has had sometimes a touch of *Schadenfreude*, especially among neoconservatives. After all, the latter never had much respect for any of the European models. But among well-meaning and non-insular Americans, the crisis in Europe, in its different manifestations, is a matter of deep concern. As for the Chinese, now the biggest creditor in the world, they must have savoured those occasions when they were called upon to help save the euro. The Chinese have a long memory of humiliations suffered at the hands of Europeans. After all, revenge is a dish best served cold and the Chinese tend to take a long view of history. But they also know that Europe is too big a part of a globalizing world to ignore.

Developments in Europe's neighbourhood have hardly helped either. Europe's neighbourhood contains mostly losers from globalization, unlike other parts of the world. Collectively, Europe had proclaimed for years its ambition to shape its immediate neighbourhood in its own image through the use of instruments of soft power, while individual European countries, mostly the former colonial masters, continued to engage in traditional power politics in the region and resorted to the use of hard power when everything else had failed. There was surely a strong element of hypocrisy hidden behind this division of labour between European institutions and member states. In the end, neither soft nor hard power worked. The provisional balance sheet is not at all positive for Europeans and the West as a whole.

Large parts of Europe's neighbourhood are now in turmoil, both to the east and to the south. The Arab Spring opened a Pandora's box. Out of it came accumulated frustration which often transformed itself into religious fanaticism leading to war. Large parts of the Middle East and the Arab world are on fire, some of the old frontiers drawn by former colonial masters are breaking down, millions of people are being displaced, and dictatorships have developed into failed states: Syria and Libya are the most obvious examples—should we also add Iraq? Western powers, European ones among them, often look overwhelmed. They are not at all sure what exactly they are willing or capable of doing, how to handle dictators and armies of fanatic jihadis, how to deal with allies who are often part of the problem and not the solution. And some at least suspect (or have already realized) that previous interventions by Western powers have further destabilized the region.

The breakdown of the old order has direct implications for Europe in particular. Energy is an old issue and it has been a key driving force for Western intervention in the region for decades. The export of terrorism is a more recent concern, but a very big one indeed. Even worse, there are apparently plenty of willing recruits at home. Meanwhile, the large numbers of political refugees and economic immigrants coming from the Middle East and North Africa risk causing a crisis much bigger than that of the euro—one more crisis that Europe can ill afford.

A rapidly increasing number of people in Europe's neighbourhood and further afield—those that have been left out of the big global transformation of the last two or three decades and now many more seeking refuge from war and persecution—are trying to cross over land and sea in search of a better future in Europe. Even in crisis, Europe looks like paradise to their eyes, and so it is. The distinction between political refugees and economic migrants is not always easy to establish. For humanitarian reasons, Europe needs to keep the door open to those fleeing war and persecution. For demographic reasons, Europe also needs a constant flow of immigrants in the foreseeable future. But the numbers of those who want to come can be truly overwhelming. European societies are not ready for such a scale of immigration and there can be no simple solution to the problem, while Europeans are again divided.

To the east, the disintegration of the old Soviet empire has not gone as smoothly as many Americans and Europeans had hoped for at the time of Gorbachev and Yeltsin. Russia under Putin refuses to behave according to norms and standards set by the West. It apparently still thinks of spheres of influence, while Brussels used to think until recently of association agreements as part of its neighbourhood policy, leaving open the prospect of full membership of the EU for all European countries sometime in the distant future. In Ukraine, those two approaches clashed. The spectre of a new Cold War with Russia looms large. It could extend beyond the front-line states, perhaps to parts of the Balkans where Pax Europaea has not yet reached. On the other hand, it is difficult to imagine any future settlement in the Middle East, if one is indeed possible, without the consent or active involvement of Russia—and also Iran. Here again, Europeans have often tried to preserve their fragile unity by doing little or simply by avoiding difficult choices.

Internal weakness and division largely determines the capacity of Europeans to collectively influence their external environment. Europe is no longer the centre of the world. Since the end of the old Cold War, it has also ceased to be the centre of attention. But a return to the Cold War would not be the best means to restore attention nor would an external enemy serve as the powerful unifying glue for European integration. Most probably, it would do exactly the opposite, thus causing further division.

Europe remains open to the world, its borders still undefined to the east, dependent for its security on the United States, confused as to how a postmodern entity such as the EU can deal with post-imperial Russia, increasingly frustrated with its diminishing capacity to influence the world beyond its borders—even those parts that are uncomfortably close to home—but also unable to control its own borders when faced with massive inflows of desperate people seeking political or economic refuge in Europe. And Europe still finds it very difficult to reconcile the needs arising from internal demographics and external pressure with political and social reality at home. Furthermore, Europe's continued prosperity remains heavily dependent on trade and security of access to energy and raw materials. It does not help that Russia continues to be Europe's main provider of energy. Linked to energy, there is the huge challenge facing Europe and the world as a whole presented by climate change. Europe has been a pioneer in the fight against climate change, although not always ready to put its money where its mouth is and finding it difficult to maintain its internal unity. It will have to do much better in future for the sake of generations to come, both European and non-European.

## A long list of questions

This book tries to explain and understand the big changes, 'the shifts and the shocks' (borrowing the title of a great book on the global financial crisis[8]), and how Europe has responded or failed to respond to them. It is about the major challenges facing European integration and Europe more generally and the forces that threaten to pull the old continent apart. It is also about policy choices.

What can we learn from the early European success story, and what were the factors that had gradually begun to undermine it in the years before the big crisis? These will be the first questions to ask in the pages that follow: the answers will require a quick *tour d'horizon* of the second half of the twentieth century. 'Anything that works will be used in progressively more challenging situations until it fails', so goes the well-known 'Peter Principle' used mostly in management theory. Can overstretch also help to explain, at least in part, the growing difficulties experienced with European integration?

The euro threatens to become the straw that will break the camel's back. Was it hubris, bad design, or bad luck that the first big test of the euro coincided with the mother of all financial crises? To answer this question, we also need to understand the context in which the early decisions were taken. Geopolitics may provide a much better explanation than economic theory.

The book will pay special attention to the economic crisis and the Great Recession of recent years (to be distinguished from the Great Depression of the 1930s). The basic question to ask in this respect is how a crisis of globalized financial capitalism was transformed into an existential crisis of the euro and European integration? And why have the aftershocks lasted so long and caused so much damage particularly in the eurozone? Who is to blame: our system of collective governance, a faulty economic strategy, or individual country failures? And who has paid the bill so far? Distributional politics is back with a vengeance in societies where inequalities keep growing. Alas, the European political system, for what it is, has great difficulty in dealing with distributional issues across borders. One reason, I suppose, is that it still largely relies on borrowed legitimacy.

The crisis in Europe has led to more economic divergence and political fragmentation. Can such different countries as Germany, Greece, and the UK continue to be part of a common European project, and under what conditions? Looking more closely at the way those three countries reacted during the crisis and how they perceive their role inside the regional system will serve to illustrate the wide diversity within European integration and the centrifugal forces stemming from it. Unity in diversity sounds like a good slogan for European propaganda, but it is often difficult to apply in practice. We may need to think more out of the box.

We shall also try to understand how the crisis of European integration in general fits into the bigger puzzle. Is it just an epiphenomenon—a secondary effect, if that long word is Greek to you—even what might be described as 'collateral damage'? After all, European integration has never had much autonomy of its own, which is, admittedly, not a politically correct thing to say for a good European. Domestic social contracts have come under much pressure in recent years—in the weaker countries, welfare policies are being cut down to size in the name of fiscal consolidation—and the number of people on the losing side of rapid economic change has increased substantially. Their perception of threat extends to the rising numbers of immigrants in their societies. Economic vulnerability in turn leads to nativism: foreigners become the threat and there are plenty of demagogues around to make the most of people's sense of insecurity in times of rapid change with strongly unequal effects on different groups of society. Not surprisingly, the domestic political order is also changing fast, especially in the weaker countries. Anti-establishment parties are on the rise and most of them are staunchly anti-European or at least very critical of present policies emanating from Brussels.

Europe seems to be in a bind: it is politically difficult to go forwards and scary to go backwards. In-between is certainly an unstable and unhappy equilibrium for all concerned. 'You cannot sustain a common currency without political union and nobody is really prepared, in deeds rather than words, to take the necessary steps in this direction', so argue the hard realists. But then, what would be the costs of going back to national currencies and the broader implications of European disintegration? Is the return to national economic policies really the right answer for Europe in today's world? And is the rebuilding of walls and fences along national borders the answer to large immigration pressures? If European integration has indeed reached the end of the road, which is what an increasing number of people now suspect or fear, what are the prospects for Europe? And indeed, what are the prospects for globalization in a world without a hegemon to impose the rules and with very inadequate forms of joint management at global level? Those who believe in the primacy of economics or technology and are always keen to argue about the alleged irreversibility of the globalization process may need to consult their history books again.

The combination of Europe's collective survival instinct, further strengthened over the years through successive tests, and its inherent tendency to muddle through may point to a quite probable scenario for the future: no big bang but a long crawl. In fact, institutions often have a tendency to survive much beyond their capacity to perform truly useful functions. Thus, the EU would continue to be around and people would continue to be paid handsomely to speak on its behalf, but with relatively little of substance to say or do. It is a real risk. A divided Europe would face a future of relative decline and marginalization, even though it may continue to be for many of its inhabitants 'the least bad of the worlds available'.[9] This scenario would fit well with the mood of complacency prevailing among many Europeans, especially among the older generations who have much more to lose and relatively little to gain. Pope Francis spoke of Europe as a grandmother, elderly and haggard.[10]

For the ageing societies of Europe, relative decline—even marginalization—may not be such a bad prospect. Whether the younger generations will be willing to put up with it is, however, an altogether different matter. And would the rest of the world allow Europe to decline in grace, if it so chose to do? Putin's Russia, Islamic jihadis—not to mention the peaceful invasion of large numbers of refugees and immigrants from its troubled neighbourhood—may not allow Europe the luxury of declining in grace.

No doubt there are much worse scenarios we could think of—and better ones, if we only dared. Sometimes, Europe has shown the capacity to surprise in a positive way. And it did precisely that on a number of occasions during the last sixty years and more during which this political experiment of jointly managing interdependence and merging sovereignties has lasted. Will Europe have the capacity to surprise us once again by redefining the terms and the purpose of the European project as a way of adjusting to a rapidly changing and not overly friendly wider environment?

It is a long list of questions. I shall endeavour to make sense out of them and provide answers, hopefully not too inadequate, in what follows. In doing so, I shall pay more attention to economic matters broadly defined, in recognition of the fact that Europe is still today more of an economic animal. My main concern, however, will be to highlight the connections between economics and politics, markets and power, efficiency and distribution, but without recourse to equations.

In the final chapter of the book, I shall attempt to pull loose threads together and look into the future. Can Europe overcome its internal divisions and face a growing number of challenges? Squeezed between rising nationalism within and the return of geopolitics without, with large parts of its immediate neighbourhood on fire, who will represent the collective European interest or just 'think European'? Free-riders, misfits, and laggards abound in times of big crises—and they do so in Europe today. I shall draw on the growing number of proposals, scenarios, and a wide range of ideas from the world of politics, as well as from the world of academia and think tanks, about the way forward for Europe. I shall then proceed to sketch out the rough outlines of a possible new European contract—you can call it a grand bargain, a pact, perhaps better a new historical compromise. Can Europe reconcile integration with diversity, growth with cohesion, governance with legitimacy, its basic values with the rough world outside? Can it reconcile the interests of the growing numbers of pensioners and the young unemployed, and if so how? I know the odds are against such a prospect today, but it is worth trying. The European project is simply too important to be allowed to fail.

This is not meant to be a book about the intricacies of European decision-making, the ways and means inside the Brussels balloon, the technical details of bailout programmes and banking union. These are all important in their own way and there is already a vast literature on each but together they form part of the bigger picture. It is the bigger picture that this book tries to look at in order to reach some conclusions concerning the state of European integration today and the key choices facing governments and citizens in relation to it. It is ambitious and risky to attempt this, I know; the reader will be the ultimate judge.

Given its wide scope, this book will be eclectic in its approach. Otherwise, one would have to begin writing an encyclopedia that would be already out of date before we reach letter B. Writing with an emphasis on current affairs always carries the risk of the ephemeral, hence also the risk of being overtaken by events even before the book comes out. Politics is determined by events and our forecasting models have done a remarkably poor job until now, although this has hardly deterred forecasters. Being conscious of this limitation, my intention is to highlight key underlying trends as well as the broader significance and implications of current issues and divisions in Europe. I also promise to avoid jargon as much as possible in the hope of addressing a wider audience and not just the specialist.

The book will be iconoclastic in places. It aims to contribute in a modest way to the growing debate across borders about where Europe is or should be heading, a debate that is engaging more and more people and not just the professionals. This growing debate is one of the few good things to come out of the long crisis. In contributing to the debate, this book may also challenge some of the established truths contained in Europe's holy books. I have always believed that a good European should be critical of established truths. The official narrative is indeed dull and outdated: it is no longer convincing. And those appointed to tell the story often make it even worse, probably because they do not believe in it themselves.

## The car and the driver

Some years back, I wrote about European integration being like a car moving uphill.[11] The French used to provide the driver, the Commission the map, the Germans paid for the petrol, and the British oiled the brakes. In bad times, it looked like a car without a driver, the map being replaced by a GPS that went on and off, the Poles insisted on taking out an insurance policy with God, nobody wanted to pay for the petrol, some clearly cheated with the bills, and they all disagreed loudly as to how many more could fit into the car.

The road has become much rougher and more dangerous in recent years. Many people believe that at long last we now have a driver and she is German. But others doubt whether she has a good sense of direction and the skills required for driving in extreme conditions. Perhaps, they may come to appreciate her driving skills more after she has left the wheel to somebody else (or to nobody). Many more wonder whether the vehicle is fit for purpose, a few want to get rid of the Greeks, while the British may be preparing to jump out. Carried away by technology, some people may be tempted to think of a driverless car. 'Just follow the market', the fundamentalists will argue, believing in the absolute wisdom of markets and the primacy of economics over politics. They are incapable of learning anything from the recent crisis—nor from history.

Surely, we must have a closer look at the vehicle and do the necessary repairs. We should think again about the driving skills required of whoever happens to be at the wheel and the conditions applying to passengers. We may also need to get rid of excess baggage in order to make seating more comfortable inside. Last but not least, we may also consider splitting the passengers into two or more vehicles running at different speeds and with different arrangements inside each one of them, just so long as we can agree on the general direction. The euro may require a separate car. Detours will be necessary along the way, even short U-turns. We are travelling into uncharted territory, hence the need to show both imagination and courage, think out of the box, and rely on trial and error. After all, this is what has always made the European journey great fun—although perhaps not for the faint-hearted.

# 2

# Ever Bigger, More Intrusive, and Less Inclusive

European integration has a remarkable record characterized by a continuous expansion in terms of functions and membership. It has continued throughout the big crisis of recent years, despite growing challenges from within and without, which is even more remarkable. What better evidence is needed of the perceived usefulness and dynamism of an organization such as the EU in its different incarnations than the accrual of ever more responsibilities, coupled with a never-ending list of aspiring members ready to submit themselves to difficult admission tests?

From coal and steel in the beginning to just about everything today—albeit with forms of cooperation (or integration) varying significantly from one policy area to the other, and from six to twenty-eight members in sixty-odd years—it is no small achievement by any standards. A European Leviathan for the non-converted, a radical attempt to reconcile national sovereignty with new advanced forms of interdependence for postmodernists, or just an intermediate stage to the United States of Europe for federalists? Views vary a great deal, and this should be, of course, welcome in a democracy. Nevertheless, Europe's nascent political system is not a democracy—not yet at least—and the centrifugal forces are now strong. Is Europe suffering from overstretch?

This chapter will offer a bird's-eye view of the development of European integration from the very beginning until the big crisis struck before the end of the noughties, with occasional references to and comparisons with the state we are in today. The main purpose of the exercise will be to understand how the implicit European contract changed over the years and how the addition of new policy functions and more members in a less favourable environment relates to weakening public support for integration. It will thus prepare the ground for a closer look at what happened during the crisis years in the chapters that follow.

## Key elements

It all began on 9 May 1950, when Robert Schuman, the French foreign minister, issued a famous declaration in which he called for the creation of a coal and steel community aiming to bring together countries that had fought on both sides of the war. The date has become an anniversary celebrated as 'Europe Day', particularly by Brussels bureaucrats who have a day off. In the immediate aftermath of the Second World War, enlightened politicians from different countries, Sir Winston Churchill most notably, had taken major initiatives for cooperation among European countries, thus drawing lessons from the terrible experience of two major wars in the course of three decades. But it was Schuman's initiative that actually changed the course of history and set the pace for subsequent developments in European integration.

It was a French initiative to deal first and foremost with a German problem, namely how to incorporate those parts of defeated Germany that had come under the control of the United States, Britain, and France after the war into the emerging post-war European order—to be precise, what was to become the Western part of this new order. The French foreign minister chose the integration option, starting with two strategic sectors of the economy. At the time, the French would have preferred a much tighter direct control of West Germany by the Allies, but that was not an option as tensions between the Western allies and the Soviet Union grew stronger.

So, Schuman went for the great leap forward and the political leaders of the young Bonn republic concurred. Italy and the Benelux countries also joined, while Britain, still the biggest power in Western Europe at the time, decided to abstain. The reasons for abstention had to do with the perception of interests of an imperial, though much weakened, Britain that always had strong stakes in Europe but never saw herself as being *part* of it. The decision to stay out was also based on a clear misjudgement of the intentions of Britain's continental partners: a rather surprising diplomatic failure of the foreign service of a country that was still running a vast empire. This failure was, however, to be repeated only a few years later at the Messina Conference that led to the creation of the European Economic Community (EEC) in 1958. Thus, European integration started with France and Germany at the centre and Britain outside, and this had long-lasting effects. Whenever France and Germany agreed, they led the process and largely determined the shape of the European project for decades to come. Britain joined later but hardly ever felt like a co-owner of the project.

The first key element of European integration had to do with the leading actors, the second with the plot. With respect to coal and steel, the interdependence of frontier regions between France and Germany—also including Luxembourg and parts of Belgium—had long historical roots. The plan therefore made economic sense. But the main purpose of the exercise was to create the basis for peace and reconciliation in Europe, and the means chosen were economic simply because any attempt to transfer power in more politically sensitive areas would have hit against the hard rock of national sovereignty only a few years after the end of a catastrophic war. In fact, defence was tried, again by the French, and it failed in their own country. Employing economic means for political ends was the second key element of the nascent European project, hence also the elaborate institutional structure provided by the Treaty of Paris of 1951 that set up the European Coal and Steel Community (ECSC),[1] a structure that could only be explained by the long-term ambitions of its authors and not by the concrete economic tasks it was meant to deliver.

The third element followed naturally. There was no popular or political pressure for European integration in the aftermath of the war, only small groups of federalists here and there. Thus, the project would have to start top-down: the far-sighted—the illuminati for those who believe in conspiracy theories—would have to take the initiative and seek democratic approval by gradually convincing and incorporating key actors into the European project, while playing down the importance of the whole thing in order not to attract too much attention. Support, if not acquiescence, would hopefully follow as more people would come to realize the benefits. European integration thus began as a plot of the few: an elitist conspiracy, if you prefer, yet with honourable intentions and remarkable results for a long time, as we can now testify with the benefit of hindsight. A kind of permissive consensus was built over the years that enabled political elites in individual countries to proceed with new initiatives and more integration. It was good while it lasted and the delivery was often impressive.

Now fast-forward to the days after the fall of the Berlin Wall in 1989. The discussions for the creation of an Economic and Monetary Union (EMU), as the next big step in European integration, were almost an exact repetition of the Schuman initiative forty years earlier. The leading actors, the plot, and the staging were the same. Yet, the performance took place in front of a different audience with different expectations. It was again a French initiative to deal with a German problem, only different this time round. President Mitterrand of France realized that German reunification was inevitable, although it was clearly not his preferred option. The UK prime minister, Margaret Thatcher, was strongly against German reunification, but she did not support the French president's second option either, namely to try to integrate a bigger Germany inside a stronger Europe. EMU was the answer President Mitterrand finally came up with. It was a plan which once again employed economic means to achieve political ends and European integration provided the setting. Chancellor Kohl of Germany spoke a similar language: EMU as a matter of war and peace in the twenty-first century. None of them cared much about the economic details, which they left to the experts (and central bankers) to deal with; they themselves concentrated more on how to sell the new project to their European partners using a mix of persuasion and side payments.[2]

No matter that the majority of Germans at the time wanted to keep their beloved Deutschmark. Their elected representatives knew better and the Maastricht Treaty for EMU was voted unanimously in the upper house (*Bundesrat*) and with an overwhelming majority in the lower house (*Bundestag*) in 1992. This followed a post-war German tradition of cross-party consensus on the big issues of European integration. Furthermore, politicians in the Federal Republic of Germany did not—and still do not—like referendums, largely because referendums are associated with the part of German history they would like to forget. In France, the referendum on the Maastricht Treaty held in 1992 scraped through with only 51 per cent of the votes cast, while the Danes and later the Swedes voted against and stayed out, each on a different legal basis. So did the British, but without a referendum. And in keeping with tradition, those in power in London misjudged again the intentions of their Continental partners. This time though, they were probably right concerning the economic merits or otherwise of the new integration project. All other members of the EU signed in.

The continuity from coal and steel in 1950 to the negotiations leading to the creation of the euro forty years later is truly astounding. The French resorted to their tried and tested formula and their main partners responded in the same way as they had done with the Schuman initiative. The wider public was not enthusiastic, although this time scepticism was expressed much more loudly than before. Now, fast-forward again to today's Europe. The conditions are very different indeed: only one protagonist is left, namely Germany, while the other, France, is desperately struggling to remain centre stage, the economic means are no longer delivering the ends, and the permissive consensus has been broken. Yet, the game goes on and all participants continue to play for high stakes.

# An ever expanding project

From coal and steel to the euro was a long distance with some big landmarks on the way. The early European project on coal and steel followed on a history of heavy government intervention and cartelization in those sectors, hence the strong powers given to the new supranational authority in the good old European tradition of managed capitalism and mixed economies. The next step leading to the establishment of a common market was more liberal in its economic approach but also much more ambitious.

During the so-called golden age that lasted for almost three decades from the end of the war to the early 1970s, Western Europe enjoyed an unprecedented combination of high growth, low unemployment, and relative price stability which has not been seen since. European integration helped to bring down national economic barriers, mainly in the form of tariffs and quantitative restrictions, and also contributed to a similar, albeit slower, process at international level through European active participation in successive trade rounds under the framework of the General Agreement on Tariffs and Trade (GATT).

With the main exception of the agricultural sector, in which the EEC, as it was then called, pursued a highly interventionist, expensive, and partially regressive policy in favour of farmers (favouring big farmers over small ones) that needs to be understood in the context of the bigger package deal for the common market, European integration served essentially as an agent of economic liberalization. Remarkably, however, this coincided with the expansion of the Keynesian state within member countries. Liberalization at the border was therefore combined with active national macroeconomic policies and growing welfare states. It was an odd fit in the eyes of the economic purist, yet one that seemed able to deliver the goods for many years. For social democrats it was a dream come true—and it increasingly gained broader acceptance—for others it was a nightmare.

I have argued elsewhere that the mixed economy and the welfare state helped to smooth domestic adjustment resulting from the opening of borders and greater international competition.[3] It also helped to buy social acceptance by alleviating the effects of adjustment on potential losers inside countries. In other words, the Keynesian domestic political contract in individual countries became inextricably linked with European integration and the slower process of liberalization at international level, creating a kind of virtuous circle as long as it lasted.

Alas, it did not last forever. The rapid deterioration of the economic environment in the early 1970s, which coincided with the collapse of the Bretton Woods system and was influenced by it, brought this virtuous circle to an end. Years of stagflation followed: a combination of low growth, high unemployment, and high inflation hitherto considered an aberration by economists. Various explanations have been offered for this dramatic shift in the macroeconomic environment that led in turn to a gradual shift in the prevailing economic paradigm in both the academic and policy worlds.

We now know that the golden age was the exception and not the rule. A rate of growth of close to 5 per cent per year lasting for almost three decades is something that Europe has not experienced before or since. In the decades that followed the end of the golden age, there have been many ups and downs with the long-term average rate of economic growth hovering around 2 per cent per annum and then dropping down to zero or below during the Great Recession. Meanwhile, the rate of unemployment continued to rise until the mid-1990s and then shot up again during the recent crisis. The picture shown in Graph 2.1 is all too clear and rather depressing: the countries of Western Europe as a whole (EU15) have experienced a long-term declining trend in real growth rates reaching zero with a corresponding increase in unemployment to double-digit figures during the period 1961–2014 for which there are comparable figures.[4]

During this time, neo-liberals gained ground at the expense of Keynesians. More market and less state, supply-side measures and deregulation became the key slogans of a political revolution led by Ronald Reagan and Margaret Thatcher, with strong ideological ammunition provided by academic economists. European institutions

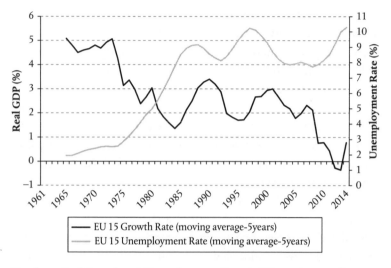

**Graph 2.1** Real Growth and Unemployment Rates in EU15, 1961–2014 (five-year moving averages)

*Source:* AMECO: Unemployment Rate (1961–1990: EU15 including West-Germany; 1991–2014: EU-15 countries). OECD: Growth Rate (GDP using exchange rates and purchasing power parities).

served as facilitators of the new economic orthodoxy, although in their own distinct way and with the usual emphasis on compromise. Politics is indeed the art of compromise, although in some political cultures compromise is a dirty word. European politics is usually the epitome of it: no surprise that this is understood and appreciated in some parts of Europe more than others.

The internal (or single) market programme was the result of these developments and it marked a major turning point in regional integration. Starting with the admission that the European common market was still very much incomplete, because of all kinds of barriers or distortions created by different national rules and regulations especially regarding services, the European Commission in Brussels under its new president, the former French finance minister Jacques Delors, a socialist, proposed a very ambitious programme to eliminate all such barriers. Mrs Thatcher and all those who complained about too little market and too much state saw it as an exercise in economic deregulation leading to a big European market without barriers and with strong competition. Delors and traditional supporters of the mixed economy saw it differently: for them, the internal market programme would involve both deregulation and re-regulation at European level.

The implementation of the programme turned the Commission and the EU into a major regulatory state[5] and in the process it entered the nooks and crannies of our societies. Free marketeers seem to be unpleasantly surprised, but how could it have been otherwise? Allowing for the centralizing zeal of Brussels bureaucrats and political zealots, which sometimes did indeed lead to excesses, it was the price that had to be paid for the creation of a European market without barriers, still an unfinished business. Who should determine the appropriate level of regulation for telecoms, the appropriate standard for protection of, say, health or the environment as regards specific products? Despite the attempt to rely as much as possible on mutual recognition, there is no magic wand that can produce the optimum level of regulation in Europe. True, what Brussels often comes up with is long and tedious. But the alternative to European regulation would be no European market at all. This is again a point that market fundamentalists fail to grasp. The right kind of regulation is a matter of ideological preference, history, and balance of interests. At European level, it is bound to be the object of intense negotiation and the result of compromise: too much for some and too little for others, although often leaving some room for national differentiation.

There was, however, one area where liberalization and deregulation, largely the product of regulatory competition, became the order of the day—and this was also fully consistent with the new economic orthodoxy extending beyond Europe and propagated by all major international institutions at the time. This was, of course, banking and financial services in general. Financial liberalization and deregulation were coupled with the lifting of all capital controls, which were also an integral part of the internal market programme and the new economic orthodoxy. This would largely shape economic developments in the years to come, leading to the big crisis.

The internal market programme also brought with it an element of redistribution at European level as part of one of those famous European package deals that are often necessary to reach consensus. Strictly speaking, it was not redistribution but development assistance for the less developed countries and regions of the EU and it was limited by the small size of the European budget. Yet, annual flows of European funds (not loans) for investment in the poorer countries represented for years between 2 and 4 per cent of their Gross Domestic Product (GDP) annually, which made a world of difference to them.

The political importance of those transfers was big: it helped to turn weaker members into major stakeholders of the European project and also made them more willing to take the risk of further opening their economies to external competition. Thus, poorer countries and regions of the EU joined the farmers as key beneficiaries of the small European budget. A different coalition of interests thus emerged. It was a strong coalition until the big crisis struck.

## All the way to the euro

The so-called 'functionalists'[6] (to employ a piece of Euro-jargon) have described the so-called cumulative logic of integration through which economic integration spills over from one sector or policy area to another and also goes deeper. You start with the elimination of tariffs and border controls. You later realize that you need to tackle all kinds of distortions created through different state interventions inside national economies. In the process, new interests are created that seek access to the markets of others and this in turn leads to the search for common rules to govern the interaction between national economic systems: the search for a level playing field, to use a sports metaphor. At some point, you will also realize that the exchange rate is the most important remaining barrier inside the common market, which also needs to be eliminated; hence, monetary union as the next step in integration. It is all very neat in theory but hardly so in practice. We now know for sure that there is nothing automatic in the process described above.

This is certainly true of the transition from the internal market to monetary union. The Bretton Woods system had provided European countries with a stable monetary order under US leadership and with the US dollar serving as the key international currency. General de Gaulle did not like this very much and fought hard in the 1960s against the 'exorbitant privilege'[7] enjoyed by the US currency, but had little success in carrying his European partners along with him. When the Bretton Woods system came to an end in the early 1970s, European policy-makers decided to establish a regional monetary order as a substitute. Only a small minority among them believed that floating exchange rates could be compatible with the European common (and now internal) market. In practice, however, they realized that it was extremely difficult to reconcile different national economic structures and policy priorities with stable intra-European exchange rates in times of growing capital mobility. In trying to do so, through successive exchange rate arrangements at European level, Germany emerged as the leading nation because of the strength of its economy and the stability of its currency. It was the first time that such a thing had happened since the end of the war, and it happened through money—not guns and tanks.

Both the first exchange rate arrangement, the so-called snake in the tunnel in the 1970s, and the European Monetary System (EMS) that followed it were cut down to size by speculative attacks in exchange markets. Therefore, the omens were not good when new discussions began about the creation of EMU around 1990. Exchange rates were the last remaining big obstacle to a truly internal market in Europe, so argued the integrationists. And more importantly, EMU became part of an exercise in geopolitics directly linked to German reunification. On the other hand, hard economic realists doubted the feasibility of the whole exercise and they had past experience to confirm their doubts. They were strongly represented in the English-speaking world.

Finally, political will prevailed over economic scepticism. The creation of the euro was the crowning act of European integration: a common currency in the final stage of economic integration, following the completion of the internal market, strong in symbolism and with broad political ramifications. It was born out of a political compromise reached at Maastricht in 1992, a compromise that reflected the strong interest of France in creating a common currency as a means of tying a reunited Germany to a stronger EU (the old Schuman logic once again), Germany's ability to set the terms of reference as a precondition for its participation, Britain's contentment with its opt-out, and side payments for weaker members.

The package agreed at Maastricht rested on two legs: political feasibility was one and economic orthodoxy was the other. In other words, the economic views prevailing at the time were married with political reality to produce the Maastricht Treaty. Monetary policy was entrusted to an independent European Central Bank (ECB) free from any political interference and with only one policy objective, namely price stability. The ECB was prohibited from acting as a lender of last resort for national governments in order to avoid moral hazard. It was also given little responsibility in terms of financial supervision, which remained with national central banks. Such responsibility was meant to be limited anyway in times of financial liberalization and deregulation. After all, financial markets were supposed to be efficient, consisting of rational actors who take decisions on the basis of perfect information, were they not?[8] That is what the academic world was saying and most policymakers were only too eager to believe them.

On the other hand, there were no provisions for internal stabilizers or transfers in the European common budget. Fiscal policy therefore remained in the hands of national governments only subject to coordination and constraints imposed at European level with the aim of avoiding excessive deficits. The contrast with discussions that had taken place two decades earlier in relation to the first attempt to set up a European monetary union was stark: much less was expected from fiscal policy and macroeconomic stabilization in general at European level, while the Germans now had the upper hand and largely set the terms of the negotiation.

The Maastricht structure was weak and unbalanced. The Europeans decided to proceed with the creation of a common currency based on flawed economics and a totally inadequate institutional and political base: the contradiction of a currency without a state, as Tommaso Padoa-Schioppa, a leading European thinker and policymaker, pointed out early on.[9] Build it as you go along would be, perhaps, the benign explanation consistent in part with the earlier experience of European integration. But for the less benign observer, it looked as if the Europeans were trying to perform a miracle.

There was an extra provision in the Maastricht Treaty, included again under strong German pressure, namely that any country that wanted to adopt the euro would have to pass a difficult entrance exam in terms of inflation, budget deficit and debt, exchange rate stability, and long-term interest rates. Clearly, the aim was to limit participation as much as possible to like-minded countries with a sound record of monetary stability. However, the Germans had not reckoned with the strong desire of most European governments to join what was very quickly perceived to be the core group of European integration. Thus, a period of stabilization policies followed the signing of the Maastricht Treaty in 1992 during which most governments succeeded in cutting down on inflation and budget deficits in order to meet the so-called convergence criteria of Maastricht. The result was that eleven countries passed the test and became the founding members of the euro in 1999—more than anybody, including German political leaders, would have anticipated only a few years earlier. Today, the number has reached nineteen.

## Distributional effects

Taking a long-term perspective on European integration, we see an ever expanding project, especially since the mid-1980s with repeated revisions of the European treaties and a rapid acceleration of integration, still with many bumps on the way. It began to reach the core of national sovereignty through the internal market and, even more, through the common currency. But it also remained predominantly *economic* in its content, despite the addition of foreign and security policy as well as justice and home affairs, where European cooperation is mostly intergovernmental and less constraining on national governments.

Economic integration led to some transfer of power from the nation state to the EU. Perhaps more importantly, it also led to a significant transfer of power from the state to the market especially in the more recent phase of integration. The reason is simple: the elimination of national economic borders substantially reduced the capacity of the nation state to influence economic developments within its territory and also its capacity to tax mobile factors of production, without the creation of corresponding powers at European level. The European project thus became economically more liberal with time and an integral part of the ongoing globalization process. Britain played a significant role in steering the project in this direction, although this did not stop most British politicians from feeling that the project was still owned by others.

Regional integration put a premium on mobility and competition. Despite the growing migration of people, partly within Europe but mostly from outside, capital continued to be much more mobile than labour and thus benefited more. The opening of economic borders coupled with growing capital mobility, rapid technological change, and the weakening of organized labour at home had important distributional consequences. It is difficult to fully isolate the effects of each factor separately, yet what we do know for sure, on the basis of a wealth of cross-country data, is that the share of capital as a proportion of national income has been steadily rising at the expense of labour during the last three decades or so. Profits have been going up while wages and salaries rose at a much lower pace or remained stagnant.[10]

Income inequalities within countries grew, with top incomes rising much faster than all others. True, the increasingly unequal effect of the market was moderated through government taxes and the operation of the welfare state, in some countries more than others. On the other hand, the lack of a European policy on company tax, not even an agreement on minimum rates, led to tax competition among countries and declining rates across the board turning tax avoidance into a cottage industry for multinationals.

The distributional effects of integration were uneven and this became increasingly obvious with time. The internal market programme further increased trade and financial interpenetration of European economies, as expected. But it also created winners and losers, much more so than in the earlier phases of European integration, by reaching new areas of activity and also going deeper. Alas, it did not also bring about the revolution in terms of productivity and economic growth promised in the marketing campaign that had accompanied the internal market programme.

The early virtuous economic circle did not last for very long, thus leaving Europe once again with modest growth, high rates of unemployment compared to the United States, and rising indebtedness. Meanwhile, competition from the emerging economies outside Europe grew stronger. The introduction of the euro later on did not change the overall picture. If anything, the effect of the common currency has been negative in terms of growth, employment, and economic convergence following an early period during which rising prosperity in the periphery had been bought mainly through borrowed money. But this takes us too far ahead into the story.

In other words, during a period of slow growth the EU became increasingly perceived as an agent of change and liberalization, with unequal distributional effects within countries and virtually no redistributive capacity of its own. European expenditure on agriculture was the exception, but hardly a model to follow in other policy areas. Thus, the burden of redistribution fell on the nation state, itself operating in a much more challenging economic environment and with less powerful instruments at its disposal than before. Unsurprisingly, resistance from losers and potential losers within countries grew.

## Numbers and diversity

Yet, there has never been a shortage of candidates to join the European club. The original six became twenty-eight in successive rounds of enlargement. Today, there are several more countries in the waiting room and others eager to be shown the green light to apply. The European project, although battered by the recent crisis, still constitutes an object of desire for neighbouring countries only too keen to join as members. The extension of Pax Europaea to the greater part of the European continent, especially to its less developed and less stable parts, has been a remarkable success in many ways. However, enlargements come at a price.

The first enlargement took place in 1973 with the accession of Denmark, Ireland, and the UK. The new members had been kept for years in the waiting room because of General de Gaulle's veto on British accession. The first enlargement sealed the victory of one form of integration over another in Europe, namely the victory of the ambitious economic project of the EEC of the Six with common institutions and political objectives over the minimalist free trade area of the European Free Trade Association (EFTA) championed by the British. But at the same time, enlargement brought within the fold the non-converted who acted on the belief 'if you can't beat them, join them'. And it did not help at all that the first enlargement coincided with the end of the golden age, thus adding to internal divisions and unhappiness as the economic environment changed for the worse. As a result, the budget and the Common Agricultural Policy became the object of recurrent disputes in European councils. On the other hand, British accession added a more global orientation to the regional bloc.

The next enlargement was to the south with the accession of Greece, Portugal, and Spain in the 1980s, following the fall of dictatorships in those countries. Democratic consolidation and modernization were thus added to the European agenda—and it worked very well for years. EU Structural Funds were among the main instruments employed, providing new members with much-needed cash to invest and develop. Membership helped the new entrants to converge economically with the more developed countries to the north. It also helped them to strengthen democracy and open up to the world. Thus, they ended up loving Europe.

Subsequent enlargements were a consequence of 1989 and the collapse of Soviet rule which produced a long list of candidates for membership. The first was a mini-enlargement without the addition of a new member: German unification extended EU membership to the five eastern *Länder* and also acted as catalyst for EMU. It was therefore a mini-enlargement with a very big effect. Next came the three neutrals who were old members of EFTA, namely Austria, Finland, and Sweden. They joined in 1995 in what became EU15. Neutrality no longer had much of a meaning after the end of the Cold War. On the other hand, the fear of being left out of an ever expanding European project trumped their concerns about loss of sovereignty and (Scandinavian) scepticism about being in too close association with the European continent. This round of enlargement went very smoothly: the three new members were small, rich, and generally well behaved.

The biggest challenge, however, was to come later with the accession of countries from the former Eastern bloc, including three former Soviet republics in the Baltics, plus the two Mediterranean islands. Almost all of those countries were much poorer than existing members, they had at best limited democratic experience, and some of them were also novices in the art of statecraft. Therefore, there were similarities with the enlargement to the south some twenty years earlier, although the size of the challenge was so much bigger. Furthermore, most of the new entrants were closer to the UK than the original members with respect to their preference for economic liberalism and limited transfers of power to Brussels. They made an exception for transfers of funds through the common budget, as long as those funds went in their direction.

The main mission of the Union further changed as a result. Having helped to establish the conditions for a peaceful and prosperous centre, European integration was turning increasingly towards the export of democracy, stability, and modernity to the less privileged parts of the continent. This new round of enlargement took many years to kick off. The first big bang enlargement brought in ten new members in 2004. They were followed by two more countries in 2007, and one other in 2013. And it is still an unfinished business with large parts of the Balkans and Turkey in the waiting room, not to mention other countries to the east—former republics of the Soviet Union, for whom the prospect of EU membership remains distant and highly uncertain.

Only a very small number of European countries have chosen to stay out, notably Norway and Switzerland, and also Iceland who has now withdrawn her earlier application. These countries are not willing to be bound by the constraints of full EU membership, although they are apparently willing to conform with a large part of EU legislation without the right to participate in the lawmaking process, as the price to pay for access to the European internal market. Sovereignty in this highly interdependent Europe has indeed become a relative concept, even for those countries that choose to stay out of the EU. But for diehard nationalists, sovereignty seems to be like virginity: either you have it or you do not have it—or simply pretend that you do.

Diversity increased with enlargement. In the first Community of Six, southern Italy was the poor relation in an otherwise relatively homogeneous economic group. In today's Union of twenty-eight, Sweden and Bulgaria, for example, inhabit very different worlds. In diplomatic language, this is called 'diversity', yet it is the kind of diversity that often clashes with the objective of common policies and closer integration, especially as long as the centre remains weak and the frontiers keep shifting outwards.

With the accession of economically less prosperous countries, European integration worked for years like a convergence machine reducing the gap between the centre and the periphery in Europe. It did so until the big crisis struck. Convergence worked for the southern members and it also worked for the new entrants from central and eastern Europe, albeit differing in degrees from one country to another. Sure, it was not just EU membership that made the difference. Other factors, both domestic and international, played an important role as well.

Take the example of Poland and Ukraine. The two countries had comparable standards of living when the communist regimes fell. If anything, Ukraine was slightly ahead of Poland in terms of per capita income. By 2013, Poland had almost quadrupled its income per capita which was by then three times that of its unfortunate neighbour,[11] even before war erupted in the eastern regions of Ukraine. But how much can we explain the different economic performance of the two countries in terms of Poland's EU membership that goes back to 2004?

The EU offers access to a large market and free movement of people and capital; it exports rules and provides benchmarks; it gives large amounts of development assistance; last but not least, it serves as an anchor and reference point for democracy and modernization. These are all very important factors that can help a country coming out of a totalitarian regime to make a successful transition to democracy and the market economy. Poland made good use of them and benefited accordingly, although not always assuring in the process a fair distribution of the benefits among all its inhabitants: inequalities have grown significantly within the country during this period. EU membership surely played an important role in the case of Poland's economic growth and modernization, but it could not be sufficient on its own to generate economic development or ensure good governance.

Compare again the experience of Poland with that of Bulgaria, a member of the EU since 2007. Back in 1990, Bulgaria was not lagging far behind Poland in terms of standard of living. GDP statistics show that Bulgaria has also enjoyed real growth since the fall of the communist regime, although less so than Poland.[12] In terms of average GDP per capita, the (remaining) inhabitants of Bulgaria are now significantly better off than under the communist regime. But in the meantime, the country has lost approximately 20 per cent of its population according to official figures and closer to 30 per cent on the basis of unofficial estimates, mostly through emigration but also through very low birth rates. This can hardly be called a successful transition.

Emigration provides a safety valve for unemployment and poor job prospects at home in general. It also contributes to the domestic economy through remittances sent home by those who have found jobs abroad. But it also deprives the country of some of its brightest and most dynamic citizens, especially among the young. Large-scale emigration can therefore make the country poorer in the long term, and not only in economic terms.[13] Large-scale emigration has also been experienced by other countries in the Balkans as well as the Baltics: the latest peak was reached during the recent economic crisis.

Bulgaria has indeed been much less fortunate than Poland with its political elites and the decisions they have taken (or not taken) in the intervening years. Corruption and administrative inefficiency remain big issues and obstacles to development. Bulgaria has also been less fortunate because its accession to the EU in 2007 was followed almost immediately by the Great Recession. On the other hand, Bulgaria has never been very visible on the radar of European policymakers and international investors (German ones in particular), who have provided a large proportion of the foreign investment in some of the new members and thus helped to integrate those economies, largely through outsourcing, in the German export machine. Bulgaria, on the other hand, never became an important part of it.

In other words, the EU surely makes a difference, sometimes a big one, but it is not and cannot be the modern incarnation of St Panteleimon (or St Pantaleon in the Western vernacular), the all-merciful healer of all kinds of disease. Thousands of pages have been written by scholars on the so-called process of Europeanization that is supposed to work through rules and osmosis bringing about a convergence of institutions, policies, and attitudes of the European periphery towards the more developed centre.[14] But we now know that Europeanization has its limits. In many cases, they are uncomfortably narrow. If, for example, after thirty-five years as a member of the EU, Greece still has a big implementation deficit of common legislation and its institutions are sometimes reminiscent of those of developing countries outside Europe, what are the prospects for late arrivals, not to mention Moldova, Georgia, or Ukraine perhaps sometime in the future? And if Europeanization is indeed a slow process with many detours, what is the price of further enlargement for the internal cohesion of the Union? This is a question that several fervent advocates of enlargement pretend does not exist, probably because they prefer a much looser European association anyway.

Numbers also make a big difference. European councils of different denominations with ten or even fifteen members still behaved like a group. Now with twenty-eight members, they are more like a mini-conference of the United Nations—and we know how effective these conferences usually are in reaching decisions. The behaviour of participants has also changed as a result: the old chemistry is gone, decision-making resembles more traditional intergovernmental negotiations, and the bigger countries are ever more tempted to strike deals outside formal channels. It is a very different Union—and it has been so for several years.

All this does not mean, of course, that enlargements should not have taken place or that the last entrant should lock the door behind her and throw the key away. Pax Europaea has real substance; it has made a big difference in the way Europeans conduct their affairs and interact with each other—and overall, this has been very much for the better. Just think of the not-so-remote past as an alternative scenario. But as the new European order extends to new territories, the capacity of the centre weakens as a result, especially when the new countries that join have weak institutions and a more loose approach to the rule of law.

It is the kind of trade-off that those who want to enlarge to Turkey, the Caucasus, and beyond prefer not to see. True, the old members have tried to link each round of enlargement with institutional reform and the adoption of new common policies as a way of avoiding dilution. But in practice, it has been very difficult to reconcile an ever expanding EU project with constantly growing numbers and more diversity internally, at least within the existing political framework and institutional set-up.

## European foreign policy: not yet

The never-ending enlargements of the EU have often been described as the most successful European foreign policy.[15] This is undoubtedly true, although there has not been that much of a European foreign policy in general to talk about. The EU has been big and influential in trade matters, with a common trade policy and the Commission acting as the joint representative of the common interest as defined after long and difficult internal negotiations. It played an important role in the various GATT negotiations and was instrumental in the setting up of the World Trade Organization (WTO), always trying to keep a delicate balance between different national interests internally and also between its formal multilateralist vows and its regionalist instincts. It has thus helped in shaping the international trade environment and its rules: the best example of strength in unity, with the EU being able to translate its collective weight in world trade into effective negotiating power.[16]

The EU28 represents today 16 per cent of world exports (Eurostat data), excluding intra-EU trade, albeit with a steadily declining share over recent decades due to the rise of China and other fast developing economies. For the first time in 2014, the EU share of world exports was second to that of China and significantly bigger than that of the United States being more open than the latter (openness being measured by foreign trade as a percentage of GDP). And when it acts as a bloc, it has strong negotiating power. For some Europeans—and for non-Europeans even more so—the EU has been too protectionist, for others it has been too open. Ideological preferences and interests of course vary a great deal, from Britain and Germany on the liberal side to France and Italy on the protectionist side. Yet, it would be difficult to deny the overall liberalizing effect of the EU on international trade over the long term.

On the other hand, for the average European country trade with the rest of Europe is what counts by far the most. At one end of the spectrum stands Slovakia with as much as 84 per cent of its total exports of goods going to other EU countries, and at the other end stands the UK with 48 per cent, still a very significant figure. Somewhere in between, we find Germany with 58 per cent of its exports having an EU destination. And if we add other European countries outside the EU, these figures increase on average by another 10 percentage points. Trade with Switzerland for an average EU country is comparable in absolute terms with trade with China: so much for globalization! This Eurocentrism has been clearly reflected all along in the attitudes of most European countries, especially the smaller ones, and it has been changing only rather slowly.

European unity vis-à-vis the rest of the world has not often manifested itself beyond trade matters, and this lack of unity has in turn been translated into much reduced negotiating power. Individual European countries, the (former) big powers in particular, still prefer to bat on their own, with limited coordination between them, in various international economic forums, such as the G7 (or G8) and G20, and also bilaterally. The presence of the European Commission at these meetings does not make much difference, especially since the common European interest remains vaguely defined. Therefore, diversity prevails over unity. But whenever Europeans succeed in adopting a common stance in international negotiations, they end up collectively as a strong player.

The hard core of traditional foreign policy and defence used to be a taboo in the early years of European integration: sovereignty concerns on the one hand and the existence of NATO on the other combined to keep such matters out of bounds until the late 1960s. European political cooperation, meaning foreign policy cooperation in the European jargon, was launched in 1970 to be succeeded at Maastricht, after the disintegration of the Soviet empire and German reunification, by the much more ambitious Common Foreign and Security Policy (CFSP). More acronyms were later added, more joint committees, and bigger tasks. In other words, some of the appetizers for a European foreign policy were already there, but where was the meat?

Individual European countries clung zealously to their national independence and prerogatives when it came to the hard core of traditional foreign policy, while responsibility for collective defence has been long delegated to the Atlantic alliance under US leadership. Most Europeans apparently still prefer being under American protection rather than trying to collectively defend themselves and bear the costs. And they have so far allowed Europe as a collective entity to engage mostly in various forms of 'soft' power, such as peacekeeping missions and international mediation, in which it has often done a good job.

There are only two carnivores left in Europe in terms of their readiness to resort to the instruments of war, namely France and the UK, countries still with global ambitions although not always ready or able to put their money and soldiers where their mouth is. The rest are herbivores, or just small countries with a foreign policy that usually does not extend beyond their immediate neighbourhood. Germany stands between the two, still very hesitant to make the transition from the latter to the former. It may be that, deep in their heart, many Europeans do not really want Germany to make this transition. Trying to construct a common foreign and security policy out of twenty-eight diverse national interests has surely not been an easy task. The gap between expectations and official pronouncements on the one hand and capabilities and delivery on the other, remains wide.[17] On some of the big issues in the past, notably the war in Yugoslavia in the early 1990s and the US-led intervention in Iraq a decade later, Europeans were deeply divided. Their big ally on the other side of the Atlantic did not help much by openly taking advantage of internal European divisions. And Russia hardly helped either, but was it ever meant to? Thus, Europeans have often tried to preserve their fragile unity in relations with the rest of the world through long and innocuous statements or simply by not doing very much.

Meanwhile, growing external immigration pressures have developed into a huge challenge for domestic political systems and for

Europe's open borders. The so-called Schengen area, borrowing the name from a small town in Luxembourg where the original agreement was signed back in 1985, is a large area comprising more than 400 million people with no internal passport controls and a common visa policy in relation to the rest of the world: another major achievement of European integration. But, together with the euro, the Schengen area is also a prominent example of the two-tier structure that has developed in the more recent phase of integration: the UK has an opt-out from both.

Open internal borders require an effective control of external borders and a degree of mutual confidence between national authorities which cannot be taken for granted, especially at a time when large numbers of refugees and economic immigrants are seeking to enter Europe's porous borders and when the terrorist threat is on the rise. The European project may indeed be inward-looking, but the rest of the world does not always oblige by letting Europeans mind their own business.

## Faltering consensus

European integration relied for many years on a generally held perception among national political elites of a win-win project combined with a wide permissive consensus among citizens across borders. European integration was dissected into different national stories[18]— narratives in modern parlance—and much of its strength used to lie precisely in the *diversity* of national narratives.

For the Germans, it was a major part of the rehabilitation process after the war, and German politicians were prepared to pay a price for it without always openly admitting that the post-war German economic miracle was very much dependent on access to a large European market without barriers. This began to change after reunification, when Germany became again a 'normal' country. For the French, it was a way of extending their influence as long as the European interest continued to be defined more or less as the French interest—and they succeeded in running the show for several decades. Italy's weak political system needed European anchorage, and so did Belgium's increasingly virtual state.

Belonging to the EU conferred respectability and status on countries that had long been treated as objects rather than subjects of European diplomacy. Small and medium-sized countries are over-represented in all common institutions and, as long as the big ones refrained from throwing their weight about, European integration provided the lesser mortals with opportunities they had never had in conditions of intergovernmental diplomacy in the past. Membership also helped to consolidate democracy in countries with a turbulent and unhappy history. It helped them to open up to the rest of the world and also served as a vehicle of modernization. Greeks and Spaniards certainly benefited much from this experience, and later so did the Poles and others in central and eastern Europe. People in these countries also greatly appreciated the inflow of large amounts of funds for development purposes, without always making the best use of them.

Membership offered security vouchers to those who felt vulnerable on the outer edges of the Union, although it could only provide a limited guarantee since security came more through the North Atlantic Treaty Organization (NATO) than the EU. Still, if you happen to live in Finland or the Baltic countries, you easily understand what it means—you also know that being in the eurozone is not only for economic reasons. In general, weak states and vulnerable countries need Europe more than the others, and those waiting outside even more so.

National narratives diverged widely with respect to the overall approach and the final objective of integration: a political project leading eventually to some form of political union for the original members and the south of Europe, or mostly an economic area that preserves as much as possible the key elements of national sovereignty for the group of countries led by the British including former EFTA members and more recent entrants from central and eastern Europe. On many occasions, creative ambiguity in official texts and declarations helped to keep everybody on board, but only up to a point. Differentiation and opt-outs for individual countries provided the instrument of last resort when the only alternative was to do nothing or very little indeed. The common currency and the passport-free Schengen area are the best examples where opt-outs for the minority allowed the majority to go forward.

Of course, this line of division between 'integrationists' and 'sovereignists' often hid considerable diversity within each of the two groups and within countries as well, as might be expected. But still, it was a convenient yardstick to separate the sheep from the goats. National narratives usually prevailed over political/ideological ones and this in itself said a great deal about the stage of political integration in Europe. In other words, a French socialist was (and still is) more French than socialist in his or her attitude to the European project and the same is true of most others. The nation state has deep roots in Europe and should not be expected to wither away anytime soon: fear not staunch defenders of national symbols!

All along, Britain stood out from the rest. Ownership of the European project remained at best limited, the European story was less convincing than elsewhere in Europe, and local interest in listening faded further over the years. Austrians and Slovaks, for example, have nowhere else to go, and they know it, while there are enough British who (mistakenly?) think they do and who continue to think in terms of 'us' and 'them'. The English Channel remains wide; if anything, it has grown wider with time.

At political party level, European integration continued to enjoy wide support among all mainstream parties across borders from Christian democrats and Liberals to Social democrats, Labour, and Greens, although they often disagreed on the specifics, as might be expected. There were a few exceptions to this consensus, British Conservatives most notably. This cross-party support for the European project was also reflected in the way the European Parliament worked for years, relying on broad coalitions of mainstream parties operating on the basis of consensus. This did not change a great deal with the advent of direct elections and the growing powers of the European Parliament. Nor did direct elections help to improve much the democratic deficit of the ever expanding European project. The fundamental reality of the European political system based mostly on indirect legitimacy through member states has never changed.

The new president of the European Commission, Mr Juncker, was indirectly elected to this post in 2014 as the candidate of the centre-right political group (European People's Party) with the largest number of votes in the European Parliament elections. It was a first, but still not the political revolution that early federalists had dreamt of. The democratization process of the European political system is likely to be slow at best,[19] which means that it will have to rely largely on consensus while continuing to produce more top-down *policies* than participatory *politics*: not an easy balancing act for European acrobats (and politicians).

Cross-party consensus among national political elites relied for years on broad permissive consensus among citizens, and it seemed to work both ways. This permissive consensus delivered support for the main objectives of European integration, although it generated relatively little interest in the specifics and had virtually no mobilizing power. For a long time, the large majority of Europeans thought that the European project was a good thing because it was seen as deliver-ing positive results, although only a small minority among them had strong feelings about Europe, knew much about what was going on in Brussels, or felt ready to mobilize for the cause.

The typical supporter of Europe and the integration project was educated and well off, he or she belonged to the political mainstream, was middle-aged or older, and willing to move. These were the people who always provided the core of support and were also among the most dynamic elements of their societies. It is not much different today. As for the young, they are the generation for whom Europe makes more sense, although not necessarily the kind of European project constructed by their parents. For the younger generations, European wars are already something from the distant past, while peace and open borders tend to be taken for granted, although prosperity less so. They want perhaps a different kind of Europe, but have no clear idea of what it should look like.

Permissive consensus was bound to change as European integration began to affect more and more the everyday lives of citizens in an increasingly competitive environment, with rapid change and growing uncertainty, also slow growth and an increasing number of losers. The losers turned to the nation state for protection because they had nowhere else to turn. Europe did not offer any kind of protection to those on the losing side. Already in the 1990s, public support for European integration began to decline and so did the number of Europeans who thought that EU membership was a good thing. This was registered in regular Eurobarometer surveys, and it was more painfully realized in some national referendums on Europe-related issues. The permissive consensus thus began to crack.[20]

European social democracy was the most directly affected by declining public support for the European project. Centre-left parties found it increasingly difficult to reconcile their pro-European policies with an integration project that became more and more identified with economic liberalization and globalization, while most of the losers and potential losers from economic change came from their own ranks. In the process, party leaders discovered to their shock and horror that significant numbers of their former voters had little hesitation about migrating all the way to the far right. They are still not at all sure how to deal with the problem.

## Referendums on Europe

Increasingly, referendums became an integral part of the politics of European integration,[21] despite the fact that referendums had not been part of the political tradition of most European countries before. And they are here to stay, it seems. This explains the reluctance of national political elites today to take new initiatives that would lead to further revisions of the European treaties. They know that referendums cannot be avoided in several countries and they are not at all confident they would win them.

The list of referendums related to European integration is very long: more than forty so far, excluding referendums held in Switzerland which has a long tradition of direct democracy and already several referendums in relation to European integration. Imagine what would happen if the Swiss were members! European referendums can be divided into two categories, namely those in which citizens of a country are asked the fundamental question, namely whether they want to join (or stay) in the EU, and the rest in which the question asked relates mostly to the acceptance or rejection of yet another revision of the European treaties, big or small. The conclusions we can draw from past experience are very different for each of the two categories.

Nine out of the ten countries that joined the EU in the 2004 enlargement held referendums on accession (and so did Croatia eight years later). The 'yes' vote ranged from 94 per cent in Slovakia to 54 per cent in Malta, with an overwhelming majority of 65 per cent and above in all the other countries. Clearly, not that many people among the new entrants had existential doubts as to whether they wanted to be part of the European project. But whatever support there was for EU membership was apparently not strong enough to motivate them to cast their vote in European Parliament elections once their country had joined. Turnouts for European elections in most central and eastern European countries have been consistently and embarrassingly low. It seems that the key thing for most people was to get in, but they never really felt themselves to be co-owners of the European project. Participation rates in national elections are usually not very high either in the relatively young democracies of central and eastern Europe. Thus, the problem goes much deeper and it is not specifically related to European integration.

The majorities registered in the referendums held in the former EFTA countries back in 1994 had been significantly smaller, but majorities nevertheless they were. The exception was Austria which fitted more into the central and eastern European pattern with a large majority in favour of accession. Clear majorities had also been registered with respect to the first enlargement back in 1973. The UK referendum held in 1975 also produced an overwhelming majority of 67 per cent for the 'yes' vote. Only the Norwegians have rejected EU accession twice, and they are unlikely to try a third time in the foreseeable future; and so did the small population of Greenland. Experience until now suggests that when citizens are faced with a clear choice of 'in' or 'out' of the EU, their answer is a resounding 'yes', with very few exceptions.

But things are very different when citizens are asked to express an opinion concerning successive revisions of the treaties. On those occasions, the answer they give is often negative. The stakes in an 'in' or 'out' referendum are pretty clear. The same should also be true in a referendum on the euro, as long as the choice presented in the question is equally clear. But being asked to vote on a long and complex legal text containing a mixed package of reforms, mostly of an institutional nature, is much less obvious. You may then be tempted to give answers to all kinds of questions that bear little or no relation at all to the text you are being asked to approve, or answer on the basis of who asks the question.

The European constitutional treaty fell between these two extremes. It was a typical example of European compromise that started with the highly ambitious goal of a proper European constitution and ended up as a long-winded treaty dealing mostly with arcane institutional changes, at least in the eyes of ordinary Europeans. Early on in the negotiations, we learned that the benign conspiracy of the Six in the early stages of integration was simply not repeatable with much bigger numbers, a very different political context, and much higher stakes. The gap between maximalists and minimalists on the big issues debated in the European Convention that was mandated to prepare the constitution was simply too wide to hide behind the language of creative ambiguity employed by diplomats and lawyers in Brussels. And there was another gap revealed later on, namely between national politicians and their fellow citizens on things European. While parliamentary ratifications of the constitutional treaty went through in most countries with comfortable majorities, the results in referendums were very different, showing much unhappiness and unease among citizens (and also a good deal of ignorance).

The constitutional treaty was not killed in the lands of the usual suspects, but in the countries of two of the founding members, namely France and the Netherlands, where people voted 'no' in the referendums held in 2005. The comparison with what had happened earlier with the Maastricht Treaty is quite telling. Denmark had voted against the Maastricht Treaty and the euro back in 1992 and stayed out. Sweden did the same more than ten years later. And so did the UK without a referendum. But monetary union went on regardless for those willing and able to join. It would not have been the same if the Maastricht Treaty had not scraped through in the French referendum or if the Germans had tried a referendum and probably failed to obtain a positive answer from their citizens. If France or Germany had said no, the common currency would have been stillborn. When Denmark, Sweden, and the UK said no, they simply stayed out. This may suggest that in European integration all countries are equal, but some are more equal than others. That much we have known all along, but inequality has grown much bigger in recent years.

The signs of public unease and unhappiness had been there for some time, but European political leaders preferred not to take notice. Thus, the negative results of the French and Dutch referendums came as a big shock. It was a political earthquake that produced a major crisis in the EU and led to a complete reversal of the Euro-euphoria that had prevailed earlier. The 'no' vote brought together the left and right of the political spectrum, an experience that was later to be repeated in several countries when Euroscepticism blazed through old ideological barriers. Concerns about the further loss of sovereignty and opposition to new enlargement and immigration mixed with anxiety about economic prospects and job losses, opposition to globalization with discontent about the weak social dimension of the European project: it was a very mixed bag.[22]

Some of those who voted 'no' wanted less Europe, and some more of it, while the majority were, perhaps, simply trying to say that they were not satisfied with the kind of Europe on offer and the way that global and European developments were affecting their lives. They were also not happy with the situation at home. There was an over-whelming rejection of the treaty among manual workers and those on the losing side of the long economic transformation linked to the breaking down of barriers and technological change. There were also many more 'noes' among young people and a higher rate of absten-tion: this came as an even bigger shock to European elites.

The 2005 referendums were a turning point in the history of European integration that marked the end of permissive consensus. What followed was a long-drawn-out collective effort by Europe's political elites to save as much as possible of the constitutional treaty in order to make the EU more functional after the big enlargement of 2004 and also better able to cope with external challenges; but how to convince their ever more sceptical publics? The result was the Lisbon Treaty that finally came into effect in 2009, after long and difficult intergovernmental negotiations and two referendums in Ireland in order to get a 'yes' majority. Europe would not take 'no' for an answer, the Irish were told—a rather disquieting message for democrats of all shades.

Ever bigger, more intrusive, and less inclusive, in the context of growing external competition, slow growth, and high unemployment. Hence also less consensual. This would be an appropriate summary of the history of European integration, still predominantly an economic affair, in the first sixty years or so preceding the big economic crisis. A remarkable success story on the one hand, the piling up of ever more functions and members in an overstretched system on the other, all in the context of a deteriorating economic and political environ-ment. A poorly thought-out and ill-prepared monetary union stood at the top of the pile. In the more recent phase, European integration became an integral part of the globalization process in an era of neo-liberalism.[23] We have lived through the consequences ever since. Chapter 3 opens with the big economic crisis that came very soon after the constitutional crisis had ended. Europeans hardly had time for a sigh of relief before the next crisis struck.

# 3

# Reality Strikes Back

Many economists expressed strong doubts about the desirability, or indeed sustainability, of a common currency shared by countries with very diverse economic structures and policy priorities, a single monetary policy but different national fiscal policies subject to some basic common rules and intergovernmental coordination, a currency with feeble common instruments and almost non-existent safety mechanisms, and last but not least a weak political base. Europe was not, at least not as yet, an 'optimum currency area' in the jargon,[1] and it was unlikely to become one anytime soon. But there were also enough economists, to be found more on the continent of Europe than among Anglo-American representatives of the mainstream, who argued that floating exchange rates in the post-Bretton Woods era were incompatible with a truly European market. 'Optimum currency areas are not given, they are created', some economists were then tempted to conclude.

Unlike the internal market, monetary union was controversial inside the economics profession and even those economists who were broadly in favour recognized that the Maastricht construction was weak and unbalanced. But that was all that was possible at the time. After all, EMU was essentially a politically motivated project and politics was meant to shape economic forces. In other words, close your eyes, pluck up courage, and take a leap—a gigantic leap indeed in European integration.

Back in 1997, before the euro was launched, Martin Feldstein,[2] a Harvard economist and former chief economic adviser to Ronald

Reagan, had warned that European monetary union did not make economic sense and was also likely to lead to political conflict within the union because of incompatible expectations among the leading actors, with negative implications for the United States as well. His warning was readily dismissed at the time by most Europeans as scaremongering and some saw behind Feldstein's critical approach American dislike of an emerging independent European political entity, employing money as its vehicle. The suspicion may have been well founded, but who can now dispute the prescience of the American economist? More than ten years after Feldstein published his article, we were to discover that monetary union would indeed produce conflict rather than unity and that the economics on which it was based was deeply flawed. Europeans have been trying to limit the damage and do the necessary repairs ever since.

## Honeymoons are not forever

Economic and Monetary Union began on 1 January 1999, with the irrevocable fixing of exchange rates between eleven national currencies, the introduction of the euro for financial transactions, and the ECB taking over the conduct of monetary policy for the union as a whole. Exactly three years later, the euro became a fully fledged currency for twelve countries (Greece having joined in the meantime), thus relegating national currencies to the dustbin of history.

The euro honeymoon lasted for slightly more than ten years in a polygamous affair with growing membership.[3] The ECB soon established its credibility and delivered a one-size-fits-all monetary policy, trying to reconcile the often diverging interests of the eurozone. It was hardly an easy task. Average inflation remained low during this period and the euro, with a wide range of fluctuations against the US dollar, soon replaced the Deutschmark (DM) as the world's second most important international trading and reserve currency, although still a long distance behind its US counterpart. Interest rates were kept low by the ECB and there was a noticeable process of convergence across the eurozone as a whole implying that country and exchange risk were no longer playing a role in the currency union. In other words, markets seemed to be convinced of the irreversibility of EMU—and this happened rather soon. It was an irrefutable sign of success, was it not?

However, output growth and productivity remained modest for the eurozone as a whole after a few good years preceding the introduction of the euro. Thus, EMU did not succeed in providing the fillip for growth and productivity that many people had hoped for, although average unemployment fell during this period (see Graph 2.1). On the other hand, EMU did act as a catalyst for further trade and financial integration across borders, as should have been expected. European financial integration was very rapid indeed after the elimination of exchange risk and national controls leading to large-scale restructuring, mergers and acquisitions, and fast growth for the financial sector. Not surprisingly, those directly involved were only too happy, celebrating the victory of unfettered markets and their rapidly growing bonuses.

Averages are, however, sometimes misleading and this has been true for the eurozone in both good and bad times. During the long honeymoon period, national economies diverged widely in terms of inflation, unit labour costs, savings, and growth and this divergence was reflected in ever-growing current account imbalances between them. Imbalances were financed in turn by capital movements going in the opposite direction, with an increasingly integrated financial sector acting as the willing intermediary.[4]

Nothing wrong with this, the unsuspecting economist used to argue—equipped, as he or she was, with a large baggage of supporting theory. After all, this happens all the time in the best of places, notably the US monetary union, and nobody bats an eyelid if Arizona or Minnesota runs a big trade deficit with the rest of the US. But when reality struck, economists and policymakers painfully discovered that the American and European monetary unions are still very different, both in terms of the policy instruments available and the perception that markets have of them when it comes to the crunch. Indeed, when the crunch did come in Europe, capital flows were immediately reversed in panic mode. And there were hardly any compensating mechanisms and no emergency exit when this happened.

In the race for competitiveness whilst still being treated as the 'sick man of Europe' a full decade after reunification, Germany succeeded in keeping wages and prices down after having substituted the euro for its beloved DM. It saved, restructured, and outsourced large parts of its manufacturing industry, or perhaps to be a bit more precise, Germany moved to a new networked supply chain model extending to neighbouring countries to the east. Germany also reformed its labour market. A stable and largely consensual political system, trade unions that put the emphasis on preserving jobs rather than increasing wages, combined with the prowess of Germany's industrial machine, delivered the goods once again. The result was regained competitiveness inside the eurozone and beyond, a more open economy with a much stronger position in a globalizing environment, albeit also a country more unequal internally and with an increasing number of poorly paid part-time jobs. The latter is apparently one of the features of economies that become fit for globalization.

Until the crisis struck, Germany kept wage and price increases down—for some years wages did not even keep pace with productivity—to a rate that even in the best of all possible worlds it would have been extremely difficult for other countries of the eurozone to follow, simply because they had neither the institutions nor the economic behavioural traits that Germany acquired in the decades after the war. And, admittedly, some did not even try, succumbing instead to the temptation of construction- and consumption-led growth financed largely through debt since they had access to ample and cheap credit in times of low interest rates and zero exchange risk inside the currency union.

Much of the European periphery, including countries in central and eastern Europe still outside the eurozone, had a party that lasted almost a decade. Domestically generated and debt-financed growth in the periphery led in turn to widening current account deficits which had their counterparts to a large extent in the ever growing surpluses of Germany—and also the Netherlands, which usually escapes attention because of its relatively small size in absolute terms.

## What went wrong?

What went wrong during the honeymoon period of the euro can be illustrated by contrasting the macroeconomic performance of Germany with that of southern European countries plus Ireland: they represent the two extremes. Graphs 3.1 and 3.2 are quite revealing. In cumulative terms, the divergence in terms of inflation and unit labour costs (average cost of labour per unit of output) between Germany on the one hand, and the south of Europe and Ireland on the other, was very big indeed for the period between 1999 and 2008. During this period, unit labour costs in Ireland rose by 46 per cent in relation to Germany. The corresponding figures were 33 per cent for Greece and 24 per cent

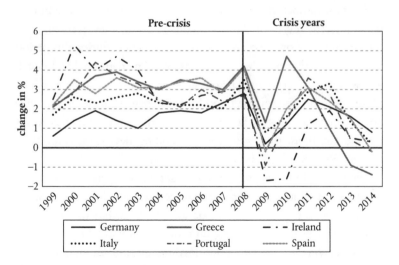

Graph 3.1 Divergence in Inflation Rates 1999–2014
Source: Eurostat. Harmonized Consumer Price Index.

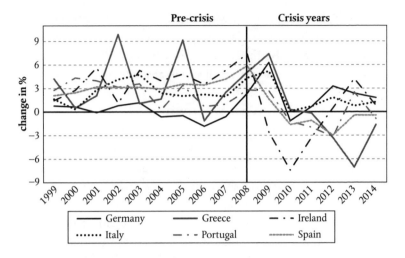

**Graph 3.2** Divergence in Unit Labour Costs 1999–2014

*Source*: AMECO. Nominal unit labour costs (ratio of compensation per employee to real GDP per person employed).

for Portugal. Unit labour costs are, of course, not the only factor that determines competitiveness, but they are an important one. Combined with different levels of domestic consumption, they were in turn translated into growing current account imbalances during this period as shown in Graph 3.3. Greece, Portugal, and Spain, more than Ireland, ended up with very large current account deficits and German surpluses shot up. The reverse trend for the deficit countries began after 2008, when the crisis hit Europe: it was both painful and divisive. As for the Germans, they succeeded in finding new outlets for their exports. We shall come back to this in Chapter 4.

The picture in terms of real growth rates for the period 1999–2008, as shown in Graph 3.4, is more nuanced. Ireland, Greece, and Spain enjoyed much higher than average growth rates. For the optimists, this was the result of a catching-up process that was all for the good: capital flowing to where better investment opportunities lie and leading to higher growth, also to higher wages and prices. They failed to notice, however, as did those who provided the necessary finance,

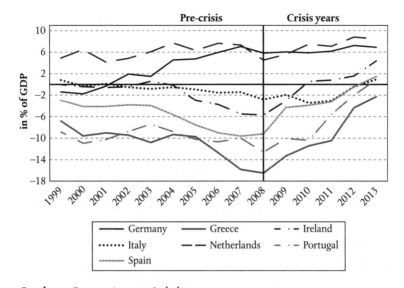

**Graph 3.3** Current Account Imbalances 1999–2013

*Source*: AMECO. Balance on current transactions with the rest of the world.

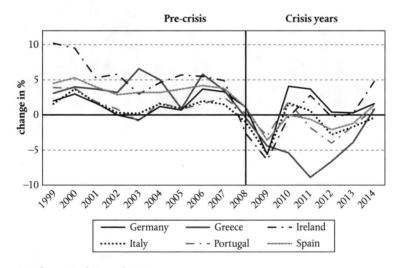

**Graph 3.4** Real Growth Rates 1999–2014

*Source*: Eurostat. Gross domestic product at market prices, 2010 reference levels.

that they were in fact feeding bubbles. Everybody clearly enjoyed the party while it lasted, but when the bill arrived they had very different views as to who should pay. During the same period, the Italian and Portuguese economies underperformed, as did Germany's until 2005 when economic and fiscal 'virtue' began to pay—and it has continued to pay throughout the crisis.

Current account deficits were financed through borrowed money that went largely to consumption and construction and/or real estate bubbles. The countries of the periphery borrowed credibility indirectly from the euro, and money directly from countries with excess savings and surpluses through the financial sector. Private debt increased very fast as a percentage of GDP (Graph 3.5): in Ireland it went up from 142 per cent in 2001 to 256 per cent in 2008; in Spain from 103 per cent in

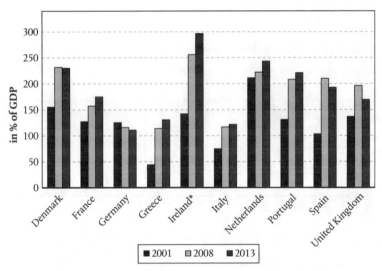

\* The data for Ireland are for the year 2001 and not for 1999.

**Graph 3.5** Private Debt as a percentage of GDP (1999, 2008 and 2013)

Source: Eurostat. The private sector debt is the stock of liabilities held by the sectors 'Non-Financial corporations' and 'Households and Non-Profit institutions serving households'. The instruments that are taken into account to compile private sector debt are 'Debt securities' and 'Loans'. Data are presented in non-consolidated terms, i.e. taking into account transactions within the same sector and expressed in % of GDP and millions of national currency.

1999 to 210 per cent in 2008, and in Portugal from 131 per cent to 208 per cent during the same period. In fact, private debt rose at a rapid pace in most countries irrespective of whether they were in the eurozone or not. In the Netherlands, private debt reached 222 per cent of GDP in 2008 starting from a high base already in 1999. In 2008, the corresponding figures for Denmark and the UK, outside the eurozone, were 232 per cent and 196 per cent respectively. Rapidly rising indebtedness was in fact a generalized phenomenon in western countries in which most household incomes grew very slowly or remained stagnant.

Greeks apparently showed more restraint with private debt, rising from a very modest 44 per cent of GDP in 1999 to 114 per cent in 2008; and so did the Italians, going from 75 per cent in 1999 to 117 per cent in 2008. But the main problem in both Greece and Italy was public not private debt. Public debt was above 100 per cent of GDP in both countries in 2008, although it had declined in Italy during the period of the euro as it had also done for the eurozone on average (Graph 3.6). And public debt was down to very low figures indeed in

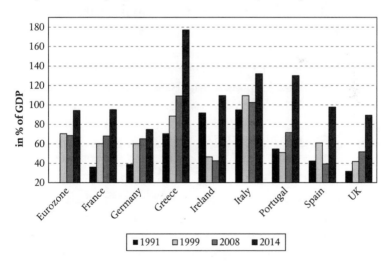

**Graph 3.6** Public Debt as a percentage of GDP (1991, 1999, 2008 and 2014)
Source: AMECO. General government consolidated gross debt.

Ireland and Spain, two countries that were hit badly by the crisis. With the exception of Greece, it is therefore simply not true that growing imbalances inside the euro and the crisis that followed were due to fiscal profligacy. However, this was soon to become the official truth.

In these times of rapidly rising indebtedness, Germany again stood out as the big exception. Private debt in Germany went down as a percentage of GDP from 125 per cent in 1999 to 116 per cent in 2008, while public debt was still at 65 per cent, despite the large (and continuing for many years) budgetary cost of reunification. But while the Germans were abstemious at home, their banks, together with banks from other countries, were lending massively to the rest of the eurozone and beyond, recycling the savings of these abstemious Germans and others and feeding bubbles in other countries. Thus, they also indirectly provided the loan finance for the further purchase of German goods abroad, hence also for German current account surpluses.

Debt always involves two parties: a simple truth that is often conveniently forgotten when the scene turns ugly. In the third quarter of 2009, total claims of French and German banks on the countries of southern Europe plus Ireland had reached astronomical figures: US $824 billion for the French banks and US$733 billion for German banks according to data provided by the Bank for International Settlements (BIS). UK banks followed with US$433 billion and Dutch banks with US$258 billion.[5] There was some geographical division of labour among them, with German banks leading in Spain, French banks in Italy and Greece, and UK banks in Ireland together with German banks.

Would they be able to get their money back? When this question began to be asked, the euro honeymoon was clearly over. It had been a long honeymoon, exciting for some perhaps, but rather dull for others. The character differences had become all too obvious during those ten years. The fundamental weaknesses of this polygamous affair had been exposed and the seeds of conflict sown. It would be anything but boring from then on.

## An international crisis turns European

However, the crisis did not begin in Europe but in a rather obscure segment of the US financial industry, the so-called sub-prime mortgage market, which got into trouble when the US housing bubble began to burst in the summer of 2007. It then spread fast like an epidemic because many of those loans of dubious quality, to say the least, had been repackaged in complex securities and derivatives and sold to other financial institutions in the Western world. German regional banks, for example, had ended up in possession of large amounts of loans granted in California to people who had virtually no chance of paying them back when house prices stopped rising there: banks in search of higher profits *today* (and the devil take the morrow), with scant attention to risk and usually little knowledge of the intrinsic value of assets bought and sold. All this was happening in the most globalized sector of the world economy.

When participants began to realize that the music and the big fiesta were about to end, fear quickly replaced greed and the interbank market seized up, since nobody knew exactly the amount of toxic assets that other banks had in their possession, and hence they were reluctant to lend. As one financial institution after another got into trouble, the US and European governments rushed to their rescue: some were too big and too important to fail while the fear of contagion was paramount in everybody's mind. The next turning point came when Lehman Brothers was allowed to go bankrupt in September 2008: a much debated and highly controversial decision on the part of the US authorities which indicated that there would be no blank cheque by the government for any bank in trouble, although it risked causing a generalized financial meltdown. And then, panic replaced fear.[6]

While governments on the two sides of the Atlantic were trying to deal with the crisis in the financial sector—being a crisis of the Western financial system only indirectly affecting the rest of the world—the shock waves reached the real economy: 2009 was the worst year since the end of the Second World War with negative growth rates registered in most advanced economies. Thus, governments were now called upon to deal with both the problem of financial institutions on the verge of bankruptcy and a deep recession leading to a large increase in unemployment. A loosely coordinated fiscal stimulus through G20 (the Group of 20 brings together the most important economies from the developed as well as the developing world) helped to prevent a repetition of the Great Depression. But while many Europeans began to think (or hope) that the worst was already behind them, the US-born crisis metastasized into an existential crisis of the euro and European integration in general.

Greece was the catalyst. It all started when the newly elected socialist government in Greece revealed in October 2009 the true figures about the budget deficit camouflaged by its predecessor in what became later notoriously known as 'Greek statistics'. This further added to panic in financial markets as they began to wake up to another kind of unpleasant reality, namely that loans to some governments could be as bad as loans granted to private individuals or other banks. And the crisis deepened further, as Greece gradually lost access to markets and had to appeal to its European partners for rescue. But there were no European provisions or instruments to deal with this kind of accident: the Maastricht Treaty had outlawed such accidents.

Soon, other accidents followed inside the eurozone when more countries lost access to markets and Europeans began to realize that the problem was much bigger than just Greece. The party in the periphery had a bad end. If the Irish accident had happened before the Greek one, perhaps the euro crisis would have taken a different course; who knows? What we do know, however, is that more than six years since people began to realize that a euro crisis was in the offing, we are still not completely out of the woods and with all kinds of injuries suffered on the way.

## Ugly Russian dolls

In order to understand the crisis of the euro, it would help to think of it in three different dimensions, namely the international, the

European, and the national, which are all closely interconnected. They are like those Russian dolls, the *matryoshkas*: you take one, open it, and find a smaller one inside. However, the trouble with this particular set of Russian dolls is that each one is uglier than the one before.

At international level, we have had the bursting of the biggest financial bubble since 1929, signalling a huge failure of markets, institutions, and democratic politics, as well as a crashing failure of the economics profession. Financial markets had been liberalized and deregulated and this was fully consistent with the economic paradigm prevailing since the 1980s, a paradigm that called for more market and less state. The Anglo-Americans provided both the political and ideological leadership, while most continental Europeans followed with a mix of anticipation and embarrassment.

Taking advantage of the lifting of capital controls, the revolution in information and communications technology, and a loose regulatory framework at national level (with hardly any regulation beyond it, including the EU), the financial industry became increasingly global and acquired an ever growing share of the economic pie and of total profits as well. This was more pronounced in the US and the UK as well as in some smaller countries, such as Ireland, Luxembourg, and Cyprus—also Iceland outside the EU—where bank liabilities reached a multiple figure of national GDP. The balance sheet of UK banks, for example, rose from the equivalent of approximately 50 per cent of national GDP in the pre-1970 period to more than 200 per cent in the late 1980s and more than 500 per cent in 2007—in Ireland in 2007 it was 700 per cent.[7] Bankers were running amok.

But how could national GDP be at all relevant as a standard of reference for global banks? This is what the apostles of the new religion mockingly asked in the good times, looking with obvious contempt at the cavemen who still thought in national terms or had some remaining doubts about the efficiency and inherent stability of financial markets. Supporters of liberalization and deregulation felt strong in their conviction until the crash came. They discovered then, to their shock and horror, that banks are international in life but national in death.[8] It all has to do with who is the lender of last resort when things go bad, and this lender of last resort remained national all through the new era of globalization. There was no international or European institution to save banks when they got into trouble.

Before the crisis, banks and other financial institutions grew bigger, recycled the large amounts of liquidity resulting from big current account imbalances at global level, took extra risks in search of higher yield in times of low interest rates, leveraged their capital several times above the threshold of prudence, and often lent with undue diligence. In the process, they acted as keen facilitators for the rapid increase in overall debt, public but mostly private, in many Western economies, thus helping to keep consumption levels high and politicians in power. Credit was a convenient substitute in times when large sections of the population did not experience any rise in incomes:[9] it was good while it lasted.

Several among the leading global banks also resorted to extensive market manipulation and fraud as regulators were later to discover with respect to interbank lending rates and foreign exchange markets among others. This led to huge fines following the outbreak of the crisis with US regulators usually taking the lead. Thus, instead of having rational actors operating with perfect information in efficient and self-regulated markets, as leading economic theorists wanted us to believe, there was greed and lack of transparency, sometimes leading to outright criminal behaviour, short-termism backed by the wrong incentives for financial managers, and the conveniently forgotten herd instinct of non-rational actors operating in conditions of high uncertainty. With the benefit of hindsight, it appears that large parts of Western financial capitalism had turned into a large casino[10] in which the insiders could circumvent the rules with relative ease— and they made huge profits as a result as the game went on. The ever more skewed distribution of earnings in advanced economies, with the US leading the pack followed by the UK, had very much to do with the increasing 'financialization' of those economies before the crisis.

Rating agencies often turned from being independent judges to accomplices, while regulators remained as innocent bystanders with a soft touch, insufficient instruments, and the wrong intellectual baggage. As for politicians, many of them believed—or very much wanted to believe—in the theory of efficient financial markets while often allowing themselves to be hijacked by financial lobbies awash with cash. It was a sad spectacle for democratic politics: poor judgement backed by ideology and lots of money.

The economics profession did not fare any better: it provided the ideas as ammunition for the political cannons. Whoever opposed the new orthodoxy was treated as ignorant or backward, to say the least. Modern economics—and the university departments practising it—showed little tolerance for alternative views. Even today, several years after the crash, the economics curriculums have hardly changed in many universities. Apparently, the power of inertia is very strong in the academic world.

When a large part of the banking system in the advanced economies came under state control, as a result of money being pumped into the system to keep banks alive, a whole ideological construct suffered a major blow. How does one reconcile neo-liberal ideology with the state coming to the rescue of financial markets that are the flag bearer of globalized capitalism? And how can one justify in political terms the privatization of large profits before the crisis, followed by the socialization of risks and losses when reality struck? This is not exactly the deal that advocates of liberalization and deregulation had prepared us for. The political effects may take a long time to unwind, especially since neo-liberalism had enjoyed such broad cross-party support in many countries before the crisis. The decline of trust in institutions and politicians is, however, already a generalized phenomenon contributing to the rise of anti-systemic parties in many countries. It is not unrelated to the bursting of the bubble and the way it has been handled since.

The countries within the euro were totally unprepared for such a crisis. But they were also very unlucky since the first big test for the new common currency came with the biggest financial crisis of the Western world for almost eighty years. The bursting of the big bubble had an international and a European dimension, inside and outside the eurozone. But the problem was much bigger for the countries sharing the common currency. They had a currency without a state, in other words without the institutions and policy instruments that would be essential to deal with such a crisis. Some people had truly believed that in the postmodern world in which they thought they lived, markets and money could do without the state, while others, the more sober ones, had simply hoped that nothing dramatic would happen as Europeans slowly built up fences to protect their new currency.

When the crisis reached the eurozone through the banks in close embrace with the sovereigns, it was painfully realized that there was no political authority with discretionary power to act on behalf of the eurozone—only constraining rules on national governments to prevent moral hazard and a slow and cumbersome intergovernmental system of decision-making, with the Commission unable to speak up for the common interest and be heard. There was no lender of last resort since the ECB was prevented from doing so under the treaty (at least no lender of last resort to governments), no single regulator or a common resolution regime to deal with financial institutions in trouble, no common budget with a size that could make a difference, and no automatic transfers between member states. Individual members had limited instruments at their disposal, no exchange rate instrument to deal directly with external imbalances, and no possibility to default on their debt. Last but not least, there was no provision for exit. Not surprisingly, political leaders in the eurozone found it extremely difficult to develop a coherent response to the crisis following the (unavoidable?) state of denial in the beginning. New instruments had to be created and legal rules to be interpreted in a rather creative fashion in order to deal with a systemic crisis that had been completely off the radar of the architects of the Maastricht Treaty.

At the same time, the crisis revealed fundamental weaknesses in individual eurozone countries as panic spread and markets became very risk-averse, which is exactly the opposite of what they had been until then. There were considerable differences among countries, although the bottom line was the same: they had all lived for too long on borrowed time and money.[11] And when the money ran out as markets seized up, the moment of truth came. The list of countries in trouble grew longer as the crisis deepened. The crisis was, of course, not confined to the eurozone, but countries outside had more instruments at their disposal, such as the UK which ended up nationalizing a very large part of its banking sector. Others, such as Hungary and Romania as well as the Baltic countries, were simply not systemic enough to affect the rest.

The worst case in the eurozone was, undoubtedly, Greece with a budget deficit exceeding 15 per cent of GDP in 2009, after successive revisions of the official figures, a big deficit being added to an already huge public debt of more than 130 per cent of GDP, an equally large current account deficit denoting a loss of competitiveness on a big scale, as well as a credibility deficit since Greece's partners realized that Greek politicians had been for some time economical with the truth and creative in the use of statistics—perhaps with the connivance of Brussels insiders and others elsewhere who were loath to spoil a good party or at the very least reticent about treading on other people's national toes.

The Greek case was an extreme example of a country living beyond its means, with the state accumulating ever growing debts and taking advantage of low interest rates under the protective umbrella of the euro, while its economy became increasingly uncompetitive through large increases of wages and salaries, low productive investment, and very few reforms. But Greece was not a unique problem inside the eurozone. Ireland and Spain had big construction bubbles for which banks—both domestic and from other EU countries and also the US—were eagerly providing the necessary liquidity, while regulators looked on and domestic politicians did (at best) nothing to stop them. Many cases of crony capitalism were later discovered in post-mortems. In Ireland and Spain, public deficits were not the problem: fiscal policy had been very prudent during the early boom years of the euro (Graph 3.6). Instead, the problem was private debt bubbles together with a progressive loss of competitiveness, clearly manifested in growing current account deficits. Little Cyprus followed a few years later with a big banking bubble of its own.

Portugal was different: its economy had been languishing for years, because it had failed to replace its old competitive advantage in textiles and footwear, lost to cheaper products from eastern Europe and Asia, with new ones in other sectors of the economy. Portugal was to a large extent the victim of enlargement and globalization and, when the crisis struck, markets became more apprehensive about Portugal's capacity to service its debt which was, however, relatively small by Greek standards.

With more than ten years of economic stagnation and having failed to adjust to an ever more competitive global environment, Italy was like Portugal writ large, but without big current account deficits. Italy also had an oversized public debt second only to Greece as a percentage of GDP and the third largest in the world in absolute figures. In the past, Italian governments had repeatedly resorted to devaluations of the national currency in order to restore lost competitiveness and they had always found it difficult to manage public finances in a usually gridlocked political system with much corruption. Italy was also a divided country, with a developed north and a heavily subsidized south always lagging behind. When market attention turned to Italy, having already swept through some of the smaller countries, everybody knew that this could be the litmus test for the survival of the eurozone. Italy was too big to fail, but also too big to save.

Not surprisingly, the crisis was not confined to the economic sphere—and how could it be, given the scale of the crisis? National political systems experienced great difficulty in handling a big and prolonged economic crisis with banks in deep trouble and unemployment on the rise, under intense pressure from financial markets on an everyday basis coupled with the pressure coming from European partners who provided the much-needed credit. In the process, all kinds of skeletons were revealed in national cupboards: political gridlock and administrative inefficiencies, clientelism, and corruption. The mix varied from country to country, but no political system came out unscathed in those countries severely affected by the financial crisis.

Behind them all stood France, the country that had led European integration for many years, yet a country increasingly disillusioned with the course that European integration was taking and very much apprehensive about the whole process of globalization. French un-happiness had been manifested at the referendum on the Maastricht Treaty back in 1992, and later on, more loudly and decisively, with the rejection of the constitutional treaty in another referendum. When the crisis hit the eurozone and market attention shifted from one country to the next, the shadow of France loomed large on the economic and political backdrop.[12]

A rich country with a quality of life (for many of its inhabitants at least) which is the envy of a good number of Europeans and others, with one of the best welfare systems, France was not doing well in terms of growth and employment. German macroeconomic perform-ance was the benchmark and France got relatively low marks in comparison to Germany in the years after the introduction of the euro, especially as regards employment figures. Furthermore, its big banks had gone global with high leverage and high risk exposure that were revealed after the bubble burst. At the peak of the crisis, French government officials lost much sleep over a possible downgrade of French sovereign debt by rating agencies that several French politi-cians had the habit of denouncing in public (and not always for the wrong reasons), fearing that France might be the next victim of panic sweeping the bond markets. Would France be able or willing to adjust to the terms of reference of a monetary union in which France was not calling the shots? Today, we are still waiting for the answer.

## Innocence lost

In previous European exchange rate arrangements, Germany had become the de facto leader with a strong emphasis on price stability on which it had repeatedly refused to compromise under pressure from its partners. The regional system broke down essentially each time some of the partners decided they were no longer willing or able to adjust their policy priorities to those set by the leader. Countries with relatively small and open economies, tied to the German mast, had little choice in practice. It was therefore up to France and Italy— also the UK when it chose to take part—to decide whether and for how long they would follow the German lead.[13]

But with monetary union, it was meant to be different: monetary policy would be decided at European level and there were common rules to coordinate and constrain national economic policies. There was perhaps also an implicit assumption in the beginning that other European countries would become like Germany in terms of its strong stance on inflation and deficits, or, even less plausibly, that Germany would be willing to meet them halfway.

Neither of the two worked in practice. The coordination mechanism set up by the treaty was not very effective. In fact, Germany and France were themselves quick to flout the rules concerning budget deficits in 2003—when Germany still ran large deficits because of reunification—and had those rules changed accordingly, thus confirming the suspicion that common rules were only binding for lesser mortals. And then, Greek politicians began to turn creative public accounting into a science, allegedly with the help of Goldman Sachs among others.[14] If the so-called Stability and Growth Pact had been implemented properly, it might have prevented the Greek public debt crisis. But it would not have prevented the Spanish and Irish bubbles, which were privately generated. The architects of Maastricht had not provided for such an eventuality.

We now know that financial systems are not self-regulating and that banks and other lenders can often be bad judges of the quality of debts they are willing to provide and of the general economic environment as well. How on earth could anybody think that German and Greek sovereign debt carried just about the same risk, as they were perceived by their lenders to do for years? But lenders also had a respectable excuse since regulators treated any kind of sovereign debt in Europe as zero risk. And how could they not have detected the property bubble in Ireland, or realized that some motorways in Spain led nowhere and new airports had hardly any passengers to fly to or from? It was not much better with easy loans provided to the Baltics that had fed the domestic bubble there, not to mention complex securities and derivatives that banks kept in their portfolios without having any real clue about what they contained. To be fair, European lenders were by no means the *most* reckless players in this dangerous game. They had strong competition from the other side of the Atlantic.

Now, we also know that common rules in an intergovernmental setting may not be at all sufficient in ensuring compliance, also that overall debt may be a much more important criterion and constraint for national budgetary policies than the ephemeral annual deficit criterion (3 per cent of GDP) that used to be employed under the Maastricht rules. The right combination of rules and discretion jointly exercised in a context of shared sovereignty may be difficult to define and politically even more difficult to implement. But hopefully, we have learned something from the experience of the early years of the euro.

Another thing we should have learned is that persistent current account imbalances in an incomplete monetary union do matter a great deal. The sudden reversal of private capital flows inside the eurozone when the crisis hit had much more in common with what had happened in East Asia during the big financial crisis back in 1997, or to countries of central and eastern Europe at the same time as the crisis hit the eurozone, than the way in which the US monetary union reacts to similar shocks affecting individual states. The irreversibility of monetary union cannot be guaranteed with an emasculated central bank, a few common rules, and many public statements. It needs much more, and this is something that Europeans have been learning the hard way in recent years.

True, these lessons and many more were still to be learned and fully digested when the European Commission published its communication in May 2008[15] in anticipation of the tenth anniversary of the euro. It was still very much upbeat in its assessment, despite the fact that the financial crisis was already gathering pace in the United States. But Europe was different and immune, was it not? At least, this is what European officialdom wanted to believe at the time—and most political leaders as well. In a celebratory mood, the European Commission produced a long list of positive developments associated with the common currency, while also admittedly expressing concern about persisting inflation divergence and current account imbalances as well as stressing the need to improve cross-border arrangements in crisis prevention. But things were very much under control, the European Commission reassured us complacently, and judged the euro to be a 'resounding success'. It was like tempting fate, the ultimate hubris, before disaster struck.

# 4

# Whose Rules and Whose Adjustment?

## Some 'unthinkables' happen

It has been the biggest crisis of European integration since the very beginning, a crisis that has put into question the survival of the common currency and much more. For all those who believed that disintegration, once started, would be like a stone rolling downhill, the good news is that the euro is still alive and with more members than when the crisis started. The bad news, however, is that Europe has paid a huge price in economic and political terms, and we are not at the end of it yet.

When, late in 2009, the international financial crisis turned into a full-scale European crisis—a crisis of the eurozone in particular—many banks across Europe were already in deep trouble. What changed then was that sovereigns began to get into trouble as well. Financial markets that apparently had not thought of risk for a long time began to realize that some sovereigns were over-indebted and that others would soon become so if they chose to rescue their banks. Rescuing their economies from a deep recession provoked by the crisis would further add to public debt.

The bursting of the bubble left many European banks vulnerable and the choice for national regulators and politicians was between letting them go under, with a high risk of contagion and a consequent financial meltdown, or saving them with national taxpayers' money, thus accepting the logic that these banks were too big (or too systemic) to fail. Given the size of the financial sector, a multiple of national GDP in some countries, saving the banks meant a big cost for the national budget and the national debt as well. Some of these banks were too big to fail, but also too big to save. When private and public debt becomes fungible, the problem shifts from one to the other. In Europe's monetary union, as it was then, saving the banks remained a national responsibility while member states no longer had access to a lender of last resort and the printing press. Hence, they had the worst of all possible worlds. This is precisely what made the big difference between the eurozone and the rest.

It also worked the other way round, namely when the state got into trouble, experiencing difficulties in servicing and refinancing its debt, and as a consequence domestic banks suffered because they were left with large amounts of debt of now dubious quality. In the era of globalization, we were thus reminded that the ties between national treasuries and private banks with headquarters in the country concerned had remained (surprisingly?) very close. At the peak of the crisis, it looked like a deadly embrace between some sovereigns and domestic banks.

The combination of national weakness and European incapacity (or unwillingness) to deal with a big debt and a banking crisis led market operators to start thinking the erstwhile unthinkable, namely that sovereign debt was not sacrosanct and also that Europe's monetary union might not be after all like a traditional Catholic marriage without the possibility of divorce. Once the risk of sovereign default and/or individual country exits from the euro— and even of a general break-up—began to look like a real possibility, capital flows were completely reversed, now moving from south to north and from east to west (or from periphery to centre) in search of safe havens.

Country risk thus reappeared within the monetary union, and the nationality of a potential borrower, state or private, influenced in a big way the rate of interest charged. This made a mockery of monetary union and risked turning into a self-fulfilling prophecy—and we know from experience that markets are very good at self-fulfilling prophecies. Constantly rising bond yields for the worst-afflicted countries, reinforced by contagion effects, raised the costs of borrowing and thus further strengthened the doubts about solvency, until the cost of new borrowing became prohibitive. And then, access to markets was effectively lost.

During this crisis, Ireland was the best example of how bankrupt banks can (almost) bankrupt a state, while Greece was the model for how it could work the other way round. Spain was closer to Ireland, and Italy to Greece—though on a much bigger scale—with Portugal somewhere in between. In the famous opening of Tolstoy's *Anna Karenina*, unhappy families are unhappy each in their own way, and this was very true of the situation prevailing in southern Europe and Ireland during the early years of the crisis. Greece's unhappiness was the first to become public, and it was rather shocking in its gory details. It thus served (conveniently?) as the basis for the official European narrative of the crisis and the strategy that followed.

The European strategy took a long time to develop following an early collective state of denial in which the Europeans first wanted to believe that the crisis would not cross the Atlantic and when unfortunately it did, that the problem in the eurozone would be confined to one country, Greece, with as little European action as possible and much penance on behalf of the Greeks who deserved their fate. As hard reality gradually dawned upon Europeans, many 'unthinkables' happened. The aim was to save individual member countries and indirectly the banks. And in doing this, political leaders thought they were saving the euro. These 'unthinkables' included policy measures and institutional reforms that had been considered beyond the realm of the politically and economically feasible only a few years previously. But crises make the unthinkable happen.[1] A more systemic approach to the crisis only began in 2012 and it has been a slow and painful process ever since.

As a result, the euro structure is very different today from the original Maastricht design and it is much more robust as a result— or so the optimists would have us believe. Meanwhile, some national economies and political systems have gone through big changes and a great deal of pain. The crisis swept the southern and western coasts of Europe. It also reached the eastern hinterland, causing much damage as far as the Baltics, although this was much less in the news in the main European capitals largely because the countries concerned had not yet adopted the euro and were therefore much less of a systemic risk.

We shall attempt to draw a provisional balance sheet about the way in which Europe has managed (or mismanaged) the crisis during the first six years or so, trying to go beyond sterile numbers and innocent averages. Who decided, who paid the bill, and who took the risk in a multinational and highly interdependent system of semi-sovereign actors, when large and painful adjustment was required? What are the broader political implications within and without, including the internal balance of power and relations with the rest of the world? And what does all this imply for the European project and Europe as a whole? They are questions that will be addressed in this and subsequent chapters.

## Bailouts that dare not speak their name

Bailouts of member countries of the eurozone were not meant to happen. They were in fact outlawed by the Maastricht Treaty in order to avoid moral hazard which, in simple words, means the risk of irresponsible behaviour when you know that, if things turn for the worse, you can always rely on others to come to your rescue. The Germans have strong views about moral hazard and they are not at all convinced about the reliability or rectitude of some of their partners, hence their strong insistence on common rules and controls designed precisely to prevent moral hazard.

We now all know that the Maastricht system did not work as expected, although everybody may not agree about what exactly went wrong. As panic spread, following the bursting of the bubble, financial markets began to doubt the capacity of one and then more members of the eurozone to service their debts. Indirectly, they also began to doubt the survival of the European Monetary Union. Greece was the first country to effectively lose access to markets in the early months of 2010. Soon afterwards, Ireland and Portugal followed. The contagion effects later spread to the bigger countries, namely Spain and Italy; even France was affected. But by then, the eurozone was ready to resort to more powerful instruments in order to stem a crisis that was already reaching the core.

When a country in the eurozone lost access to markets, the choice was stark for the government concerned. Should it try to adopt drastic measures at home without really knowing how far it would need to go to placate panic-driven markets? Should it let banks default or go for public debt restructuring, which is a more polite word for default? Should it consider instead the nuclear option of exiting the euro, thus trying to recover some of the policy instruments lost? Or, should it try to persuade its euro partners to circumvent the rules and bail it out in the name of European solidarity, while also politely reminding them that this way they would be saving the euro and their banks as well? The collective instinct of survival prevailed in the end. Or was it rather the interest of the more powerful countries that prevailed? We shall return to this sensitive question later. The result in any case was a series of national bailout programmes that dared not speak their name for the simple reason that they had been technically outlawed. Brussels and national lawyers helped to provide the legal formula once the political decision was taken. The bailout programmes included harsh domestic measures for the debtor countries.

The first one was for Greece: a three-year programme of €110 billion agreed in May 2010, a new world record in terms of financial assistance going to a modest-sized economy. The second one was for Ireland in November of the same year for a total amount of €86 billion, following strong arm-twisting of the Irish by their eurozone partners and the ECB.[2] Then Portugal followed with €78 billion in May 2011. A big taboo was thus broken and Europeans were forced to submit to hard reality—and repeatedly so. A second programme of €130 billion was agreed for Greece in 2012 and a third of €86 billion in

August 2015. Greece thus became a permanent feature of the European crisis in contrast to Ireland and Portugal which have already exited their respective programmes. In the meantime, Cyprus had been granted €10 billion in March 2013, a relatively large amount for the size of the country, and Spain had been given a credit line of €100 billion in order to recapitalize its banks. Spain has since then successfully exited its different and milder programme on schedule, and Cyprus has now done the same.

What happened in all cases was that financial flows through official channels replaced private flows that were now going in the opposite direction. Thus, Greece substituted the biggest part of its debt previously owed to private creditors with debt owed to governments and international institutions, while Ireland and Spain bailed out their banks (and indirectly the creditors of those banks, domestic and European) with money they borrowed from other European governments and international institutions. In other words, national bailout programmes were also indirectly bailout programmes for banks.

The eurozone intervened when the countries concerned could no longer handle the problem on their own. The direct cost of rescuing Irish banks after the bubble burst was close to 40 per cent of Irish GDP, although the final cost is expected to be smaller after the state has sold nationalized bank assets. This cost fell on domestic taxpayers and the Irish state was forced to seek external financial assistance through the bailout programme. In relative terms, the direct cost of rescuing banks was smaller for other countries. However, if the indirect effects in terms of output and jobs lost are also included, the overall bill for the crisis becomes very big indeed for Europe as a whole.

No country was spared, although some were much more affected than others depending on the relative size and past recklessness of their banks. For countries outside the eurozone with their own currency and central bank, the big difference was that they had more instruments at their disposal to deal with the problem compared to euro members with their hands tied. During the early phase of the crisis, the UK benefited from much lower interest rates than Spain, both countries experiencing a serious banking crisis at home and comparable levels of spiralling public debt. The explanation was rather simple: unlike Spain, the UK borrowed in its own currency and had access to a lender of last resort, namely the Bank of England—and that made a big difference.[3] It is also worth adding that the UK proved to be much more decisive and effective in dealing with its banking crisis than many of its Continental partners.

Breaking one taboo sometimes acts as an incentive for breaking others as well, like a release mechanism for all kinds of inhibitions. The early bailout programmes were strictly intergovernmental agreements involving the debtor country and the other members of the eurozone; the Commission was really absent, not to mention the European Parliament. Governments took over as a group and threw the celebrated Community method of decision-making out of the window. They started with bilateral loans. Later on, the mechanisms created to deal with crises, which had been previously exorcised as the agent of moral hazard, were again based on intergovernmental agreements outside EU law. They were meant to ensure ultimate control for creditors. The same remains true today of the European Stability Mechanism (ESM) established in September 2012 as a permanent firewall for the eurozone with a maximum lending capacity of €500 billion. This was a crucial step in safeguarding the stability of the common currency, yet in the form of an intergovernmental organization based in Luxembourg and operating under international law.

In fact, creditors went even further. They brought in the IMF to contribute part of the financial assistance and to be directly involved in the surveillance of the implementation of the programmes, together with the European Commission and the ECB, in what came to be known as the troika. For a monetary union that aspires to become a political union, bringing in the IMF to help deal with an internal problem of the union was hardly flattering and certainly not reassuring as regards its officially proclaimed ambitions. Would the United States call in the IMF to help if Louisiana lost access to markets? We then discovered what we should perhaps have known all along, notably that Greece and Portugal were indeed very different from Louisiana.

It was a big blow to the credibility of the European project and its crown jewel, the euro. Adding insult to injury, the Germans, by far the most powerful among the creditors, made it abundantly clear that one important reason they insisted on the IMF being involved was that they did not trust the European Commission with the task of designing and executing the adjustment programme that came with the financial assistance to the country in need. They went even further by repeatedly trying to use the IMF to impose their own point of view on the other members of the troika.[4] Neither European institutions nor the IMF came out stronger from this experience, to put it mildly.

Adjustment programmes were meant to restore fiscal sustainability through rapid reduction of budget deficits, which in most cases were in turn the product of the crisis. Adjustment programmes were also meant to restore competitiveness through a comprehensive and in places extremely detailed list of structural measures to be adopted by the borrowing country and closely monitored by the respective troika. Devaluation was, of course, not an option inside the monetary union and countries with adjustment programmes had to go through the much more difficult route of internal devaluation by trying to push wages and prices down.

In the first Greek programme, the terms imposed by the creditors were not only comprehensive and detailed—to the point of micromanagement—but also punitive and economically unrealistic—*pour décourager les autres*. But it did not really work. Programmes for other countries followed, while the terms for Greece have been repeatedly revised in order to make the servicing of the debt more palatable for Greece's imploding economy and also make it (look) more sustainable.

In the long process of integration, Europeans have accepted, albeit sometimes reluctantly or even inconsistently, that shared sovereignty is indeed the price to pay for a high degree of interdependence and open borders. New candidates have also realized that the price of membership comes with tens of thousands of pages of legislation that they need to incorporate en masse without asking too many questions—perhaps just a few about the correct translation of terms into their own language.

Countries with adjustment programmes during the financial crisis were in for a new experience:[5] it proved highly damaging for the domestic political class and also in terms of popular trust in democratic institutions, in some countries more than others. Domestic politicians had to accept and implement—lock, stock, and barrel—a comprehensive economic programme, including many unpopular and often ideologically inspired measures, that was partly if not entirely designed by their creditors on a take-it-or-leave-it basis to be monitored by the respective troika: a kind of latter-day Europeanization decided by those who controlled the purse. National ministers of debtor countries were obliged to negotiate with officials from the three institutions, who were essentially accountable only to governments of the creditor countries, and those hapless ministers were often seen at home as obeying orders in order to secure the next tranche of financial assistance. Hundreds of pages of new legislation had to be bulldozed through national parliaments with precious little time for debate. It was not exactly a feast of democracy.

How much economic sovereignty (or democracy) can you afford, if you are bankrupt? Countries with experience of IMF programmes in the past knew that the answer was 'Not much'. European countries with adjustment programmes, in or out of the eurozone, renewed that experience in recent years with representatives of European institutions also being directly involved—and that made a big difference for relations inside the Union as a whole. Insufficient domestic ownership of the respective adjustment programme, coupled with poor implementation, of course made matters much worse. The contrast between the Irish and the Greek experience is indeed telling: members of the troika needed heavy police escort in Athens but hardly any in Dublin.

And when all else failed, capital controls were introduced in Cyprus in 2013, and two years later in Greece, to stem deposit outflows from domestic banks when confidence hit rock bottom. Capital controls used to be another unthinkable inside the monetary union and Europe's internal market as well, but no longer.

## One taboo proves harder to break

When a big bubble bursts, as it did in the United States and Europe in a series of explosions starting in 2007, what is left behind is a large pile of debt, both private and public.[6] With the major exception of the UK and the Scandinavians, Europeans have been much slower than the Americans in, first, recognizing the problem and, second, trying to deal with it. They have resorted instead to the time-honoured tradition of kicking the can down the road, buying time, perhaps also hoping for a miracle to happen. They have, of course, been terrified of the political cost. The Americans were more effective in dealing early on with their banking crisis through bailouts followed by re-regulation as well as restructuring and recapitalization of banks in distress. But they also proved much more reluctant to deal with the big 'house of debt'[7] accumulated by US households since the early 1980s. This attitude reflects, one presumes, the balance of power that exists between creditors and debtors in the United States, even more so in Europe.

Attitudes have certainly evolved during the crisis and new European legislation makes it clear that in the future bank shareholders and creditors, even large depositors, will be expected to bear the main burden when things go wrong: bail-ins of shareholders, creditors, and depositors, as the jargon goes, rather than bailouts with taxpayers' money will be the rule. Who pays when things go wrong? That is the key political question and it has been so throughout the crisis, applying not only to the distribution of costs between bank shareholders, creditors, and depositors on the one hand and taxpayers on the other, but also between countries. Not surprisingly, it has been very divisive and the interests of the strongest have mostly prevailed. The new legislation meant to deal with moral hazard, as it applies to banks, took effect on 1 January 2016. But the Single Resolution Fund that is meant to deal with any banking crisis in the future will only become operative some years later.

Another reason for Europe's unwillingness to deal more decisively with the banking crisis and the large debt overhang has to do with the fragmentation of public responsibility in this domain until very recently along national lines, despite the high degree of integration of banks already reached in the marketplace before the crisis. Europe's slow and reluctant response also has to do with the way decisions were (and still are) taken (or not taken) at EU level: too cumbersome a process and with too many veto players.[8] Those representing the interests of creditors have been by far the most powerful veto players in the eurozone during the crisis and they are the ones who have been calling the shots. In this respect, the crucial difference between the US and the European monetary unions is that in Europe creditors and debtors have been divided mostly along national lines in a still embryonic political system in which the protagonists are the member states, whose role has been accentuated as a result of the crisis.

Some decisions taken in the early years of the crisis have left an indelible imprint on subsequent developments. One of them is surely the initial decision about the way to deal with the Greek problem, the biggest and most enduring of all. When the true figures were revealed in the late months of 2009, Greece was shown to have a close-to-impossible combination of public debt, budget and current account deficits. Given the size of economic adjustment required, made much worse by a very weak administration and a dysfunctional political system, the awkward question at the time was whether the country was illiquid or insolvent—hardly ever an easy question to answer. The staff of the IMF (some at least) suggested that Greece was insolvent and hence they were unwilling to get involved in a programme unless the problem of debt was dealt with. They were, however, overruled by the board where Europeans continue to have a very strong presence and have had a monopoly in appointing the managing director since the birth of the IMF. The collective decision of the eurozone followed suit:

Greece was declared illiquid not insolvent, hence the first bailout programme agreed in May 2010.

Hardly anybody, including notably the ECB, was prepared at the time to contemplate the alternative, partly for reasons of principle but mainly because they were not ready to take the risk concerning the effects of a Greek debt restructuring on European banks, some of which were Greece's biggest creditors. European banks were still very fragile, markets were panicking, and European officials wanted to avoid a European Lehman. According to figures from the Basel-based BIS, the total exposure of Western banks to Greece in the third quarter of 2009 was more than US$210 billion, out of which US$79 billion was for French banks and US$43 billion for German banks.[9] It was in this context that the decision was finally taken to proceed with a Greek bailout. It was accompanied by an adjustment programme based on unrealistic assumptions and projections that quickly proved to be completely off the mark, and not only because of procrastination or ineptitude on the Greek side. The result was that the Greek economy imploded.

The sanctity of European sovereign debt, repeatedly proclaimed by European political leaders and central bankers, was, however, violated later on through the restructuring of Greek debt held by the private sector as part of the second programme. This happened in early 2012. In the meantime, many foreign holders of this debt had the opportunity to offload large chunks of it, thus cutting their losses. They did exactly the same with much of the sovereign debt of the euro periphery, taking advantage of ECB purchases of government bonds in secondary markets. Between the third quarter of 2009 and the fourth quarter of 2012, total exposure of French and German banks to the euro periphery had been reduced by 38 per cent and 51 per cent respectively. German banks proved faster in this race, which may also help to explain the increasingly more assertive attitude adopted by German governments as the crisis unfolded.

When the restructuring of Greek sovereign debt finally took place, Greek and Cypriot banks and pension funds were among the main victims. In fact, the restructuring of Greek debt was largely responsible for the banking crisis in Cyprus that ensued—as well as a big negative wealth effect amounting to close to 25 per cent of Cyprus' GDP—while other European banks had already insulated themselves from the contagion effect. And Greek banks, which had not done so, or to put it more correctly, *could* not have done so, saw their capital being wiped out and then had to be recapitalized with European money borrowed again through the Greek state. Thus, the net effect of the haircut on overall Greek public debt was significantly reduced.[10] And because this debt, now held almost entirely by Greece's eurozone partners and the IMF, continued to be unsustainable as the Greek economy sank, interest rates charged on this debt were reduced and maturities prolonged by Greece's creditors, while the latter continued all along to proclaim the sanctity of debt repayment.

Approximately 70 per cent of the total financial assistance provided to Greece through the two bailout programmes of 2010 and 2012 has been spent on servicing, repaying, and restructuring old debts, and another 20 per cent has been spent on the recapitalization of banks following sovereign debt restructuring: a policy of 'extend and pretend', as critics prefer to call it,[11] which will continue with the third programme agreed in 2015. There is, of course, something surreal in all this, although explainable in terms of the domestic politics of the key creditor countries, Germany in particular, where politicians have never dared to tell their citizens the bitter truth, namely that the money they lent to other countries in the eurozone was also money to save their own banks and some of it at least may never be paid back. European taxpayers and the IMF have thus become the main holders of Greece's public debt which is now much bigger as a percentage of GDP than when the crisis started for the very simple reason that GDP has collapsed (Graph 3.6).

In September 2008, when the financial crisis was at its peak, although it still remained a national problem within the eurozone, the Irish government at the time decided to guarantee all the deposits and debts of heavily exposed Irish banks and their subsidiaries abroad.

Its successors came to regret this decision—and Irish taxpayers even more so, since they are the ones who have to foot the bill. More than two years later, another government in Ireland tried to restructure the bank debt owed to senior creditors, mostly big banks in other European countries, but the ECB threatened to cut off all liquidity to Irish banks if the government went ahead: a threat that, if acted upon, would have led to sudden death for the Irish banking system. Subsequent efforts by the Irish along those lines continued to meet a wall of resistance from their official European creditors.[12]

The ECB was concerned about the effect that such a bail-in would have on the still fragile European banking system. Total exposure of Western banks to Ireland was much bigger than their exposure to Greece: US$193 billion for German banks, US$192 billion for UK banks, and US$74 billion for US banks in the third quarter of 2009. In opposing the bail-in of other big creditors—mostly European—to Irish banks, the ECB had the support of political leaders from countries where those creditors came from, notably Germany and the UK but also France. In less diplomatic language, one might argue that the ECB had mostly the interest of creditors in mind. It was once again deemed proper that the taxpayer in Ireland should pay for bad loans given by Irish banks with money they had borrowed mainly from other European banks.

Yet, when the banking crisis in Cyprus led to a European/IMF programme for the island state in March 2013, that programme included a bail-in provision for bond-holders and larger depositors of one of the big Cypriot banks. Other bail-ins of banks followed in Slovenia and Portugal later on, although not including deposits. European attitudes on the subject had clearly evolved in the meantime, while European banks had become stronger and less worried about possible contagion effects from the crisis in Cyprus. It also so happened that Russian oligarchs and other more ordinary mortals were among the main victims of the haircut. Cyprus was accused of operating for years as a convenient offshore centre for Russian money (if so, was it really the only one in Europe or elsewhere?) and it had in fact first tried Russia for help before turning to its eurozone partners. Geopolitics is complicated in that part of the world. And double standards are not so rare in European politics.

Six years into the eurozone crisis, public debt as a percentage of GDP is now considerably higher than it was when the crisis erupted. Public debt for the eurozone as a whole rose from 69 per cent of GDP in 2008 to 94 per cent in 2014 (Graph 3.6). France is very close to the eurozone average having also gone through a large increase in its public debt during this period (almost 30 percentage points). Belgium is once again above the 100 per-cent mark. It thus happened even in the best of families: the rescue of domestic banks, together with measures to soften the recessionary impact of the crisis, has been very costly for the public purse. But has the UK, outside the eurozone, done much better? Public debt in the UK more than doubled as a percentage of GDP between 2007 and 2014, reaching 89 per cent. Even in Germany, the preacher of austerity, public debt reached 75 per cent in 2014, which is much higher than the Maastricht mark (60 per cent) for good behaviour.

Of course, the situation is much worse on the periphery. The figures for Greece were 109 per cent in 2008, 127 per cent in 2009, and 177 per cent in 2014. Italy followed with a public debt at 132 per cent of GDP in 2014, and Portugal with 130 per cent. As for Ireland, its public debt jumped from 24 per cent in 2007 to 110 per cent in 2014: the cost of rescuing Irish banks and dealing with the collateral damage on the economy has been truly monumental. And Spain did not do much better either: its public debt rose from 36 per cent of GDP in 2007 to 98 per cent in 2014. Meanwhile, deleveraging in the private sector across Europe has continued at a very slow pace. The champions of private debt are to be found mostly in the north and not in the south of Europe, with Germany being the main exception and a paragon of virtue (Graph 3.5).

As long as growth in Europe continues to be slow and inflation remains close to zero, even if interest rates also remain low thus reducing the cost of servicing, the debt problem will simply not go away. It will be like an albatross hanging from the neck of younger generations of Europeans. The fact that Europe has become divided between creditor and debtor countries during the crisis certainly does not help. The fact that a large part of sovereign debt is now owed to governments and European institutions does not help much either.

## Austerity rules

Many rules have changed and many 'unthinkables' have indeed happened during this long and deep crisis. The governance of the euro has changed as a result and relations between the eurozone and the rest of the EU as well. According to the official narrative adopted—or rather imposed by creditor countries and Germany in particular as a corollary to national bailout programmes and the setting up of new common financial mechanisms—the crisis had been the product of fiscal laxity, leading to large budget deficits and unsustainable national debts, translated in turn into ever-growing current account deficits. Common rules in the eurozone's decentralized system of national fiscal policies had proved to be weak and very poorly implemented, so the story went. This story did fit Greece well, and to a limited extent also Portugal, but Ireland and Spain not at all. However, political narratives can often afford to take liberties with the truth which is inconveniently more complex than they pretend it to be.

Consistent with the official narrative, new legislation was introduced in successive batches in order to make the rules of economic surveillance for eurozone countries much stricter and sanctions stronger and more automatic. The aim was the same as before: budget deficits should be below the 3 per-cent GDP limit, while public debts above 60 per cent had to be progressively reduced. In fact, the so-called Fiscal Compact of 2012 went much further, requiring member countries to introduce domestic legislation, ideally enshrined in national constitutions, which would ensure balanced budgets in perpetuity. Thus, structural deficits (an economic term to denote fiscal deficits adjusted for the economic cycle, albeit still difficult to define and agree upon among economists) have hence acquired the force of law. Is it fiscal virtue in legal clothes or a kind of policy straitjacket in a European system that is turning into a madhouse?

Rules were made much stricter in order to discourage large public deficits and debts and thus reduce moral hazard in a currency union which was now being forced by events to establish jointly funded financial mechanisms to deal with crises. Present and potential creditors therefore wanted to make sure they would not be called upon in the future to bail out irresponsible partners: a perfectly legitimate concern, one might think. Yet, it apparently did not also occur to them to ensure that the burden of economic adjustment within the monetary union was more or less equally shared among member countries.

Symmetry of adjustment might have implied that countries would be called upon to take action in times of very low growth and zero inflation and/or when those countries also happened to run persistently large surpluses in their current account, instead of just waiting for deficit countries to deflate. No way, was the answer given. It was clear that in the eurozone's brave new world, Keynes has long been dead and forgotten. In the rather unkind words of Wolfgang Münchau of the *Financial Times*, 'German economists roughly fall into two groups: those who have not read Keynes, and those that have not understood Keynes.'[13] Perhaps it all boils down to deep cultural and historical differences as Jürgen Stark, former board member and chief economist of the ECB, argues.[14]

Admittedly, new legislation made provisions for correcting macroeconomic imbalances in individual countries. Such provisions are, however, much less constraining than those referring to budget deficits. Furthermore, the yellow alert is triggered when current account deficits, an indicator of a macroeconomic imbalance, reach 4 per cent of GDP, while the corresponding figure is 6 per cent for surplus countries. Presumably, that is because surpluses are considered better than deficits and also because it so happens that German surpluses (surprise, surprise!) had been for some years close to the 6 per-cent figure—and they are now above it. The European Commission, as the legal enforcer of these rules, has consistently shown remarkable understanding and tolerance for big German surpluses within the monetary union. The message is thus clear for all concerned.

Fiscal austerity became the name of the game at a time of economic slump in Europe that produced the Great Recession. Of course, most of the eurozone countries of the periphery had very little margin of manoeuvre in terms of fiscal policy. It is also true that fiscal consolidation was and still is required in many European countries and further afield. Ageing populations, rapidly rising health costs, unsustainable pension systems, and the large increase in sovereign debt resulting from bankrolling the banks after the bubble burst do not leave many governments with much of a choice in the medium and long term.

True, but this does not necessarily mean that the whole of Europe should have taken the road of fiscal contraction in conditions of low demand and scarce liquidity. The fiscal contraction imposed on European economies, especially between 2010 and 2012, was excessive and further aggravated the economic downturn: this is an almost consensus view among economists, while most of the exceptions are to be found among German economists.[15] But creditor countries begged to differ, and they were able to impose the rules and the overall economic strategy. Diplomatic gloves were off and big countries often muscled their way around in ways that European councils had not been accustomed to in the past. The European balance of power game thus got much rougher.

The new rules for economic governance in the eurozone[16] were adopted through intergovernmental channels: creditor countries, Germany very visibly so, were in the driver's seat. This is true of how decisions in general have been taken throughout the crisis, with relatively little role left for institutions such as the European Commission or Parliament. This is what academics often refer to as 'executive federalism'.[17] On the other hand, the Commission has been given an increased role in the monitoring and implementation of new rules. The Commission in the guise of policeman enforcing unpopular rules is arguably a mixed blessing for an institution that serves in the best of times as an easy scapegoat for national governments.

The Fiscal Compact, officially known as the 'Treaty on Stability, Coordination and Governance in the Economic and Monetary Union', deserves special mention. It came into force on 1 January 2013 and at the time of writing it applied to twenty-five countries of the EU, not just the eurozone. This is in fact characteristic of other intergovern-mental agreements reached during the crisis with the aim of strength-ening the euro: all eurozone countries were naturally directly involved and some outside also voluntarily joined, although never the UK. The aim of the Fiscal Compact is to create internal automatic correction mechanisms within member countries that will ensure that EU fiscal rules are adhered to, strengthened by the threat of sanctions and with the European Commission in the now familiar role of the watchdog even more than before. The new treaty also provided for regular euro summits, thus taking another big step in endowing the eurozone with its own institutions.

The Commission has been given the right to request changes in national budgets before national parliaments have the chance to debate them, while the Commission's recommendations and fines can from now on be overturned only by a majority of member states. Thus, it was hoped that the sanctity of balanced budgets would be firmly established and room for wayward national behaviour appro-priately constrained. To quote Martin Wolf of the *Financial Times*: 'member countries are free to do precisely as they are told'![18] The new rules for economic governance are indeed playing a dangerous game with democracy.

Germany insisted that this was a precondition for giving the go-ahead for any kind of common financial mechanism, while the new treaty also helped indirectly to free the hand of the ECB to intervene more actively in support of banks and sovereigns. When the subject came to the European Council, the UK threatened to veto unless its financial institutions (for which, read 'the City') were excluded from new EU legislation. The answer it got then was that the rest would proceed instead with an intergovernmental treaty outside the EU legal framework, which is precisely what they did in the end. Thus, the threat of the UK veto foundered and the new treaty went ahead with twenty-five countries. Only the UK and the Czech Republic opted out, and the Czechs have also signed since then. This was a major turning point for relations between eurozone countries and the UK.

An intergovernmental treaty outside the EU legal framework, yet employing all the institutions and instruments of the Union in the pursuit of its stated objectives: it was an exercise in legal acrobatics essentially forced upon the rest by the threat of the UK veto, yet also very characteristic of how the European project evolved during the crisis. And there was more. The new treaty came into force not when all signatories had properly ratified it, as had been the practice until then, but as soon as a minimum of twelve members of the eurozone had done so. This could serve as a useful precedent for future treaty revisions in trying to circumvent veto threats and speed up the process of implementation.

The new treaty was driven through the labyrinth of the European decision-making process in record time, which clearly indicates that where there's a will there's a way, even within Europe's proverbially slow system, but only as long as a powerful leader makes sure that the will and the way are properly connected. In this mother of crises, Europe had found such a leader in Mrs Merkel, the German chancellor, although not everybody is so convinced of the wisdom of her European strategy, if indeed there was one behind the long series of cleverly crafted tactical moves.

But what happens when European legal rules come into collision with national political reality? Experience suggests that it is not always the latter that gives in, especially when bigger countries are involved. In 2015, the new fiscal rules went through a tough political stress test when the Commission and the Eurogroup were called upon to apply them to France and Italy among others. Creative interpretation of otherwise strict rules was then required to the obvious consternation of those who had designed them in the first place. But will such creative interpretation also apply to smaller countries and lesser mortals, or is it just the privilege of big ones?

## Structural reform with an ideological prefix

The other main component of the European strategy that gradually took shape in response to the crisis was structural reform. It was seen as the means to make national economies more competitive, although common rules were less binding than with respect to budget deficits. Structural reform is, of course, a mixed bag of very different measures, including the liberalization of services and the opening of closed professions, the elimination of administrative obstacles, pension reform, privatization, and the liberalization (usually meaning just deregulation) of labour markets. No doubt several European countries need nothing less than wide-ranging reforms to break the stranglehold of vested interests and also to correct institutional failure. How much can be imposed from outside in the name of Europeanization is, however, a moot point. National elites need to take ownership of such reforms, but existing elites are often part of the problem and not the solution. Can or should countries import a wide range of reforms from Brussels?

Even with the best will in the world, it is extremely difficult for any government to engage in a wide-ranging reform programme and fight with organized domestic interests to get it through while at the same time pursuing a very tight fiscal policy. It is perhaps no coincidence that labour reforms under Chancellor Schröder were introduced at a time when Germany was running large budget deficits, while subsidies to the citizens of former East Germany were as generous as ever. On the other hand, the gains from structural reform are mostly long term, while the political costs are immediate: a combination that most politicians want to avoid at all costs. The president of the European Commission, Mr Juncker, put it very aptly in his previous incarnation as prime minister of Luxembourg and also president of the Eurogroup: 'We all know what to do, we just don't know how to get re-elected after we've done it.'[19]

Proponents of structural reform start from the premise that a comprehensive programme of liberalization measures will open the economy to competition and thus increase efficiency, which in general terms may be correct but it is only part of the truth. In the real world, especially in a democracy, a great deal of political capital needs to be invested for structural reforms to become effective; hence, the need for targeting and prioritizing reforms.[20] This simple idea often seems to have escaped the attention of Brussels technocrats descending on national capitals with their baggage full of reform proposals and often with the zeal of missionaries.

And this is not the end of the story. Many of the structural measures appearing on Brussels' favoured list, notably labour market reforms and privatizations, have a strong ideological bias. In times when growing inequalities within countries are recognized to be closely linked not only to globalization and technological change but also to the weakening of collective bargaining and to labour market deregulation, European economic orthodoxy simply calls for more of the same, at a time when even the IMF is beginning to have doubts.[21] Europe has therefore ended up with a partisan programme for which there is precious little legitimacy in several of the countries directly concerned. This European orthodoxy has had a more wholesale and stricter application to countries going through adjustment programmes. Although the new rules for economic governance apply to everybody, there are much tighter rules and enforcement procedures for countries with adjustment programmes, including those outside the eurozone such as Hungary, Romania, and Latvia (before Latvia joined the euro).

'Beggars can't be choosers' would be perhaps too cynical an explanation. For countries of the eurozone that no longer have the option of devaluing and therefore need to go through an internal devaluation, more flexibility in the labour market was seen as the way to bring wages down and thus restore competitiveness. The measures included in their adjustment programmes therefore implied a much more flexible model of labour relations than those found in Germany,

Austria, or the Scandinavian countries for example. The weakening of collective agreements required from countries with adjustment pro- grammes, together with many other provisions included in these programmes, such as Sunday shopping for example, would have created little short of a political revolt in Germany. The official explan- ation is that differentiated measures are needed to deal with economic divergence in a monetary union. But is it the right policy, and how much democracy can or should be sacrificed on the altar of the euro?[22]

## Who runs the show?

National bailout programmes were considered as the instrument of last resort to rescue countries in trouble and European banks as well, while the new rules for economic governance were meant to prevent such crises from recurring in the future, thus also rendering the use of new financial mechanisms virtually unnecessary. Surely, there was logic in the argument, although in practice it was not powerful enough to convince and calm down markets that were increasingly concerned about sovereign risk and the deadly embrace between sovereigns and banks. The danger of sovereign insolvency turning into a self-fulfilling prophecy was very real, while financial fragmen- tation along national lines remained. This could not continue for very long, especially since the crisis had now reached the core.

When it came to the crunch, it was left to the ECB to calm down the 'animal spirits' of financial markets, and it did so by insistently (and insidiously?) stretching the limits of the legally and politically possible for a central bank that had been meant to act like a central bank in a straitjacket according to Maastricht rules. Instead, it ended up acting (within limits) as the lender of last resort for banks and sovereigns in the eurozone. In the process, it chose its steps and public statements very carefully, always sensitive to the prevailing political balance of power and economic orthodoxy, since the two often go together.

True, central bankers are meant to be non-political, but in the midst of an escalating crisis which threatened to blow apart the entire euro project—and not only that—and with no other institution in the eurozone capable of acting fast and decisively, the ECB was called upon repeatedly to perform difficult acts of acrobatics. It has been a fascinating spectacle to watch the masterly performance sometimes given by Europe's leading central banker. However, the ECB did not avoid making extremely sensitive political decisions nor did it avoid making political enemies. This therefore raises awkward questions about legitimacy in a monetary union in which there is really no political counterpart to the central bank (that is, if you exclude the German finance minister!).

The first big step was taken when the ECB started to lend on a big scale to European banks in trouble. It continued with the purchase of government bonds in secondary markets, thus trying to circumvent the legal prohibition of directly lending to governments. The main argument employed by the ECB in support of its operations was the need to restore the unity of financial markets and the credit channel within the monetary union that had suffered by strong market perception of country risk. And the ECB was always careful to insist on the link between fiscal consolidation and structural reform on the one hand and its own monetary interventions on the other, especially for countries benefiting the most from those interventions. It thus tried to mollify its critics among creditors by paying its respects to the main tenets of the prevailing economic orthodoxy in Europe.

The big turning point came in mid-2012. The crisis had already spread beyond the small countries of the European periphery, reaching Italy and Spain; France had begun to look vulnerable as well. It was therefore make or break as Europe's political leaders became increasingly and painfully aware that ad hoc and country-specific measures would no longer be enough to deal with a systemic crisis. And systemic crisis it was indeed, despite repeated statements to the contrary by politicians who had simply tried to wish it away.

At the euro summit of June 2012, political leaders agreed that 'it is imperative to break the vicious circle between banks and sovereigns'.[23] It was a path-breaking statement and led to a major political decision, namely to proceed with the creation of a European banking union about which the first discussions can be traced as far back as the 1960s.[24] You could call it a revolutionary decision had it not to do with banks: revolution and banks are a contradiction in terms, are they not? It was surely the most important decision since the launching of the euro. And it made it easier for the president of the ECB, Mario Draghi, to take the next step one month later by announcing in London, Europe's main financial centre yet outside the eurozone, that '[W]ithin its mandate, the ECB is ready to do whatever it takes to preserve the euro. And believe me, it will be enough'.[25] Markets did indeed believe him.

I am not sure whether this proves or disproves the theory about rational actors in financial markets. Academic economists may have a lively, albeit not necessarily very fruitful, debate on the subject. However, what we do know for sure is that with this simple and straightforward statement, the president of the ECB helped to restore calm in the markets without even having to deliver on his promise (or threat). Markets simply believed him and speculation against the weaker countries calmed down as a result. Thus, the worst of the euro crisis was over, and Draghi was clearly the boss as far as markets were concerned.

The next big step by the ECB was taken early in 2015 with the announcement of a large quantitative-easing programme, having already tried several conventional and unconventional measures of central banking, including negative interest rates, while the prospect of deflation loomed close. The quantitative easing programme meant that the ECB would spend more than €1 trillion purchasing government bonds and securities in secondary markets, thus following the example already set by other central banks during the crisis, including notably the Federal Reserve, the Bank of Japan, and the Bank of England. It was the 'big bazooka' that many people had been eagerly waiting for to fight against deflation and very slow growth through a massive injection of liquidity into the system. Quantitative easing has, however, awkward distributional effects since it favours (and subsidizes) those who own assets. In times when there is growing awareness of widening income and wealth inequalities, this presents certain problems, to say the least.

At the time of writing, quantitative easing by the ECB has not yet succeeded in raising significantly the rate of inflation in the eurozone, still uncomfortably close to zero. Will the next step in unconventional measures be so-called helicopter money?[26] And how will orthodox zealots react? In the meantime, large purchases of sovereign bonds have given a welcome breathing space to several governments. They also provided an effective shield against contagion, when the rest of the eurozone decided to face up to the challenge presented by the radical-left government in Greece in the early months of 2015.

Such decisions were not at all uncontroversial, which had also been true of earlier decisions by the ECB. They were often taken by majority within the governing board where all national central banks of the eurozone are represented. Compared to its counterparts in the US and the UK, the ECB has been indeed slow and timid in its actions during the crisis. But considering the legal constraints imposed on it by Maastricht and the continuous rearguard action—especially by German central bankers and politicians, not to mention the German constitutional court—Europe's federal bank has indeed travelled a long way. In the process, it has played a key role in saving the euro, while surely antagonizing many Germans. It also antagonized Irish, Greeks, and Cypriots who were probably considered to be politically more dispensable. Central banking and power politics is a fascinating game to watch from a safe distance.

A letter from the president of the ECB asking for domestic reforms as a precondition for central bank support triggered the resignation of the Berlusconi government in Italy in 2011, ushering in an internationally respected economist, Mario Monti, as the new unelected prime minister of Italy. Although relatively few Europeans are likely to have shed tears on the departure of Mr Berlusconi, the political symbolism (and more) of what happened was, however, rather disconcerting.[27] Does the ECB determine the limits of democracy and sovereignty in this brave new world? And what if democracy produces outcomes that are incompatible with the joint management of inter-dependence in Europe, or that may be incompatible with good admin-istration in the country concerned? These are really awkward questions that many Europeans, especially among officials in Brussels, prefer to ignore. They are, however, indicative of the still wide gap between policy and political integration in Europe today.

Jean Pisani-Ferry, a French economist and leading expert on European issues, concluded[28] on the basis of the number of telephone calls made at the peak of the euro crisis by the then US Secretary of the Treasury, that the president of the ECB was the person that mattered most, followed by the German finance minister. Those representing institutions such as the Eurogroup, consisting of the finance ministers of the eurozone, and the Commission were far behind. This ranking order sounds entirely plausible—and the situation has hardly changed since then. A central banker and a national minister running Europe's monetary union was not exactly what the fathers of EMU had in mind.

## Who runs the risk?

The ECB pumped liquidity in times of low confidence and slow demand, but it also crucially helped to recycle funds from the centre to the periphery, thus complementing the role played by governments through the bailout programmes at a time when private funds were flowing massively in the opposite direction.

As a result, inside the 'Eurosystem', comprising the ECB and all national central banks of eurozone countries, some national central banks have ended up with large debtor positions with the ECB and others with the corresponding surpluses. Italian banks, for example, borrowed money from the Banca d'Italia, which in turn borrowed from the ECB, and used this money to lend to private companies or buy (mostly) Italian sovereign debt, while private money from south-ern Europe flowing to German banks in search of a safe haven, or money earned by German exporters, ended up as deposits with the Bundesbank and then as claims on the ECB.

This merry-go-round of money is quite normal and nothing to worry about as long as you continue to think of the eurozone as an irreversible monetary union, like the US, in which the federal bank performs its traditional role. After all, nobody pays any attention to interstate bank balances in the United States. But, if you think there is risk of a break-up, to be followed very likely by massive defaults in countries with new and depreciating currencies, then you surely have good reasons to worry. The German and Dutch central banks have big creditor positions with the ECB matched by the large debtor positions of central banks in southern Europe and Ireland.

This is precisely what a well-known German economist, Hans-Werner Sinn, brought to public attention first in 2011[29] by presenting creditor and debtor positions along national lines in the so-called Target 2, which is the interbank payment system comprising the ECB and national central banks of the eurozone. Then the common folk in Germany began to realize that the Bundesbank had a net creditor position sometimes as high as €800 billion with the ECB—which is a great deal of money even by German standards—matched by large debtor positions of the central banks in the periphery. Were the savings of hard-working Germans at risk inside the European monetary union? Thus, Mr Sinn opened up another Pandora's box.

In a multinational monetary union, which is still very far from a political union and in which marriage for life is not yet a given, the distribution of risk was bound to become a very hot political issue. And it very much did so inside the eurozone in the midst of the crisis. Who decides and who pays are key political questions with which many economists feel extremely uncomfortable. Who runs the risk is another one, especially in times of high uncertainty such as those that Europe has lived through in recent years. These are all extremely relevant questions to ask in trying to understand how Europeans have tried to manage the big crisis and the conflicts that have arisen in the process.

The road to a European banking union provides another good illustration. It took a few years for Europeans to agree that, short of a fiscal union that still seems to be a political impossibility,[30] the creation of a banking union would be necessary in order to break the deadly embrace between sovereigns and banks. For a banking union, you need a common rulebook for financial institutions, joint supervision of banks, a common resolution regime for when things go wrong for a particular bank and a common deposit insurance scheme as well. These are meant to be the main elements of a European banking union to be built in stages.

But having agreed on the general principle, European political leaders still had to tackle some difficult questions on the road towards a banking union. How much and what kind of regulation? What should be the division of labour between European and national regulators, and which banks should come under European supervision? Who would be entitled to decide to close down or restructure a bank deemed to be insolvent, and if so, under what conditions and who would bear the cost? Who would take the risk for insuring deposits? In other words, who decides, who pays, and who runs the risk in a banking union?

We now already have a common rulebook and a Single Supervisory Mechanism (SSM) for around 130 'significant' banks in the eurozone operating under the aegis of the ECB, having been preceded by the most serious stress test up to that point for the financial institutions concerned; previous stress tests had been hardly credible. We also have a Single Resolution Mechanism (SRM) of sorts, again based on an intergovernmental agreement under international law. But the responsibility for the recapitalization of banks, if so required, will still rest essentially with national authorities during a long transitional period until the Single Resolution Fund (SRF) gets going with a sufficient capital base of its own. And we still have no agreement as yet on a joint deposit insurance scheme.[31]

True, the eurozone has travelled a long way, although it is still far from a properly functioning and sustainable monetary union. The remarkable reversal of the process of financial integration that happened during the crisis, with the de facto redrawing of national boundaries for the banking sector, still holds. One of the main stumbling blocks on the road towards a more complete monetary union has been the (understandable) reluctance of potential creditors to share risk for sovereign or bank debt. Thus, each new step, small and unsure, in the direction of mutualization of risk within the eurozone was taken once everything else had been tried and had failed. Meanwhile, with further policy integration inside the eurozone, the gap between the latter and the rest of the EU has been steadily growing wider, the UK being a case on its own.

## And who pays the bill?

Those who did not believe in extraterrestrial economics knew all along that adjustment to a post-bubble and post-crisis world would be painful and most probably protracted, for some countries of course more than for others, depending on how bad their starting point was. And it was only to be expected that the main burden would fall on the deficit/debtor countries, even though there was a systemic component of the crisis that should normally be dealt with collectively and with a fair distribution of the burden among all members.

Adjustment did take place in the deficit/debtor countries, which were left with no real alternative by markets and EU partners alike—and it was quite fast. The turning point was around 2008–9. In the years that followed, the pre-crisis divergence in terms of inflation rates, unit labour costs, and current account imbalances inside the eurozone was completely reversed (Graphs 3.1, 3.2, and 3.3). The countries of the periphery used the fiscal brakes often in conditions of financial strangulation, bailed out the banks, squeezed wages, imposed drastic welfare cuts, liberalized markets, and reformed at least in part. Competitiveness was hence restored and, coupled with the squeeze in domestic demand, helped to eliminate gradually the deficits in their current accounts.

Meanwhile, German overall current account surpluses continued regardless, and so did those of the Netherlands. What happened during the crisis years was a gradual shift of those surpluses from trade with the rest of the EU to trade with the rest of the world. In the case of Germany, the share of the current account surplus made up by trade with other EU countries was 86 per cent of the total in 2008 (and most of it was in fact with the rest of the eurozone). It came down to 42 per cent in 2013.[32] Thus, the German addiction to surpluses continued unabated, with high domestic savings and low demand, as well as a favourable exchange rate, courtesy of the eurozone. A separate German currency could not have done the trick for long. And the eurozone as a whole became more Germanic not only through the adoption of German-inspired rules and policies but also by running surpluses vis-à-vis the rest of the world.

The price paid for adjustment by countries on the periphery of the eurozone was, on the other hand, very big indeed (Graphs 4.1 and 4.2). Between 2007 and 2014, Greece lost 26 per cent of its GDP and unemployment reached 26 per cent. The Greek experience was comparable to the US experience during the Great Depression. The loss of GDP for Italy, without an adjustment programme as such, was 9 per cent, and more than 7 per cent for Portugal during the same period. Spain followed with a negative 5 per cent, while Ireland succeeded in regaining the ground lost in the earlier years of adjustment. In 2015, only Greece was still suffering from negative rates of growth, having shown signs of economic recovery the previous year that were nipped in the bud by political developments at home. In contrast, both Ireland and Spain have been recovering fast in the more recent period. But unemployment was still very high in the Iberian peninsula, and youth unemployment was much higher throughout southern Europe, which meant that some of these countries risked losing a whole generation and not just a decade.

Emigration for many people in the worst-affected countries provided the only way out. As a result, southern Europe and Ireland saw some of

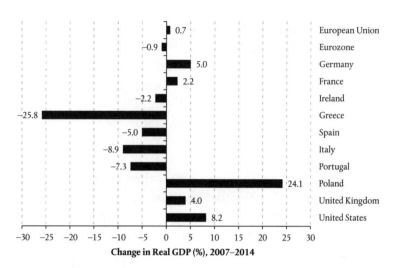

**Graph 4.1** The Impact of the Great Recession: Real GDP 2007–2014
*Source*: Eurostat, OECD (for the United States)

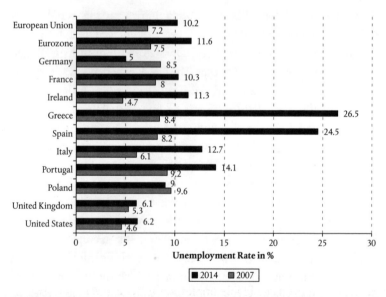

**Graph 4.2** The Impact of the Great Recession: Unemployment Rates 2007 and 2014
*Source*: AMECO

their best educated and most dynamic citizens, especially among the young, leave for other countries in Europe and beyond. The loss of precious human capital will also have long-term negative effects on the economy, the political system, and society in these countries.

The countries of southern Europe and Ireland were not the only ones to go through this shock treatment following the bursting of the bubble. When capital flows were abruptly reversed, other countries still outside the eurozone were forced to go through a similar experience. Latvia is such a case, often presented by the apostles of European economic orthodoxy as an example to follow in other parts of Europe. This small Baltic country was faced with an economic meltdown in 2008, after years of financial inebriation with very rapid growth financed with borrowed money from abroad. And it then went through a tough and front-loaded adjustment programme with financial assistance from the EU and the IMF.

The goal of macroeconomic stabilization was soon achieved and growth returned, while Latvia was also able to keep its peg to the euro against expectations.[33] The country was later rewarded with full participation in the eurozone in 2014 and its former prime minister, Mr Dombrovskis, became vice president of the new European Commission in charge of the euro, presumably in recognition of his earlier efforts at home. Yet, the price that Latvia paid was big: it lost almost a quarter of its GDP in two years, it dismantled a good part of its already lean welfare state, while unemployment skyrocketed and large numbers of its young and most mobile citizens voted with their feet. Latvia's GDP in 2014 was still 5 per cent below what it had been in 2007, admittedly an unsustainable level of prosperity financed by the Baltic bubble. But can Latvia really serve as a model? Not many countries have such small and open economies, nor (luckily for them) do they have the long and painful Soviet legacy that may indeed influence the citizens' tolerance of pain. If this is indeed the model, we may be in for more highly unpleasant experiences in Europe.

Things have not been that bright for the rest of Europe and the eurozone either, with only a few exceptions. The year 2013 marked the end of a long, double-dip recession in Europe, but recovery has been modest in most countries since then. By the end of 2014, real GDP in the eurozone as a whole was still below what it had been back in 2007 (Graph 4.1) and unemployment was close to 12 per cent, with an increase of 4 percentage points since 2007 (Graph 4.2). Comparisons with the United States were not at all favourable, as shown in these two graphs. It was Europe's Great Recession, by far the worst since the Second World War, although experienced very differently by individual countries. Economic divergence in Europe has grown very much as a result.

The German economy did pretty well by comparison with a gain of 5 per cent in real GDP during the same period and with unemployment falling below 5 per cent. Virtue rewarded was how many Germans viewed their country's performance, and not without some justification. As for France, it continued to occupy an intermediate position between the relatively successful centre and the embattled periphery. Outside the eurozone, the UK had a fast recovery and a good record in terms of unemployment, although critics often point out that low rates of unemployment in the UK are partly due to many poorly paid and/or part-time jobs, which in turn reflected rising inequalities. Only Poland stands out with a remarkable performance in terms of GDP, although less so in terms of unemployment.

## Toxic politics and flawed economics

What conclusions can we draw? Opinions, of course, differ, as do interests. With the exception of unreconstructed 'austerians', to be found predominantly (and not surprisingly) in creditor countries, most observers and analysts tend to agree that adjustment in Europe as a whole, and the periphery in particular, during the crisis has been much more painful and much longer than needed[34]—and they also agree that the prospects for the future are not very good either. The explanation lies with over-restrictive and front-loaded fiscal policies all around, insufficient monetary stimulus in the early period in conditions of depressed demand and scarce liquidity, collective denial on the subject of debt and banks, which in turn prolonged the uncertainty in financial markets and the fragmentation along national lines, and last but not least, the incoherent nature of euro governance which often sounded like an uncoordinated and cacophonic orchestra with one instrument often covering all the rest. Judging from results, it would be difficult to give the eurozone even a pass mark for what admittedly proved to be a very difficult test, a test for which euro members had clearly not been prepared.

Peter Hall, an expert on Europe and professor at Harvard, has compared the response to the euro crisis to a transnational Ponzi scheme 'in which the European Union (EU) lends funds to national governments that are then sequestered to pay the interest on previous loans from the EU, while those governments borrow to bail out banks that are in turn lending to them with the encouragement of the ECB'.[35] It is both ingenious and pathetic, depending on how generous you may want to be with those responsible.

In addition, European policy measures have been invariably late, always less than required, and implementation has left much to be desired. The euro decision-making system is very slow and cumbersome; it is not designed to deal with emergencies. In contrast, financial markets are extremely fast, though following the instinct of the herd and hence not always wise, to put it mildly. The eurozone has been able to react fast only when Germany, with or without France, had a clear idea of what it wanted and was ready to lead the others, although not always (indeed, some might argue rarely) in the right direction and sometimes resorting to arm-twisting. Narrow self-interest usually prevailed and European solidarity suffered commensurately.

The politics was slow and toxic, and the economics was flawed. The IMF belatedly recognized that the speed of fiscal adjustment for countries with adjustment programmes was excessive, admitting that the so-called fiscal multipliers (measuring the effect of fiscal contraction on economic output) proved to be much bigger than anticipated.[36] European institutions have found it much more difficult to recognize mistakes. In fact, in the early years of the crisis, all macroeconomic predictions by official institutions for the countries with adjustment programmes were completely off the mark. Deficit/debtor countries had to cope with incompatible objectives: on the one hand, they went for internal devaluation as a means of restoring competitiveness, which in turn led to deflation and further reduction in nominal GDP, and on the other, they tried to reduce their debt as a percentage of GDP. Alas, miracles do not always happen. Nominal and real GDP fell, while public debt rose rapidly as a percentage of it: Graph 3.6 is all too clear.

The burden of adjustment fell almost entirely on the deficit/debtor countries, especially those with adjustment programmes. The price paid in terms of lost output and jobs is very high. There will be a further price to pay as unemployment becomes long term. The burden of adjustment would have been less if surplus/creditor countries had been willing to boost domestic demand and accept a higher rate of inflation at home. They were not. They argued instead that deficit/ debtor countries were entirely to blame for the sorry state they were in, and hence they had to pay the price by adjusting. The crisis was about individual countries, not about the eurozone as a collective unit, they argued. And the policy conclusion followed, because creditor countries had the capacity to impose their point of view. Furthermore, there were no rules to ensure a minimum of symmetry in the distribution of the burden of adjustment in the eurozone.

The distribution of the burden of adjustment between deficit and surplus countries in a system of fixed rates was first recognized by Keynes as an important issue during the Bretton Woods negotiations before the end of the Second World War. When there are no jointly agreed rules, the will of those with stronger staying power will inevitably prevail: these are the surplus countries. Despite repeated efforts, mainly by the French, to ensure some symmetry between the two sides in successive stages of European monetary integration,[37] the burden of adjustment has continued to fall almost exclusively on the deficit

countries. It has not been at all different with EMU. The economic effect
is deflationary.

While the burden of economic adjustment fell on the deficit/debtor
countries, it was the surplus/creditor countries that had to take the
credit risk by providing or underwriting financial flows to the former
through official financial assistance or indirectly through the ECB. It was a
pact with the devil for all concerned, a pact of which the main beneficiaries were the banks. They were protected with money and guarantees
from European and non-European taxpayers through national governments, European institutions, and the IMF. Thus, the distribution of pain
after the bubble burst was very different from the distribution of gain in
good times, something which was an issue more within countries than
between them.

Just think of the following counterfactual. It was spelt out eloquently and rather convincingly by Barry Eichengreen and Charles
Wyplosz,[38] two well-known economists. It goes as follows: European
leaders recognized early on that Greece's debt was unsustainable and
forced a restructuring as a condition of external assistance. To protect from moral hazard, the lending banks had to accept the consequences instead of being bailed out with European taxpayers' money.
The IMF proceeded with an assistance programme to Greece on the
basis of the agreed debt restructuring, which meant that the fiscal
consolidation effort would be significantly smaller for Greece. The
latter also proceeded with structural reforms, but the priority was to
liberalize product markets rather than the labour market. Meanwhile,
France and Germany nationalized their worst hit banks, and so did
Ireland and Spain. They bailed in unsecured creditors while protecting small depositors. The unavoidable restructuring of banks was
coupled with the early introduction of European banking union to
help restore confidence. And the ECB helped with early cuts in
interest rates and aggressive quantitative easing. Last but not least,
Germany gave a helping hand by relaxing its fiscal stance and accepting a higher rate of inflation which made adjustment easier for the
other countries. Also taking advantage of low interest rates, it proposed

a bond-financed programme of investment in infrastructure across Europe, which stimulated growth.

This way the crisis could have been over before 2013: look at the US. Europe, however, decided otherwise, because narrow, short-term interests prevailed and also because instead of trying to deal collectively and effectively with the systemic problem at hand, Europe's leaders engaged in a blame game. And Europe is still not out of the woods.

# 5

# The Priest, the Sinner,
# and the Non-Believer

## A divided and unhappy church

Divergence has grown during Europe's crisis and divisions have
run deep. Europe had not been so divided for a very long time:
creditors versus debtors, centre versus periphery, eurozone versus the
rest. We had long wished for a proper European debate on European
issues, and we really got it with the crisis: a European debate that
crossed borders and was no longer limited to elites and the illuminati.
Because it was a democratic debate, it covered the whole spectrum from
the sublime to the ridiculous. And it turned very ugly on many occasions, with recriminations crossing borders that Europe was meant
to break down, while stereotypes—mostly national—came back with
a vengeance.

Markets often set the tone, especially in the early years of the crisis,
and politics followed. Triple As and PIGS was how the division was
presented in markets: on the one hand, countries that still enjoyed
triple-A rating from those agencies that had completely misread the
financial health of banks and governments alike before the crisis; on
the other, countries that saw their ratings plummet and their access to
markets restricted if not completely denied, countries referred to with
the acronym of PIGS that stood for Portugal, Ireland, Greece, and
Spain—or PIIGS to include Italy as well. Politicians happily engaged in
slanging matches with their counterparts in other countries and so did

many journalists in the popular media, stoking the fires of nationalism and populism. Ugly scenes often took place in European councils; insults were followed by bullying. Might often turned into right and the weak suffered what they must, as Thucydides told us many centuries ago.[1] This was certainly not what the European model was supposed to be all about. But the stakes were very high and diplomatic niceties were thrown out of the window.

Perhaps inevitably, it was not just a clash of interests and ideas about how to resolve the crisis. It was also very much a blame game with a morality tale attached to it about the good and the bad: the devout observer of Europe's morality code and the sinner. The two extremes in this moral blame game were occupied by Germany—the paragon of virtue who set the rules, also the alpha male (female?) among the triple As—and Greece—the ultimate sinner, the 'piggiest' of PIGS. Exchanges between these two extremes sometimes got completely out of control. Germans referred to lazy and cheating Greeks, who should sell their islands or the Acropolis to pay for their debts, and Greeks reciprocated by making nasty references to Germany's Nazi past. It did not help at all that the Nazi occupation of Greece during the Second World War had been one of the bloodiest. Many people had long hoped for these terrible memories to be buried for good under the mountain of European integration. But when crisis struck and politics turned nasty, demagogues and others who should have known better began to dig. It was extremely unpleasant and also dangerous.

Germany became the leader and the priest of a divided European church and tried to set the code of conduct. In the meantime, France had lost her sangfroid, becoming increasingly afraid of markets and of losing her triple-A-rating, which she did indeed lose in the end. She was also increasingly afraid of being left behind by Germany and thus tried to hang on to the old special relationship which had steered European integration for decades but now increasingly served to disguise Germany's strength and France's weakness. As for the embattled periphery of the eurozone—the sinners who were now being called upon to redeem themselves by putting their economy and their finances back in order—their response varied from obedience (in an effort to emerge from their state of penance as soon as possible) to challenging those rules (usually not successfully) or simply pretending to abide by them. The pragmatic Irish concentrated on the former course of action, while the Greeks tried a combination of different strategies without much consistency; admittedly, they had the hardest form of penitence to go through. And everybody else desperately tried to avoid ending up like the Greeks.

The eurozone became the centre of European politics during the crisis, with creditors turning against debtors, while the countries outside it increasingly felt marginalized and frustrated, worried about the broader consequences of a possible euro break-up that would surely reach them as well, also concerned that their interests as members of the European internal market would be trampled upon by the majority of euro members. The UK felt most strongly about this new situation: a country that had never been a true believer in the European project (convinced Europhiles have always been a small minority in the UK), happy in its early decision not to join the euro but certainly not immune to the negative effects of the euro crisis, and with a Conservative-led coalition government since 2010 that did not seem to mind all that much being no longer at the 'heart of Europe'. The UK was like the non-believer who, having previously chosen to be a member of the church for practical rather than spiritual reasons and having paid membership dues, was now behaving as if he was really getting bored with services and might consider walking out.

Divergence and diversity in Europe increased very much during the crisis. The question was therefore bound to arise at some stage whether Europe's broad church could actually accommodate so many different members; hence the talk about Grexit and Brexit. Would the priest try to keep everybody in, and with what kind of incentives? And how far would he be willing to accommodate diversity or sin? The centrifugal forces in today's Europe are strong; they are also increasingly evident within countries in the form of regional, race, and social divisions. Meanwhile, Europe's troubled neighbourhood is creating new challenges and further divisions inside Europe. Putin's Russia, the refugee crisis, and terrorism—terrorism being in part also locally produced—are the most important ones. A new East–West division is being added. The happy days and years that followed the fall of the Iron Curtain, when ardent believers in the European project were convinced that history was definitely on their side, were over.

## Germany: successful, but reluctant to lead

The word crisis does not exactly describe the experience of most Germans in recent years—that is, until refugees began to arrive in very large numbers in 2015. After all, unemployment had been at a record low, growth may have been slow but was still positive (unlike the experience of many other European countries), inflation was low and public finances under control, which allowed those in power to plan for surpluses in the years to come. Last but not least, the current account surplus remained as large as ever. For most Germans, economic crisis was therefore something terrible that so far had happened to others; yet, uncomfortably close to home and constantly in the headlines, forcing them to take big credit risks in order to save partners in distress, some of whom (they felt) did not really deserve to be saved. Germans suspected that at least some of their European partners were trying to get their hands into German pockets: their precious savings were at risk. And on top of all this Germany is an ageing society.

Germany is a world economic power, the world's third biggest exporter. It does not want to lose out to tough and globally competitive emerging economies, hence the competitiveness argument is very strong in Berlin. German politicians had been trained to speak mostly of business and law rather than grand strategy and geopolitics. For years, the chancelleries of European big powers spoke sotto voce of German provincialism. Therefore, Germans have had to learn fast in an effort to translate economic power into ever growing political presence on the international scene, albeit always within the constraints of soft power.[2]

Germany has become the main interlocutor in Europe for Americans, Chinese, and Russians alike. Relations with Russia present Germany with a particular challenge because of geography, history, close economic ties, and energy dependence, hence the effort made by German representatives to steer a middle course between unrepentant cold warriors in Europe and those only too ready to bow to Russian blackmail: hardly an easy thing to do. Germany, together with France, has been leading negotiations with Russia on Ukraine. It has also played an active role in negotiations with Iran.

Germany is economically bigger and stronger than its partners— and it is more successful than most. It managed a difficult and very costly reunification by integrating the new *Länder* of the former communist East Germany into the Federal Republic, and it went through painful reforms when the country was still considered 'the sick man of Europe'. True, it has become more unequal in the process, but this is still manageable through the operation of the German welfare state. Its institutions, largely designed by the Allies after the Second World War, have passed the test of time with flying colours: a decentralized system with many checks and balances reinforced by a strong consensual element in German political culture. If anything, consensus may have actually gone too far, thus allowing little room for an effective challenge to established views or dogmas.[3] Consensual Germany is convinced it knows best, but could it be wrong?

For years, Germany enjoyed remarkable political stability. The lid was kept on xenophobic and anti-European populism, despite the combination of self-righteousness and scapegoating beyond Germany's borders that characterized much of the domestic debate. In other words, the centre held pretty well in Germany and this surely had much to do with the fact that the political system continued to deliver the goods. Nothing works like success.

The role of personalities was also very important. Chancellor Merkel proved to be a master in leading, managing, and assuaging the concerns and fears of her fellow citizens while keeping the euro system and debtor countries alive—but only just.[4] She has been in power much longer than any other political leader in Europe, although some people begin to wonder whether the refugee crisis will become the straw that finally breaks the camel's back. Anti-immigration feeling is on the rise, the Alternative für Deutschland party, which sprang up as a reaction to the euro crisis, is gaining strength in opinion polls, and more Germans now seem ready to abandon political consensus and correctness. How much, or how fast, will this shift in public opinion translate itself into a policy shift within the mainstream parties, notably Mrs Merkel's own party, leading eventually to a change in leadership?

Personalities have played a key role during the European crisis, which turned Germany into the indispensable nation[5] and the lender of last resort. Mrs Merkel and Mr Schäuble, the German finance minister, have dominated the European scene not only because they represented Germany or because of their longevity in office. Merkel and Schäuble carried weight and enjoyed respect from their European colleagues. The former proved to be more of a skilful tactician than a strategist, allowing things to get to the edge before acting, in search of the *ultima ratio*, as she liked to put it, for domestic political reasons. The latter, a convinced European but with (one suspects) a preference for a smaller Europe, had a very clear but dogmatic view of how Europe's monetary union should work, a view which he tried (mostly with success) to impose on everybody else. If, or rather when, Merkel and Schäuble leave the scene, it will be almost like the end of an era in European politics.

Throughout the euro crisis, German politicians and institutions set the limits of what was doable at European level: usually not enough to deal effectively with the crisis and at the very last minute. People in the rest of Europe also had to wait eagerly for the decisions of Germany's federal constitutional court in Karlsruhe, which set the limits of legality for the ESM, established in 2012, and the ECB, although at some point German high judges decided to ask the European Court of

Justice for an opinion as well. If the German example were to be imitated by constitutional courts in other countries, would the European system not grind to a halt?

Germany had leadership—like greatness in the famous words that Shakespeare gave to Malvolio—thrust upon her during the recent crisis.[6] And German politicians often gave the impression that they felt uncomfortable with it, not only because of the big financial costs associated with leading Europe out of the crisis. Leader is a word that translates badly into German: *Führer* carries very negative connotations inside and outside Germany. The Franco-German vehicle was therefore seen as a convenient one to continue to use during the crisis. On many issues in the past, Franco-German leadership had worked because the two countries started from different ends and met somewhere in between, allowing room for other countries to chip in with their own special interests. This is one way of presenting a typical compromise on which Europe's successful model of integration had been built. But now, Paris was weak and Berlin had strong views about what was needed.

Austria, Finland, and the Netherlands were only too happy to follow German leadership during the crisis. They were often joined by countries in central and eastern Europe which had toughened out the painful transition from communist regimes. Several of them were now very much dependent on the success of the German export machine, or were just part of it. It was a new coalition in Europe with an undisputed, yet unhappy and often reluctant, leader facing debtors who were weak and divided: the *sauve qui peut* instinct usually prevailed among the latter.

## Indignant and with strong views

Many Germans always had their doubts about monetary union, especially about the company of some of their European partners. I remember an unusually frank public discussion with a senior adviser of the German chancellor a few years after the signing of the Maastricht

Treaty. He tried to explain the reticence of Germans in abandoning their beloved Deutschmark, the symbol of the post-war economic miracle (*Wirtschaftswunder*), for a European common currency by comparing his fellow Germans to a couple who took extra care in the upbringing of their only beloved daughter only for her to be asked, when she became a young woman, to 'join a brothel'. Apparently, this is what he thought of some of his Mediterranean (and other) partners in the EU with respect to their approach to economic policy and public finances in particular.

Judging from what actually happened inside the euro some years later, he may after all think that he was right about Germany's unnatural cohabitation (as he would see it) in a currency union with countries that do not share the German stability-oriented approach to economic policy—and many of his fellow Germans would agree with him. But, at best, they confess to only half of the truth. They tend to forget Germany's export-led growth which in the years of the euro has benefited from the competitive advantage that Germany built vis-à-vis its European partners who no longer have the possibility to devalue and from an exchange rate vis-à-vis the rest of the world that has certainly been much lower than the exchange rate of an independent Deutschmark would have been. They also forget the benefits of lower borrowing costs (in fact negative for some time now) since Germany turned into a safe haven within a eurozone in crisis. And last but not least, they prefer to leave out of the picture the role of German (and other) banks in feeding the bubble in the first place. This is a subject not much discussed in Germany as a whole, and even less by German politicians. To put it very bluntly, the Germans have been extremely successful in producing and exporting high quality products but not very wise in the way they invested their savings and surpluses abroad.

When the crisis broke out, most Germans were really shocked at being called upon to contribute to bailout programmes of countries in distress. They referred to the Maastricht Treaty that was meant to prohibit such bailouts, while the economically more sophisticated talked about 'moral hazard'. They were indignant, but also economical in their expression of solidarity. The German taxpayer had already shown much solidarity vis-à-vis his or her compatriots in East Germany, following reunification, and was not at all keen on repeating the same thing for Greeks, Irish, and Portuguese—or Italians in the future. Pomerania is close to home, but not Algarve or Crete: it was stretching solidarity too far.

On the other hand, it is interesting to compare German and, say, French attitudes to bailouts of other European countries. The German quota in bilateral loans and also contributions to the ESM is 27 per cent of the total. The French contribution is 20 per cent, which is not small at all and translates into tens of billions of euros. But it became a big political issue in Germany and hardly an issue at all in France. The Dutch and the Finns in particular behaved like the Germans, while the Italians and Spaniards, who also paid their relatively big national quotas for the bailout programmes of other countries while borrowing at higher interest rates than those charged to countries on the receiving end of official assistance, hardly made any fuss either.

If you have been selling austerity at home for years, it is understandably difficult to convince your fellow citizens to be generous to foreigners or fellow Europeans. German political leaders therefore had a hard sell with bailouts of other countries. The cynic may also point out that countries in the south, including France, have been more sympathetic to other countries in distress because they feared that they might end up in the same position themselves—and they also had their over-exposed banks to think about. And this is again an argument with some validity. These arguments are not, however, enough to explain the stark contrast in the attitudes of different countries. We may need to add cultural differences to the pot of explanatory factors. After all, cultural differences have deep roots in Europe and they continue to play a significant role in intra-European politics.

The experience with European monetary integration clearly suggests that Germany enjoys a strong structural advantage in any system of fixed exchange rates based on its long tradition of stability-minded policies, consensual politics and industrial relations as well as on the strength of German industry. In European exchange rate arrangements preceding monetary union, Germany had always emerged as the leader and had refused to compromise on its main policy priorities whenever it came to the crunch, thus forcing other countries, those with some degree of autonomy, to leave in the end. This was perhaps not so clearly understood by President Mitterrand and his advisers in their push for EMU and the negotiations leading to Maastricht.[7] They had apparently hoped it would be different with a proper monetary union. But the union we have ended up with still operates like the old gold exchange standard of the interwar period, with some allowance made for the expanding role of the ECB—and this expanding role is precisely what Germany has tried to resist all along or to constrain.

Is Germany a model for other European countries to follow? There are certainly many things to learn from a country that is successful in many respects and has a successful economy. But there are also limits to exporting successful models to other countries by stealth or force.[8] Economic zealots should be aware that economic logic does not always prevail over history or politics. Furthermore, the argument that everybody should do like the Germans is fallacious. The combination of competitive advantage and the savings surplus at home explains the large and apparently never-ending current account surpluses of Germany. The rest of Europe and the world have put up with these surpluses. Is it likely that the whole of Europe, or just the eurozone, would be allowed to behave like Germany for any length of time? And do we really expect the United States to be the consumer of last resort for all of us? China will certainly not accept such a role for itself; after all, it has been behaving all along like Germany.

Many German economists form a school of their own, strongly influenced by so-called 'ordo-liberal'[9] ideas, a school of thought which puts the emphasis on rules as opposed to discretion. Germany is a country with a strong legal tradition and this is also manifest in the conduct of her economic policy, which is often run by lawyers. In addition, the emphasis on rules that provide the basis for a well-functioning market economy, with a welfare dimension added to it (*Soziale Marktwirtschaft*), also relies heavily upon lawyers. Price stability, sound public finances, competitive markets, and rules to set tight boundaries on policy discretion, with a strong moral undertone, have unsurprisingly been constantly emphasized by German representatives throughout the eurozone crisis. Germans were opposed to the ECB extending its role as lender of last resort, and were also opposed to any kind of mutualization of risk. 'Transfer union' became a term that haunted many Germans. They argued instead that if all countries were to put their house in order and respect the rules of the game, the euro would be safe once again. 'Do it like us' was in fact what Germans were telling their partners. They argued that painful adjustment for countries that had veered off the track of virtue was the necessary price to pay for a return to stable money and sound finances. The problem was individual countries and (lack of) respect for rules, they insisted, rather than a systemic problem which only began to be recognized belatedly and very reluctantly.

The official German stance drew much criticism, especially from Anglo-American disciples of Keynes in the worlds of academia and policymaking.[10] On the other hand, criticism was rather subdued in official European meetings, apparently for fear of antagonizing the leader: a true sign of the times. In any case, Germany did not budge (or not much, and only at the very last minute) and the German finance minister accused his critics of living in a parallel universe.[11] The crucial question, however, remains: whose parallel universe was closer to reality? The European debate often sounded like the dialogue of the deaf. Was it a clash just of ideas, or of interests as well? Again, this is a difficult question to answer, because ideas and interests are closely entangled, and this was certainly true during the crisis of recent years. What it largely boiled down to was about who would pay the bill of economic adjustment in the post-bubble world.

The eurozone ended up being 'governed by the rules' and 'ruled by the numbers'.[12] Rules and numbers were meant to eliminate moral hazard and constrain discretion in the conduct of national economic policy. The rules of good behaviour were determined at European level, the product of intergovernmental negotiations in which the role of Germany was paramount, and member states were expected to conform. European rules were thus increasingly pronounced with a rolling 'r', as in German. And the legitimacy of the European project was further undermined, especially since the latter was now delivering pain rather than gain in many parts of Europe. Liaquat Ahamed, a Pulitzer-winning author, reached the conclusion in a study on the IMF during the crisis that the organization had the capacity to draw lessons from its mistakes and acknowledge them. He argues that 'By contrast, the Germans appear to be totally without doubt. So convinced did they seem of their rectitude that they came across as rigid and dogmatic—dare I say it, Germanic'.[13]

Thus, the country that had learned to think of the European project as being inseparably tied up with its own national project and that had so many of its intellectuals arguing cogently and with passion for a federal Europe—perhaps more so than in any other European country—ended up during the big crisis as a defender of intergovernmental methods and no longer shy of throwing its weight around. It was a different Germany from what its European partners had been used to in the past, and the 'German Question' was brought back in a new form.[14] True, German politicians regularly paid their dues to the ultimate goal of European political union although safely placed somewhere in the distant future: 'God give me virtue, but not yet', in the famous words of St Augustine.

Was it disillusionment with the way the European project had developed and disillusionment with feckless partners? Was it the delayed effect of reunification that had liberated Germany from its shackles? Was it because of the new generation of German politicians for whom the Second World War was already far behind and a cross they were no longer prepared to bear? Or, was it just a temporary aberration during a long emergency? The answer may become clearer as the European project staggers on. But there is little doubt that German heavy-handedness on occasions and a dogmatic approach to economic policy has alienated people in Europe and beyond and has been deeply divisive.

The emergency meeting in July 2015, when the Germans, exasperated with the new radical government in Greece, tried to push the country out of the eurozone, may prove to be a turning point in this long saga of euro negotiations. German tactics at that meeting came as a real shock to many people and most notably to political leaders in France and Italy. A German Europe is not a sustainable proposition nor is it desirable for most Europeans, including Germans. A leading team player, who often leads by example and assumes the responsibilities that come with leadership, would be a workable and indeed desirable proposition. But such a proposition would require that other players also rise to the challenge, notably France.

## Greece's success story shattered

Critics of German 'ordo-liberalism' used to ask jokingly what is worse: a German lawyer or a German economist. And during the crisis, they have come across the true, yet unexpected, answer. Worse than a German lawyer and a German economist is a Greek politician, they now know. The combination of German rules-based economics and Greek clientele politics has been a disastrous combination, although much more for Greeks than for Germans.

Greece represents approximately 2 per cent of the eurozone in economic terms. Yet, the amount of time, effort, and money spent on Greece during the crisis has been out of proportion to this—and with not much success to boast of. However, it is not the first time in its modern history that Greece has attracted much more international attention than its relatively small size would justify, starting with the first major war of independence against the Ottoman Empire back in the early nineteenth century, and continuing with efforts to create a modern European state on Balkan territory, successive stages of territorial expansion and international defaults, heroic resistance to the

Axis powers, and a civil war which precipitated the direct involvement of the United States in post-war Europe.[15]

Greece is a small country with an extremely heavy baggage of history; strategic location; a cosmopolitan elite with a strong presence internationally in the arts, sciences, and finance, not to mention shipping; a disproportionate number of very rich people; large inequalities; and a state that is still more Balkan than modern European. It has a long history of foreign intervention that has largely shaped its own development and has created in turn the conditions for a strong sense of victimhood among Greeks who constantly look for external scapegoats. Nevertheless, modern Greece succeeded in being on the right side of history when it came to strategic decisions and choice of allies, including the two major European wars in the last century. The same applies to Greece's direct involvement in the European project going all the way back to an early association agreement with the EEC soon after the signing of the Treaty of Rome in the 1950s and full membership since 1981. A clear choice was thus made early on regarding the kind of Europe Greece wanted to belong to. Greece's European credentials are strong, although with a mixed track record: rich on strategic decisions and often poor on delivery.

Greece's remarkable transformation during the second half of the previous century from economic underdevelopment and deeply flawed democratic institutions to a fully-fledged democracy and a high standard of living (being classified among the top twenty-five countries in the world by the United Nations before the crisis) was a real success story. And it was a story closely interwoven with its participation in the European project. Membership of the EU provided the anchor of stability, often the benchmark, if not the catalyst, for modernization and development; it also provided some of the funds. This has also been true of other countries that joined after Greece, and it is part of the European success story.

But Greek politics has been clientele politics all along. Political parties distribute money and favours to voters/clients and they maintain a close, two-way relationship with the privileged few. This was bad enough—although Greece was not unique in this respect—but if anything, the problem has grown worse in more recent years. The quality of the Greek political class steadily deteriorated, the *enrichissez-vous* culture became dominant after many years of rapidly rising prosperity, while membership of the euro came to be perceived as a provider of cheap money rather than an agent for reform. Successive Greek governments pretended their public finances were in order and reforms were under way, while their European partners pretended to believe them. Nobody wanted to spoil a good party.

Should Greece have joined the euro in the first place? And can countries such as Greece and Germany, with very different levels of development, different economic structures, and different political economies, coexist in a system of fixed exchange rates with very little in terms of compensating instruments? In the years of undiluted optimism and innocence, everything seemed possible. For Greece, the moment of truth came when the international bubble burst, leaving her exposed and over-indebted. After several months of denial, Greece's lenders agreed on a rescue programme, knowing only too well that in rescuing Greece they were also rescuing European banks and the euro. It was not at all easy for any of them, facing as they did much resistance at home. In Slovakia, the government fell in an attempt to get through parliament the first bailout programme for Greece. On the receiving end, the Greeks faced an economic disaster at home with little bargaining power vis-à-vis their European partners, short of employing the kamikaze threat of blowing themselves up together with the rest, which they wisely decided not to use at the time.

Greece ended up with successive bailout programmes that contained large amounts of financial assistance (the largest ever received by one country) with strict conditionality that stretched from every aspect of fiscal policy to a wide range of structural reforms. Greeks had to change everything and fast: that was the logic. In the process, troika representatives became experts on Greek banks, pharmacies, taxis, and all kinds of minute detail of Greek everyday life, and they tried to set the rules: the kind of treatment reserved for colonies in the past.

Admittedly, a good number of Greek politicians did little to gain the respect and trust of Greece's lenders in the meantime.

## Economic and political implosion

The economics of Greece's successive adjustment programmes was deeply flawed and the politics was even worse.[16] It will most likely in due course become a case study in precisely what should *not* be done in such circumstances. It all started badly: an insolvent country that everybody chose to treat as illiquid because of fear of contagion, with very large internal and external imbalances as the result of gross domestic mismanagement yet financed for years by bankers and fund managers who should have known better, with limited policy instruments at its disposal as a member of the monetary union, weak institutions, poor tax collection, and a political culture in which consensus remains a dirty word and populism is rife. By 2010, Greece was a bankrupt country to which rescuers arrived from abroad in a punishing mood, with unrealistic expectations and an obstinate refusal to recognize that the Greek problem was also part of a much bigger systemic problem of the eurozone.

Between 2009 and 2014, Greece reduced its budget deficit by 13 percentage points of GDP, in a front-loaded programme of fiscal consolidation which was a record for any developed country for decades. This happened at a time when domestic bank liquidity was drained and speculation on sovereign debt default—and later Grexit—was intense, thus undermining any attempt at restoring stability or attracting investment. Last but not least, it was a time of deep recession and uncertainty in Europe as a whole. Greece also went through a long and painful internal devaluation, with wages and salaries being squeezed downwards and inflation rates turning negative since 2013 (Graphs 3.1 and 3.2). External competitiveness was hence restored the hard way (Graph 3.3): imports plummeted, partly because of the change in relative prices but mainly because of shrinking domestic demand, while exports did not increase that much in an inward-looking economy. The trend established during the years of irresponsibility in terms of inflation, unit labour costs, and current account imbalances was therefore dramatically reversed.

A wide range of reforms was also enacted, including pension reform and deregulation of the labour market, although these were often introduced half-heartedly and with repeated attempts to weaken their effect by politicians who were hostage to client-voters. The extent of change should not, however, be underestimated. It was a legislative and regulatory tsunami that hit virtually every sector of the economy and every section of society. The reform programme was ideologically loaded in places, too wide-ranging, often with the wrong sequencing and with little attempt to prioritize—as if you could change a country from outside and from above in a short space of time. This may be possible in textbooks, but is very difficult in practice even in a dictatorship. Greece's lenders imposed much conditionality and each time the Greek side failed to deliver, they imposed more: there is, perhaps, some logic in madness.

The area where reform proved to be the most difficult to introduce and implement properly was public administration and the general functioning of the state, which remains today the biggest obstacle to economic development in Greece. If anything, the Greek state today is more dysfunctional than it was at the beginning of the crisis: repeated cuts in personnel and salaries, combined with piecemeal reforms and little domestic ownership, have so far delivered the opposite from what had been expected.

Meanwhile, the economy imploded and so did the political system. With a loss of a quarter of its GDP and with unemployment approaching 30 per cent—youth unemployment being around 50 per cent—and with public debt as a percentage of a rapidly declining GDP being much higher than it was when the crisis broke out, Greece's adjustment can hardly qualify as a success. For the average Greek, real income after tax was reduced by 40 per cent during the crisis. Of course, averages hide large differences, especially when unemployment is so high. And, if all that was not enough, Greece became the main point of entry into Europe for very large numbers of refugees and immigrants from Syria, Iraq, Afghanistan, and other countries in trouble, crossing through Turkey. Under such conditions, it is perhaps (pleasantly) surprising that the country is more or less in one piece and with democratic institutions still functioning. Some of its European partners seem tempted to close the borders around it and turn Greece into a big refugee camp: that would be the final blow.

The economic implosion was followed by a political implosion. Just when it looked as if the Greek economy had reached rock bottom and the first modest signs of recovery began to appear in 2014, the old political order reached its limits under the burden of a deep and prolonged economic crisis, corruption and inefficiency, and the humiliation caused by an economic adjustment imposed from abroad.[17] The main elements of a classical Greek tragedy were all present: hubris followed by nemesis—with many demagogues along the way. The combination of denial from within and dogmatism from without created a vicious circle. Greece is still not out of it.

Until 2009, Greece's two biggest political parties, which had been alternating in power for more than three decades, used to receive a combined share of the vote of around 80 per cent, plus or minus. In the first of two successive elections in 2012, their combined share of the vote had fallen to slightly more than 30 per cent. They recovered partially in the second election of that year, brandishing the threat of an anti-systemic party coming to power, and governed together until January 2015. And then the threat became reality. They were replaced in power by a radical-left party, Syriza, coming from the fringes of the political system, a party which back in 2009 represented only 4 per cent of the electorate. It was a democratic revolution of sorts, with strong populist undertones,[18] taking place in the extreme conditions prevailing in Greece at the time. And Syriza chose to govern in coalition with a small party of the nationalist Right: an unorthodox marriage in Orthodox Greece.

Syriza came to power with a declared mission to change Europe, not just Greece. It challenged the domestic system, broadly (and vaguely) defined, and it also challenged Europe's policy of austerity. In doing so, it set up an alliance with other anti-systemic parties of the Left gaining popularity in the embattled periphery of Europe, most notably the Podemos party in Spain, itself the product of the Indignados protest movement that had sprung up during the crisis. The tectonic plates of European politics thus began to shift in a way that had not been seen for decades and nobody could predict what kind of earthquake would follow.

But Syriza had hardly any experience in the exercise of power and precious little knowledge of how the European system worked. It completely misjudged its own bargaining power and the balance of forces inside the eurozone, treading in European negotiating forums with the diplomatic grace of an elephant, while the Greek finance minister[19] during the first crucial months in power—an intellectual with rock star ambitions—completely mistook the Eurogroup for an academic seminar. Mr Schäuble and company were not at all pleased and they decided to teach the rebellious Greeks a lesson that was also addressed to all those who wanted to challenge the prevailing economic orthodoxy In Europe.

Presented with a German plan for Grexit and no credible plan B from their side, the Greek government finally gave in. In July 2015 it accepted a third adjustment programme with conditions that were clearly worse than those it had (successfully) asked the Greek population to reject in a referendum held a few days earlier. It was a complete mess: a democratic charade while the economy started sinking again in conditions of total uncertainty and with capital controls now being imposed to stem the flood of money leaving Greek banks in search of safe havens abroad. A big setback for the new, totally inexperienced government of Greece, it was also a setback for those advocating a different economic policy for Europe. And the spectacle of the Greek prime minister, Mr Tsipras, negotiating until early in the morning with Chancellor Merkel the details of the latest Greek programme, in the presence of the French president and the president of the Council, summarized only too well the new political reality in Europe.

Greece is still in the eurozone and likely to remain there, perhaps against the odds, for two basic reasons. One is that the large majority of Greeks believe that an exit would make things even worse for them: this political fact has constrained the actions of Greece's new political leaders who are not exactly in love with Europe—at least the Europe they know. The second is that a critical mass of key policymakers in Europe are still convinced that if only one country leaves the euro, the bonds of marriage will no longer be seen as unbreakable for the others—and then all hell would be let loose. But both reasons may not hold for ever, if euro membership continues to be associated with pain rather than gain. Is Greece a misfit in the eurozone, and if so, is it the only one? If the answer is yes to the first part of the question, it is certainly no to the second. There is a systemic problem, not just individual misfits, and on top of that, wrong policies. When the crisis first broke out, some of Greece's lenders wanted to treat it as a unique case—and they have repeatedly tried to do the same ever since. Greece remains the weakest and most vulnerable link of the euro chain: extreme in several respects, but not unique.

Monocausal explanations can hardly do justice to the truly sad story of a country that came tumbling down from the peak of success and self-confidence, fed in part by borrowed money, to being treated almost as a basket case in the course of only a few years. In the process, the old domestic order, very much imperfect though it may have been, has broken down. And Greece is a broken country. Greeks are demoralized and see no credible way out of a long and very deep crisis. But it will be up to them to find their way out, although they will certainly need a helping hand and a sense of realism from Europe. At the time of writing, the prospects were still not good on either side. The lessons from the crisis have not yet been fully digested and national politics inside the eurozone seem to be as incompatible as ever.

## Britain's Europe

If Britain had chosen to do so, it could have played a leading role in European integration from the very beginning and could have shaped the European model much closer to its own image. And luckily it did not, ardent supporters of European unity would hasten to add today, less interested in political correctness than they might have been some years back. Britain joined late in what has always looked from London like a business affair, based mostly on a narrow calculation of economic benefits and costs: an arranged marriage if you prefer, certainly not an affair of the heart.

The European project has never incited much enthusiasm in the British Isles. In the words of Winston Churchill: 'We are with Europe but not of it. We are linked but not comprised. We are interested and associated, but not absorbed.'[20] In his famous Zurich speech in 1946, Churchill spoke in favour of the United States of Europe, but Britain was not meant to be part of it. Nothing much has changed since then, many people would argue today on both sides of the Channel. Britain's political elite has always been divided on European integration and not terribly interested in it, with some notable exceptions. When the Conservatives led Britain into the Common Market, as European integration characteristically used to be referred to for many years on that side of the Channel, Labour was against. And then the roles were progressively reversed, ending up today with a strongly Eurosceptic Conservative party and a mildly pro-European (albeit with a vocal Eurosceptic minority) Labour party that does not usually want to talk much about Europe.[21]

All along, genuine Europhiles have remained a small, persecuted(!) minority within Britain's two big parties, the Liberals (now Liberal Democrats) being the only consistent and strongly pro-European political force in the country, yet small. With a mostly Europhobic tabloid press owned by foreigners (not Europeans) and persistently low levels of public support for European integration (always among the lowest registered in Eurobarometer surveys), Europe has never been treated as a vote winner by Britain's political class. If anything, it has been like a poisoned chalice[22] that has led several prominent British politicians to their premature political death. True, Britain was a late entrant to a club where the basic rules had already been set by others and it then had to fight successive battles in the name of reform to change the rules as regards the European budget and the much-hated Common Agricultural Policy. However, the problem goes much deeper: many British people and their political representatives simply do not consider themselves European.[23] Not surprisingly, they are not at all keen to transfer power and money to European institutions or indeed share their destiny with foreigners on the continent of Europe.

Nevertheless, once it joined, Britain succeeded in playing a determining role in important areas of European policy, such as the internal market, trade, enlargement, and foreign and security policy. For years, it used to find allies among those who appreciated British pragmatism, liberal views, and a strongly pro-Atlantic policy, as well as among those who looked for a counterweight to France (or France and Germany together), and last but not least, in countries outside the Union, eager to become part of the European project, who saw Britain as a champion of further enlargement. Given its relative weight as a country that had run a huge empire until a few decades previously, the quality of its political leadership and civil service, with the Rolls Royce of foreign and diplomatic service in the Foreign Office,[24] Britain's influence in European affairs was hardly surprising. Britain commanded respect, even from those who disagreed, and in turn it respected the rules once adopted, unlike some of its continental partners for whom new legislation was just one more stage in the negotiation and obeying the rules a relative matter. The differences in political cultures and legal traditions, not to mention institutional capacity in rule implementation and enforcement, were bound to cause more friction as integration deepened.

Britain has traditionally been on the liberal side in economic terms, keen on safeguarding the interests of the City of London as an international financial centre almost irrespective of the political colour of those who happened to be in power, and with a more global outlook than almost anybody else in Europe. At the same time, it has consistently tried to put its foot on the brakes and restrain the pro-integration zeal of its partners on different fronts, resorting to exceptions and opt-outs when everything else has failed. British exceptionalism has become more pronounced in the more recent phase of European integration and it has led to more isolation.

Many Conservatives blamed Thatcher's demise in 1990 on a conspiracy of pro-Europeans inside the party and turned more Eurosceptic, while sterling's forced withdrawal from the European Exchange Rate Mechanism (ERM) in 1992, when Mr Soros won his bet and some billions at the expense of the Bank of England, was traumatic. To make matters worse, France and Germany were at the time leading the way towards monetary union; this was certainly one big step too far towards integration for the British—and they opted out. The decision on EMU was a major turning point in Britain's relations with the rest of the EU. Other opt-outs followed, notably from the passport-free Schengen area, large parts of justice and home affairs, and the Charter of Fundamental Rights. The British felt increasingly uncomfortable with the accelerating pace of integration in Europe and decided to distance themselves. The arrival of New Labour, led by Mr Blair, the most European-minded prime minister since Edward Heath, did not fundamentally change the domestic scene because Blair never really tried to do so, despite constantly repeating his priority to keep Britain 'at the heart of Europe'.

The next big turning point came with the euro crisis. In (many) British eyes, Europe and the eurozone in particular were totally incapable of managing the crisis, stagnating economically yet integrating further, becoming more undemocratic in the process and run by Germans: a terrible combination indeed. Furthermore, Britain felt marginalized in a Union where the euro was at the centre, and risked becoming the recipient of policies (and failures) decided elsewhere. And it became increasingly isolated. On the Fiscal Compact, it was left in a minority of two with the Czechs. In the campaign (not very wisely) launched against the nomination of Mr Juncker as president of the Commission in 2014, the British prime minister could only rely on the support of Mr Orban in Hungary. 'Perfidious Albion' had apparently lost its knack of forming alliances on the European continent: isolation is often a self-fulfilling state of mind.

Meanwhile, on the domestic front Euroscepticism was growing. The UK Independence Party (UKIP) on the ultra-nationalist Right[25] succeeded in drawing support mostly from those left behind during the big economic and social transformations of recent decades, combining nostalgia for the (often mythical) past with a strong denunciation of European constraints on British sovereignty. And most important of all, its leader, Mr Farage, played up the issue of immigration which he identified with membership of the EU. Net migration from the rest of the EU has indeed increased substantially since the accession of central and eastern European countries, and much beyond the expectations of former Labour governments which had chosen not to make use of transitional periods allowed for by the accession treaties. Immigration provided the fodder for populism and anti-Europeanism in the UK, as it did in other European countries.[26] And UKIP succeeded in winning the largest number of votes cast at home in the European Parliament elections of 2014, although with a high rate of abstention.

In the Conservative camp, an increasing number of MPs had already decided that the most effective way to deal with the mounting challenge from the Right would be to adopt much of the vocabulary of the challenger. Under the leadership of Mr Cameron, the Conservative Party distanced itself further from the European political mainstream. In government, it called for a reformed Europe, yet often behaved as if European affairs were not of direct concern to it: the eurozone crisis was a matter for members only to resolve and the crisis in Ukraine was an issue for the French and Germans to handle; as for the refugee crisis, Britain could always put up the fences. In the words of the former president of the European Council, Herman Van Rompuy:

'How do you convince a room full of people, when you keep your hand on the door handle? How to encourage a friend to change, if your eyes are searching for your coat?'[27] And while the Conservative Party was shifting further to the right, Labour elected in 2015 a new leader, Mr Corbyn, from the far Left. In Britain's polarized political set-up, Europe does not easily fit in.

There are in fact many different kinds of Britain today:[28] a very international economy with a deregulated jobs market that attracts many people from the rest of the EU and beyond, with institutions and universities that are more open than anywhere else in Europe (speaking the lingua franca surely helps), a multi-ethnic and multicultural society, and London as the most global of cities, alongside New York. Yet Britain (or, its greater part) is also an increasingly parochial country, with England withdrawing into a 'Little England' mentality, while Scotland diverges politically, is more pro-European, and still thinks of divorce. Britain is in many ways a divided country with growing inequalities; it is not, however, unique. The sources of anti-Europeanism in the UK are not unique either. Europe often serves as a scapegoat for a variety of ills related to globalization or just modernity. Again, this happens in the best of families. However, anti-Europeanism was bound to play a much bigger role in a country that has always felt ambivalent at best about its commitment to the European project.

Espousing globalization the way Britain has done contributed significantly to internal divisions and inequalities. Between global London and little England, there may be narrow space left for Europe. Only a small minority of British politicians (but many more intellectuals[29]) have ever seen the European project as a means of collectively managing and taming globalization, a means of projecting a common model and defending shared interests and values in a rapidly changing world where the relative weight of individual European countries, the UK included, is rapidly diminishing. This is arguably where much of the political problem lies in Britain's attitude towards Europe.

## What is the real question?

In January 2013, Prime Minister Cameron announced in his Bloomberg speech[30] that he intended to ask, if re-elected, for a renegotiation of Britain's terms of membership of the EU on the basis of which he would later call an 'in' or 'out' referendum to be held before the end of 2017. A comprehensive review of EU competences and how they affect the UK had already been launched by the Foreign Secretary, intended to highlight the alleged over-centralization of powers in Brussels. It was a painstaking exercise and very comprehensive, as was to be expected from the British civil service. But having produced no spectacular results in political terms, the final report was quietly set aside.[31] After he won an (unexpected) outright majority in the 2015 election, the prime minister then proceeded to outline the UK's demands in the renegotiation. Thus, more than forty years after the 1975 referendum, history is repeating itself: another renegotiation of the terms of EU membership for the UK, again for internal party reasons (this time it is the turn of the Conservatives), and with narrow terms of reference, exactly as before.[32]

Much ado about nothing? Or a huge political gamble with high stakes? It is arguably both. The terms of reference of the renegotiation were totally disproportionate to the stakes associated with the final verdict. They were presumably meant to make the case more easily winnable which would then justify a decision to campaign for Britain to stay in. Harold Wilson had done exactly the same back in 1975. Of course, the choice presented to the British people in the referendum is not as simple or straightforward as it may appear, but referendums do not allow for complicated answers. The real choice is not black or white. A vote to remain in the EU means essentially a vote for continuing with the UK special status, a kind of semi-detached EU membership with several important exceptions, including most notably the opt-out from the euro (and a few more added as a result of the renegotiation). A vote to leave would most likely be followed by an even more difficult and long negotiation to define, among other things, the conditions of

Britain's access to the internal or single market. Britain simply cannot ignore its close economic (and political) interdependence with the rest of Europe. The experiences of Norway and Switzerland, countries that have negotiated their access to the large European market from outside, are not very encouraging—but perhaps Britain is different.

The popular verdict on Britain's membership of the EU will also have an impact on its own internal unity, since the chances of Scotland leaving the rest of the UK would greatly increase if the latter ceases to be a member of the EU. Thus, the country could be sleepwalking towards a real disaster: being cut off from its continent and then being dismembered. Of course, English Eurosceptics would treat this as pure scaremongering. On the other hand, the result of the referendum is bound to have an effect on the future course of European integration. An eventual Brexit would be a serious blow for an EU already buffeted by successive crises. It would also make it even more difficult to imagine Europe developing into a major actor in a multipolar global system. Last but not least, Brexit could be a precedent for other countries to follow, although there are no obvious candidates at present.

To cut a long story short, the stakes are very high indeed for the UK and also for the rest of Europe. Will it be the endgame[33] in the long and troubled relationship between Britain and the rest of Europe? Perhaps so, for one generation at least. But whichever way one may choose to dress it up, the choice is really between a special status inside the EU or some kind of preferred status outside: the former leaves options open for the future and a guaranteed place at the table, while the latter opens Pandora's box.

The list of British exceptions inside the EU has grown longer with time. It is, however, the euro that makes the crucial difference: the difference between the core group and the others. Britain has many good reasons to stay out of the euro, but there is also a political price to pay in terms of reduced political influence in European affairs, assuming that there is indeed a British interest in exercising such influence. The euro could break up at some stage under the weight of its own internal contradictions, as old Marxists would have put it. But do not bet on it. The experience of recent years in the midst of a huge crisis should have taught some lessons to all those who see the end of European integration as being just around the corner. And is it really something they wish for? Would the break-up of the euro (and all that would come with it) *really* be in Britain's interest?

The British government has asked for a formal exception from the 'ever closer union' objective enshrined in the preamble of the Treaty on European Union, first introduced in the Maastricht version of the treaty back in 1992. Very significantly, this non-binding wish is followed by the phrase 'in which decisions are taken as closely as possible to the citizen in accordance with the principle of subsidiarity'. 'Where is the meat?', the pragmatic British might have asked, but apparently pragmatism has its limits even in the UK. However, behind anodyne phrases, behind flags, hymns, and all kinds of symbols, there is a wide gap between Britain and many of its European partners concerning the expectations that each has from European integration. While the British prime minister speaks of 'network Europe' and cooperation in a common market, the large majority of his partners already share a common currency and take further steps in economic policy integration. Some even dare talk of political union, although federalist rhetoric has been significantly toned down in recent years. The gap is wide and goes far back in time. Compared with the past, the main difference today is that the UK is apparently willing to let others go ahead, if they wish, as long as they let the UK opt out. In other words, Britain has chosen to be at best on the outer periphery of European integration. When faced with a hard choice, very few countries, even among those outside the eurozone, would be ready to follow the UK example.

The wide diversity in terms of structures and political objectives in the EU28 requires further differentiation of policies and rules applying to members as long as everybody recognizes that rights go with obligations: no free lunch, in other words. The UK renegotiation has not gone far enough in this respect, because of political and time constraints. Europeans are apparently still not ready or able to think out of the box and take more radical steps away from the one-size-fits-all model of integration. Further internal differentiation and flexibility will be required in the future, especially if the EU is to have more enlargements.

But, as always, the devil lies in the detail. For example, Britain wants a less regulated and more competitive Europe open to global economic forces. This is not meant to be a special UK interest: a reformed EU without unnecessary rules and regulations would be good for the whole of Europe, many British politicians argue. But, of course, the beauty of regulation is in the eye of the beholder and it depends on history, institutions, and political preferences among other things. On this issue, Britain is not short of allies, more because of a shared belief that the EU may have indeed gone too far in appropriating regulatory powers for itself than because of a pronounced further shift towards economic liberalism. The European Commission is already trying to reduce EU red tape. On the other hand, given the experience of the last twenty years and more, it will not be credible to argue in favour of decentralized and light touch regulation when it concerns financial markets.

Britain has decided to stay out of European monetary integration for economic and political reasons, irrespective of whether it finally decides to stay out of the EU. And it wants to make sure that its interests with respect to financial markets in particular are not trampled over by the eurozone members. This is, of course, a perfectly legitimate demand which may justify additional legal guarantees. However, there is a much bigger issue here that lawyers are not able to address. Is London confident about the future of the City as an offshore financial centre outside EMU and in an increasingly regulated international financial environment?

Britain also wants measures to reduce net migration from the rest of the EU and the welfare benefits associated with it. This is indeed a burning political issue which has acquired a completely new dimension because of the refugee crisis. Britain has been for years a prime destination for migrant flows now outcompeted only by Germany, and populists have a field day especially among the poorer and lower skilled members of society who feel more directly threatened. The British government is therefore asking for more restrictive application of welfare benefits to immigrants and for limits to free movement applying to new members in the future. It has decided not to question the principle of free movement of people for existing members, thus heeding the clear warning issued by its European partners who still consider the free movement of people as an inalienable right of EU membership. However, if conditions of wide economic divergence and high unemployment in large parts of Europe persist, coupled with strong immigration pressures from outside, this inalienable right may not remain so for very long.

One can only hope that the debate leading to the referendum will help to make people wiser about things European and Britain's place in Europe: such a debate has been long overdue.[34] But throwing (often meaningless) figures at each other would surely not be the way to do it: the pros and cons of Britain's participation in the European project, what kind of participation in what kind of project, do not easily lend themselves to precise measurement. It would be a great pity if the opposing camps pretend otherwise. The rest of Europe wants Britain to stay and long experience from previous referendums across Europe suggests that, faced with a choice of 'in' or 'out', British citizens will probably vote for the status quo rather than for an uncertain future, more out of fear of the unknown than out of love for what is on offer. Alas, this seems to be the way many Europeans today feel about the common project—and not without justification. But we no longer live in normal times and we also know (once again, from experience) that referendums can sometimes produce unexpected results for reasons that may have little to do with the actual question asked.

In a country with a proud history, many people seem to believe that if only they could pull up the drawbridge that connects the island with the European continent, Britain would be restored to its old global power status, striking deals with other big powers and competing successfully in global markets. Perhaps they overestimate the relative weight of the country and its negotiating power and thus prefer to ignore the warnings coming from Washington or even Beijing. More importantly, they often confuse the constraints on sovereignty imposed by EU membership with the constraints that result from growing European and international interdependence. They may choose to do away with the former, but are they able to do away with the latter? That is the real question that many British Eurosceptics prefer not to answer.

# 6

# Still Holding Together, But...

If we were to travel back in time, back to the turn of the new century, we would find a confident Europe ready to take its destiny into its own hands. It was the time when European political leaders were constructing a new order for the old continent on the basis of principles and values that had guided the regional project for fifty years and more.

EMU had already begun in 1999 with more members than anybody would have dared to predict some years earlier, when the previous European exchange rate system collapsed and Mr Soros humiliated the Bank of England. The creation of a common currency opened a new phase in European integration; the sky was now the limit. And a European constitution was meant to follow soon, opening the way for the United States of Europe—or so hoped a still-active and ever-conspiring minority of federalists. As for the British, they could no longer restrain the integration zeal of their partners and followed reluctantly, waiting for an opportunity to put their foot on the brakes again. But they were also keen on the big-bang enlargement of the EU. The more the merrier, the British thought, and the looser the organization that would result from such an enlargement. Of course, they usually avoided saying as much in public—as did people on the other side of the Atlantic who feared that a strong and united Europe might challenge US supremacy after the end of the Cold War. Those were the days.

Yet, enlargement was also the epitome of Europe's soft power: exporting peace, democracy, modernization, and regulated capitalism to the former communist countries of central and eastern Europe. In fact, European soft power was meant to extend beyond European boundaries, thus providing a solid base for a common European foreign policy. It was the moment of triumph of the European project and Europe's political leaders could have been excused an excess of self-confidence. In their first attempt to define the European Security Strategy, in a document adopted at the European Council of December 2003, they began by stating that 'Europe has never been so prosperous, so secure nor so free'.[1]

So much has changed since then. Europe has been buffeted by successive crises, each more difficult than the last. It is no longer particularly confident—on the contrary. It is certainly much weaker in economic and political terms, while security has become a big issue once again. The European model (or models) has lost much of its shine in the process. But in these very difficult times, Europe has remained in one piece and free—albeit illiberal ideas and practices are spreading in parts of the continent. Will Europe continue holding together despite strong forces that threaten to pull it apart, and if so, in what shape or form? It is a very demanding stress test indeed for the 'oldest'[2] region in the world.

## The European paradox

The early European success story had been based on an elitist, yet benign, conspiracy led by the French, later in close cooperation with the Germans, with support from virtually all mainstream parties in participating countries with the exception of the UK, and relying on a wide permissive consensus of citizens who supported European integration as long as it was seen to be delivering the goods. Some countries were (naturally) more equal than others in the way they influenced decisions. But small countries were over-represented in European institutions and the less developed ones treated regional integration as a convergence machine and a provider of funds as well. It looked like a good deal for all concerned and ever more countries wanted to join in. Permissive consensus was, however, gradually eroded as the European project became bigger, more intrusive, and less inclusive in an economic environment that had turned more competitive and less favourable. Thus, a gap gradually opened up between elite and popular perceptions on Europe, which looked manageable for a while. But with the debt crisis leading to the big crisis of the euro, some of the fundamentals of regional integration began to change along with European politics. We have ended up with a very different Europe as a result.

Germany has become the undisputed leader in the person of Chancellor Merkel, centrifugal forces have grown much stronger, and intra-European politics often turned ugly. Trust between Europeans and popular trust in political leaders and institutions have reached unprecedented lows and European integration has become an increasingly divisive issue. In different ways, growing economic divergence between and within countries has been translated into political divergence, if not polarization, though the cause has not only been of an economic nature. The rise of nationalism has gone hand in hand with growing Euroscepticism in its strong and light varieties. To top it all, a common European foreign policy drawing mostly on soft power came in for some rough treatment by all kinds of bullies, or simply because soft power was not really what it was meant to be. The world around Europe has changed a great deal, and in most cases not for the better.

With the benefit of hindsight, it is now clear that European integration suffers from overstretch. It is, however, an overstretch that has been largely imposed upon Europe by external events, most notably the collapse of the communist order to the east of the old Iron Curtain, which brought about both monetary union and the near doubling of EU membership. It may indeed be difficult for dedicated Europeans, especially those who have made a profession of Europe (and there are quite a few of them living within the Brussels balloon), to admit that regional integration in its later phase went too far and too fast, but there are strong signs pointing in this direction. Common institutions have experienced great difficulties in coping with constantly expanding members and functions, while citizens across Europe have become increasingly reluctant to accept the intrusion of ever more decisions and rules adopted in faraway places by people they do not easily identify with.

The institutional and legitimacy deficits of the European construction became only too apparent in times of crisis. Brussels has repeatedly shown itself to be structurally incapable of dealing fast and effectively with a major crisis—and there have been quite a few of them in recent years. Comparisons with the United States are mostly unflattering. But is it fair to compare an emerging political system such as the EU—a loose confederation at best—with a mature federation, even with all its inherent gridlock, like the US? The comparison needs to be made for the simple reason that the European system, highly decentralized though it remains, has been called upon to manage a common currency and police common borders among other things—and it has not been up to the task, if not for want of trying.

The euro is clearly the most extreme form of European overstretch: a common currency with a very inadequate institutional structure in its original design, incompatible membership, and an extremely weak political base. Admittedly, it is not at all obvious what kind of intra-European exchange rate regime would best suit a European internal market—surely not a system of floating exchange rates, especially when markets run amok as they often do. But to think you could manage a currency shared by very different countries and economies with a common, yet tightly constrained, central bank and a few rules to restrict the autonomy of national economic policy was really bordering on the naïve.

Arguably, the main problem with the euro has been not so much one of overstretch as of a collective denial of the political, economic, and institutional consequences of the decision to share a common currency. Sylvie Goulard, a dynamic French MEP and academic, has compared national governments to spoiled children who seem to want contradictory objectives: the benefits of European integration without the constraints on national sovereignty, competitiveness without painful reforms, a strong EU with weak institutions.[3] This is a very apt description of European reality that seems to apply particularly to French governments. It is quite remarkable that the French, the main force behind European monetary integration all along, have three times now repeated the same experience. They used the currency as the means to tie the Germans to the European mast and ended up with the Germans driving the boat, even reluctantly, and the French are not at all happy with the direction it takes. With monetary union, French strategic thinking has not been at its best, to put it mildly, and contradictory objectives have been a large part of the problem.

EMU's poor design and divergent membership, combined with wrong policies during the Great Recession, have cost Europe a great deal. The distribution of the cost between and within countries has often turned European politics toxic. But Europe was also unlucky, since the first big test of the euro coincided with nothing less than a huge generational crisis of Western financial capitalism.[4] A whole era of financial deregulation leading, and in turn accelerating, the process of economic globalization came to an abrupt end with the crisis of 2007–8. And with it came crumbling down the so-called Washington Consensus[5] on economic policy promoted zealously for many years by Western governments, steered by the United States, and Western-led international institutions such as the IMF and the World Bank. The West lost face and it also lost its intellectual supremacy when financial markets imploded. Given the magnitude of the crisis unleashed, one might have expected much stronger political repercussions to follow in the countries directly concerned. But history suggests that such repercussions may take a long time to unwind fully. We may be caught in the midst of a major political transition; the end of an era, perhaps? We shall return to this subject later.

During the crisis, continuous efforts have been made to strengthen the governance of the euro and improve on the weaknesses of the original design—still an incomplete task. In doing so, two major obstacles had to be overcome. One was the widening gap in terms of the perceptions and interests of participating countries as to the appropriate rules to be adopted and policies to be followed. Repeatedly, German leadership acted as a bulldozer in order to reach an agreement, leaving behind a great deal of frustration among those who were forced to follow. The counter-argument would be that without German leadership no agreement would have been possible. On the other hand, better governance of the euro generally implied more centralization and hence further transfer of powers to European institutions, such as the ECB and to a lesser extent the Commission. If there was already a problem of overstretch and a democratic deficit in European decision-making, this could only make things worse. 'Deal with the democratic deficit first' might be the answer, but nobody among the protagonists really showed any interest in embarking on such an exercise. After all, they are just politicians who have been repeatedly lynched by reality, are they not?

The new governance structure of the euro may be more effective but is hardly more legitimate. The increasingly intergovernmental nature of European decision-making, the transfer of more powers to central institutions—especially the ECB run by politically non-accountable central bankers—as well as the ever more binding constraints on national economic policy resulting from tighter eurozone rules, have further reduced the power of national parliaments. Alas, the European Parliament has not been very successful until now in filling the democratic vacuum created. The EU constitutes the most advanced case study of the so-called 'globalization paradox' analysed by Harvard economist Dani Rodrik,[6] who has argued rather convincingly that faced with the 'trilemma' consisting of globalization (global markets), sovereignty, and democracy, countries today can only choose a combination of two out of three at a time—unless they happen to be the hegemon, I might add.

As a result of many years of regional integration, Europe has reached a very high level of interdependence managed through shared sovereignty. Democracy has always been the weak link, since the constraints on national democracy resulting from integration have never been adequately compensated for at European level.[7] During the recent economic crisis, many Europeans felt they were losing both sovereignty and democracy and they were told it was for the sake of the euro. The European version of Rodrik's paradox is by far the most advanced and hence also the most difficult to deal with. The euro has added a new dimension to the European paradox, which became all too obvious during the recent crisis.

## Domestic losers and broken contracts

What the recent crisis has also done is to make the division between winners and losers from European integration and globalization (the two being closely interconnected and almost indistinguishable in the eyes of the losers) sharper than ever.[8] This division cuts right across all member countries. Those who benefit from open borders and high economic interdependence—and most are naturally keen supporters of European integration and globalization—can be found in Germany, France, and Sweden, as well as in Spain, Greece, and Slovakia. They belong to a cross-border coalition of Europeans, informal yet powerful: a cosmopolitan elite broadly defined whose members are usually well educated, mobile, and well off. They are the clear winners in a rapidly changing world that offers many opportunities to those willing or able to take advantage of them, yet also a world of 'radical uncertainty'[9] in which a growing number of people face worsening job prospects and stagnant—or indeed declining—living standards, people who see themselves on the losing side of change. These two large groups hardly interact or understand each other. Our societies are divided: those who win often do not think much of national borders while the losers are ever more tempted to seek protection under the national umbrella. This umbrella may be full of holes. Some people already realize this, others don't, but they know of no other means of protection to turn to. The debt crisis, followed by the Great Recession and the crisis of the euro, has greatly exacerbated an already existing problem.

In the earlier stages of integration, Europe acted mostly as an agent of economic liberalization breaking down national economic barriers and freeing the forces of competition, while the nation state was responsible for stabilization policies and redistribution at home—a division of labour that has been aptly described as 'Keynes at home and [Adam] Smith abroad'.[10] Rapidly rising levels of economic prosperity across the board were combined with a more equal distribution of income within countries: it was Europe's golden age. Problems began around the mid-1970s, when growth and productivity rates in Europe went down while unemployment rates moved in the opposite direction. Soon afterwards, income inequalities within countries also began to rise, thus reversing the previous happy trend.

The Oxford-based economist Tony Atkinson attributes the growing income inequalities of the last thirty years or so in the developed world (more in the US and the UK than the rest of Europe) to a combination of factors, namely globalization, technological change (especially in the information and communication sectors), the growth of financial services, changing pay norms, the weakening of trade unions, and the reduced role of the redistributive policies of the state through taxes and transfers.[11] Most of these factors are man- (or woman-)made; they are not the product of forces of nature (or technology) beyond the control of human beings. This is a key point: it is political decisions and choices that have been largely responsible for the more unequal societies we now live in. It has been the era of neo-liberalism, of more market and less state, of growing individualism and the weakening of societal bonds. In its more recent phase, it has suffered from big market failures and political failures. Interestingly enough, the predominance of social democratic and labour parties in most European countries for a rather long period preceding the bursting of the big bubble in 2007–8 had not made any noticeable difference to the prevalence of neo-liberal ideology for the very simple reason that the European centre-left had bought into it.

In a path-breaking book entitled *Capital in the Twenty-First Century*,[12] drawing on a wealth of data since the eighteenth century from many countries, the French economist Thomas Piketty draws the conclusion that market economies, if left to themselves, contain powerful forces of divergence because wealth accumulated in the past tends to grow more rapidly than output and wages, thus creating a self-perpetuating circle of widening disparities of income and wealth: a time bomb for both social cohesion and political stability. According to Piketty, it was the two world wars that massively destroyed accumulated wealth in Europe followed by high rates of growth during the golden age, when Europe was still catching up: they temporarily reversed this long-term trend. We have been back on it during the last three decades or so.

True, inequalities in most European countries are not as bad as in the United States where the gap between top and bottom incomes has widened dramatically during this period. The top 1 per cent in the US now account for almost 20 per cent of gross income in the country and 58 cents of every dollar of real income growth between 1976 and 2007 went to the top 1 per cent of US households[13]—so much for spreading widely the gains from competition in global markets. In fact, the more you narrow down the privileged few, notably the top 1 per cent within the top 1 per cent, the more glaring the disparity. In Europe, income inequalities are wider in the UK, which has many similarities with the US (the relative size of the financial sector being one of them), as well as in the south and in the central and eastern countries that were formerly communist.

As long as the 'catching-up' process continued in the south and large amounts of development money flowed from European Structural Funds, Europe remained for people in these countries an object of desire. It largely ceased to be so when the big crisis hit and Europe was transformed almost overnight into a policeman of austerity in times of negative growth, rising unemployment, and successive cuts in already lean welfare systems. Many of those living on the southern periphery therefore turned into losers in a big way. In the Baltics and the Balkans, many people suffered a similar fate during the crisis. But the prospect of catching up with the more prosperous countries of western Europe continues to act as a magnet and EU development money is still flowing in, while the bad memories of the communist era are still alive. And when all other alternatives have been exhausted (or almost), emigration remains an option for the young Latvians, Bulgarians, or Romanians.

A big threat to the European project today comes from growing discontent in the old and more developed member states where domestic social contracts have come under increasing pressure in times of low or zero growth, economic austerity, high unemployment, and ever more precarious, part-time jobs. Inequalities have been on the rise virtually everywhere and the feeling of injustice (and powerlessness) has been stronger than ever among an increasing number of European citizens. Having not benefited much in the times of plenty, they deeply resented being forced to shoulder the main burden of adjustment during the Great Recession. They blamed bankers and politicians, globalization and European integration, and they blamed 'the system' in its different national incarnations and names. They did so much more in France than in Germany: growth but mainly unemployment statistics in the two countries can provide much of the explanation. French domestic politics will be a decisive factor for European integration in the next few years, and not for the first time.

Those people who fear going under in our societies consider Europe as an agent of economic liberalization and fiscal austerity and consequently do not see much in it for them, unless they happen to be on the receiving end of the generosity of Structural Funds and the Common Agricultural Policy: a relatively small minority today in the old member countries. The division of labour between Europe and the nation state is therefore no longer working: the gains from open borders are unequally distributed in an unfavourable economic environment, while social protection provided by the state is getting weaker with time. The implicit European contract has been broken.

Under these conditions, Europe has come to be seen by losers and potential losers alike as part of the problem and not part of the solution—and they have turned against it. In times when distributional politics once again reached the top of the agenda, Europe has had little to offer to people who believe that the economic odds are against them. Some years back, the European Globalization Adjustment Fund was created with a view to helping the adjustment of those who lose their jobs as a result of global competition.[14] In practice, it proved to be one more symbolic gesture of the sort that Europe specializes in. Such gestures only help to widen further Europe's credibility deficit among the more vulnerable members of society.

It may not be that different with European programmes to fight youth unemployment, announced with much fanfare at European councils but lacking in concrete measures and money. The intergenerational contract is not working either. In most western European countries, the younger generation will inherit a heavy debt burden from its parents—not to mention the environmental burden—and will expect to live less prosperously, in ageing societies with slow growth prospects. It will be the first time since the end of the Second World War that this has been the case. In the south in particular, the spectre of a lost generation looms ahead. Unemployment among the young today is about double the average rate in Europe as whole, i.e. more than 20 per cent; it is 40 per cent in Italy and close to 50 per cent in Greece and Spain. As things stand today, the young will be the main losers from a growth model that used to be based on debt and with dual labour markets to protect the interests of insiders, i.e. mostly those from the older generations.

## Immigrants and refugees

In a period of growing social discontent, immigration has turned into a hot political issue, reaching boiling point in some European countries. According to Eurostat, approximately one person out of ten living in an EU country on 1 January 2014 had been born abroad (approximately 52 million out of whom 33.5 million from non-EU countries). The figures were slightly higher than the average in the UK and Germany, almost 16 per cent in Sweden, and as many as

43 per cent in little Luxembourg, where it related mostly to people from other European countries. Big European cities had become very multicultural: 37 per cent of people living in London had been born abroad, 27 per cent of those in Munich, and 25 per cent of those in Paris.

Immigration in the EU has grown since 2000, with a further accelerating trend during the economic crisis, and reached a peak in 2015 when unprecedented numbers of refugees and irregular immigrants began to arrive on dinghy boats on Greek islands close to the Turkish coast. Between 2008 and 2013, 2.9 million new immigrants entered the UK, attracted by job opportunities in a very flexible labour market and a more dynamic economy, at least in recent years, not to mention the advantage of being able to speak an international language. Approximately 700,000 Poles live in the UK today. Since 2011, Germany has been catching up fast by attracting an increasing number of mostly young, educated people from European countries in crisis, and more recently having opened its doors to Syrian and other refugees. Germany is now far ahead of other EU countries in terms of absolute numbers of new immigrants.

Freedom of movement inside the EU constitutes one of the fundamental freedoms that are enshrined in European treaties—and indeed one of its sacred cows, as Mr Cameron discovered the hard way in trying to restrict internal migration from the rest of the EU in the context of the renegotiation of UK membership. For many years, it used to be a freedom that few people made use of inside the EU. What has changed in the last ten years or so has been the accession of countries with much lower levels of economic development, and then the economic crisis. Numbers have shot up as a result. For young people in the Baltics, also Bulgaria and Romania, and increasingly in southern Europe, the greatest advantage of EU membership may be the freedom to emigrate: a mixed blessing at best for their countries of origin and often a cause for concern for countries on the receiving end.

Immigration from outside the EU is an altogether different matter: there is no legal obligation to allow immigrants in, except for those legitimately seeking political asylum, although the distinction between political refugees and economic immigrants has never been easy. Economists usually refer to the benefits of labour migration, especially for countries with ageing and declining populations such as the large majority of European countries today. What could be better for stagnant labour markets and welfare systems under stress than the injection of a good number of young immigrants eager to work? It is surely a strong argument. But then comes the warning from those who fear that European societies may soon go above the threshold of tolerance for change and for the 'Other'. Several countries may have already reached that point: growing opposition to immigration and xenophobia very quickly transits from protest to organized political expression, and this is precisely what has been happening in many parts of Europe. Immigration has a big impact on the domestic politics of many European countries. In 2015, it became the number one issue of concern for most Europeans (according to Eurobarometer data), more in the north than in the south where they had many other problems to contend with.

Within countries, this concern has been even more pronounced among the weaker and more vulnerable members of society. The people with strong feelings against globalization also tend to have strong feelings against immigration, which is in turn closely identified with EU membership. They tend to be male, older, with lower education and income.[15] They have turned anti-European, xenophobic in general, and they do not have much time for political correctness. Similar things have been happening on the other side of the Atlantic on the way to the presidential election of 2016. Fears of 'social dumping' and 'welfare tourism'—meaning that immigrant workers tend to offer their services at much lower wages than locals and are also suspected of scrounging on national welfare systems—have combined in several European countries with concerns about national identity and cultural homogeneity. Economics combined with culture often make for a heady mix. And there are plenty of demagogues in every country ready to exaggerate numbers and stir up feelings of insecurity, especially among those who feel under threat in a rapidly changing economic and social environment. In such conditions, nationalism serves as a convenient mobilizing force: the formula has been tried many times before all over the world.

Irrespective of the model adopted—ranging from a strong assimilation policy *à la française* to 'letting a hundred flowers bloom' in the multicultural Netherlands, Sweden, and the UK—integration of large ethnic and religious minorities has not proved to be a smooth operation in any European country.[16] Some minorities integrate more easily than others. We therefore need to recognize that, although cultural diversity is indeed enriching, it is not always politically easy to manage, especially in times of crisis when economics comes to be perceived as a zero-sum game. Good intentions combined with political innocence can do a great deal of damage.

Former imperial countries have a longer experience on the receiving end of migration, dating back to the 1960s in the fallout of empires and decolonization. Germany started importing large numbers of *Gastarbeiter* (guest workers), mostly from Europe including Turkey, at about the same time to help build the German economic miracle, and then discovered that many of these workers came to stay and brought their families along. And Sweden has long been particularly generous with its immigration policy, especially as regards asylum seekers.

For the countries of southern Europe and also Ireland, large-scale immigration is a relatively recent phenomenon. Having been for long periods of their modern history large exporters of labour to other more prosperous European countries, as well as to America and faraway Australia, they reversed roles in the years of plenty preceding the crisis. Geography and history of course played a big role. Albanians and Bulgarians came to Greece and also to Italy which became a favourite destination for immigrants from the Balkans and Africa, while Latin Americans went to Spain and people from all over arrived in large numbers at the shores of Ireland. And when the crash came, roles were reversed once again.

In some respects, the countries of central and eastern Europe for the last twenty-five years or so have had a similar experience as southern Europe and Ireland during the first decades after the end of the Second World War: large-scale emigration as a way out from poverty and unemployment combined with relatively closed and conservative societies at home. And suddenly in 2015, refugees and other immigrants began to arrive in large numbers in south-eastern Europe. The countries of central and eastern Europe wanted to have nothing to do with them: they wanted emigration not immigration—especially not from people of different cultures or religions—and their leaders said so in no uncertain terms.

Almost 1 million refugees and irregular immigrants were estimated to have landed in Greece alone in 2015, coming in search of the European dream or just a safe haven. The island of Lesbos, which became the main point of arrival for immigrants crossing from the Turkish coast, exemplified Greece's contradictions: a weak state along with strong manifestations of solidarity from non-governmental organizations and local inhabitants ready to offer a helping hand to people in need. The traditional route via Italy—in particular the small island of Lampedusa close to the Libyan coast—had shifted eastwards as the composition of refugees and immigrants changed. They now included large numbers of Syrians fleeing the civil war in their unfortunate country, and also Iraqis, Iranians, Afghanis, Pakistanis, and people from North Africa and as far south as Sudan and Eritrea. There are many more (temporarily?) hosted in Turkey and Jordan, plus large numbers of internally displaced people in Syria ready to move further, not to mention millions of others desperately keen to escape from Europe's poor and troubled neighbourhood. Meanwhile, people-smuggling has become one of the fastest growing industries providing finance for criminal networks.

Europe will have a hard task in the months and years ahead to reconcile its humanitarian values and traditions (also its long-term economic interest, some people would add) with the need to preserve social and political stability at home, where anti-immigration parties and protest movements have been rapidly gaining strength, and their discourse has already entered mainstream politics. Coming in the wake of the Great Recession, the refugee crisis thus risks succeeding where the euro crisis has so far failed, namely in breaking Europe apart. One million refugees in a year for a continent of 500 million people is surely not that much. Compared to what has happened in a small country such as Jordan where refugees from the war in Syria represent almost 20 per cent of the population, it is trivial. However, the political climate in Europe is very tense, solidarity among countries is in short supply, and the numbers of potential refugees and immigrants are indeed staggering.

For once, Chancellor Merkel threw caution to the wind and took the moral high ground by opening Germany's doors to refugees, in stark contrast to most of her European counterparts. In 2015, Germany welcomed more than 1 million refugees, more than all the other European countries put together. In doing so, Mrs Merkel was, however, accused by other European leaders of deciding unilaterally to open the floodgates while also stretching the limits of what German society and local authorities could take. Some people suspect that the refugee crisis could be Chancellor Merkel's political undoing. If so, it would be a heroic exit.

At European level, the refugee crisis has raised two very important issues. One has been about burden-sharing among member countries and the other about policing Europe's common borders. As refugees and immigrants set out on the long journey from the Greek islands to central Europe, with Germany as their favourite destination, transit countries suddenly had to deal with hundreds of thousands of desperate people whom local authorities tried to push on as quickly as possible to the next frontier. The European Commission, with the strong support of Germany and France, tried to get member countries to agree on national quotas for the relocation of refugees, as a way of alleviating the burden on those most directly affected—notably Greece, Italy, and Hungary, as key transit countries on the international migration route, as well as Germany and Sweden (the two countries with the most open-door policies). The reaction from governments in central and eastern Europe in particular was strong and often ugly. A new division was thus created in Europe, this time along the east–west axis. And although a European agreement on the relocation of refugees has been reached by qualified majority with some countries kicking and screaming, it has been extremely slow in its implementation. Only some 200 people were relocated by the end of 2015. Thus, intra-European solidarity went through another very difficult test and, once again, it was found wanting.

European countries reintroduced border controls and erected fences to stop the human tide from entering their own territory. Such measures were not compatible with intra-European open borders under the Schengen agreement, although they were supposed to be temporary. Another one of the main achievements of European integration thus came under threat. But as with the euro before, the threat of a break-up touched a sensitive nerve in the right quarters and it could end up being the catalyst for further integration. In December 2015, the European Commission, with the support of Germany and France once again, made a truly daring proposal for the creation of a European border and coast guard to police Europe's common borders (the Schengen borders to be precise). It would have more money and staff than its predecessor Frontex, which had already been overtaken by events, and, strikingly, it would have the power to intervene on the territory of a member country on the external borders of the EU, even without that country's permission.

If agreed, this would be another major step in European integration under pressure. A common force to police the borders of an (over) extended empire and with the power to overrule member states on their own territory: who would have guessed that only a few years back? There are some interesting parallels to draw between the refugee crisis and the euro crisis. Is there an inexorable logic of cumulative integration that ties up with the everlasting conspiracy of federalists? The answer is that the Franco-German couple, in close cooperation with the Commission and a few other countries, is trying hard to defend the common project under very adverse conditions. The proposal for a common border force is, of course, controversial especially in the eyes of governments that risk being overruled in the future as regards the protection of their own borders. Neither the Germans nor the French would ever have accepted such a thing. Conveniently, their own national borders are inside the Schengen area. It is also unclear what the policing of external borders may actually imply when European border guards are faced with sinking boats of refugees and immigrants in the Mediterranean or the Aegean Sea. Policing of external borders will not be enough to stem the tide of immigration. The unpleasant truth for Europe is that there is no simple or effective answer to the problem.

Another parallel with the euro crisis was that Greece was again cast in the role of catalyst or scapegoat. Greece became the main point of entry of refugees and immigrants coming via Turkey and experienced enormous difficulties in handling such numbers. Thus, some Europeans began to flirt with the idea of shutting Greece out of Schengen, which would leave a large number of refugees and immigrants stranded on Greek territory, while also sending a powerful message to potential new arrivals that Greece could be their last stop. Grexit thus appeared in a different form this time: it concerned the borders and not the currency.

## Security and high politics

The refugee crisis has surely not been made any easier by the rising threat of jihadis, home-grown or imported, who draw their inspiration and mostly receive their training in military camps in Syria where large chunks of territory, also of Iraq, have been under the control of the Islamic State (IS).[17] A succession of terrorist outrages in European cities and elsewhere over the years perpetrated by people waving different flags, yet all in the name of radical Islam, culminated in the coordinated attack that took place in Paris in November 2015, and more recently in Brussels. European authorities are preparing for the worst and for the long haul knowing full well that a few thousands of their own citizens have come under the spell of IS and might be ready to take their lives together with those of innocent victims. And more may be trying to enter Europe hiding inside the otherwise peaceful flux of refugees and immigrants escaping from violence and poverty back home. The refugee crisis has therefore become an internal security issue as well, and this hardly makes it any easier to deal with.[18]

Europe's neighbourhood is shaking: the tectonic plates are shifting fast and the tremors are felt all over Europe, while the continent is trying at the same time to deal with the growing problem of alienated immigrant youths who have developed a deep hatred for the Western way of life. Not only Europe's open borders, but also security and political stability at home are at stake. The end of the Cold War created the illusion that EU countries could export Pax Europaea not only to the rest of the continent, through EU membership, but also further afield by offering incentives to neighbouring countries to become 'more like us': soft power on the cheap, this is what many Europeans dreamt of in their mental postmodern world.[19] Alas, it has turned out to be more like a nightmare from which Europeans find it extremely difficult to escape. Short of EU membership, which has not proved to be a panacea either, all other policies addressed to Europe's neighbours have largely failed to deliver. Both carrots and sticks employed have simply been too weak to have much of an effect.

Thus, Europeans have been learning the hard way about the difficult dilemmas and narrow constraints of trying to exert influence outside their borders, even in their immediate neighbourhood: not a comfortable conclusion to reach for some countries that still have memories, though distant, of ruling the world. On a different scale, the Americans have been going through a similar experience in the more recent past, when US hegemony has repeatedly hit against tight domestic as well as external constraints. Trying to rule the world has been an increasingly difficult and frustrating experience with some big failures: remember Iraq?

The Arab Spring has not produced the democratic transition that many people in the West had hoped for. Autocratic regimes are still around in most countries, bloody civil wars are being waged, post-colonial borders break down, and much of the conflict in the wider Middle East is rapidly being transformed into a major religious war. It risks being both extremely violent and long—more so if Iran and Saudi Arabia continue to be engaged in it, even if fighting by proxies. Meanwhile, the Palestinian issue remains as far from being resolved as ever and Israel is not at all in a hurry to move towards a two-state solution. Will it ever be? Regional politics in the wider Middle East today is truly awful, the prospects are not good either, and the intervention of foreign powers has not usually made matters any better.

In November 2014, Ms Mogherini took over as 'High Representative of the European Union for Foreign and Security Policy' (which also comes with a sizeable European diplomatic force and budget), yet with relatively little in terms of common strategy and collective commitment to back it up. The terms 'High Representative' and 'European External Action Service' for the diplomatic force are quite indicative: Europeans are not exactly sure, or not yet in agreement, as to what they really want. A common European foreign and security policy is still a long-term ambition at best.[20] Europeans have played a very constructive role in the Iran nuclear negotiations. In contrast, they have felt collectively impotent all along as regards the Israeli–Palestinian conflict. They were deeply divided on the Iraq War between 'old' and 'new' Europe in the famous words of Donald Rumsfeld, then US Secretary of Defense, who did his best to make the division true and stronger. More recently, the refugee crisis and terrorist attacks have forced Europeans to become more actively engaged in trying to bring about an end to the bloody war in Syria. They have high stakes in the restoration of peace in the region, certainly higher than the United States which enjoys a long safe distance from the scenes of war. Yet, Europeans have limited capacity to help restore peace in their neighbourhood and also to insulate themselves from the consequences of war, including notably the arrival of large numbers of refugees and immigrants.

Europeans have had to negotiate with Messrs Erdoğan and Putin, two leaders with strong autocratic tendencies who have switched from love to hate for each other following the downing of a Russian fighter plane by the Turks on the border between Syria and Turkey. The latter controls the gate through which the flood of refugees enters Europe, while the active engagement of Russia now looks like a necessary condition to reach any kind of settlement in Syria. Mr Putin has skilfully demonstrated to his European and American interlocutors that he still has strong cards to play; they had thought (or hoped) otherwise. Here again, the leading role from the European side has been taken by Germany and France. Mrs Merkel does more of the negotiation and Mr Hollande does more of the war game. Germany and France have an implicit division of labour in this respect: sometimes it works.

On the eastern border, things have not been much easier. Russia under Putin has tried to make sure—and so far largely succeeded—that the hard reality of spheres of influence in its shared neighbourhood with the EU would not give way to European soft power employing the instrument of association or partnership agreements, with the prospect of EU membership in the very distant future. Small countries close to Russia again feel under direct threat and they do not think they receive enough support and solidarity from their European partners: the Balts feel most strongly about it for obvious reasons of history and geography. In Ukraine, European policy in the earlier phase was literally hijacked by a small group of member countries who chose to ignore Russian sensitivities—albeit the sensitivities of a bear, as they would contend. But when it came to the crunch, with Mr Putin upping the stakes, Europeans collectively were unwilling or unable to put their money (and whatever power they had) where their mouth was.

Did the Americans do any better on Ukraine? Hardly so, would be the honest answer.[21] At least, in a damage limitation exercise,

Europeans and Americans succeeded in preserving their fragile unity on sanctions against Russia, following the Russian annexation of Crimea and the rebellion/invasion in the eastern regions of Ukraine. Once again, Chancellor Merkel was mobilized to limit the damage in cooperation with the French. As for the Brussels bureaucracy, they seem incapable of thinking or acting strategically: high politics is clearly not their forte.

## Fear not love

European overstretch, successive market and political failures, deep divisions caused by the economic crisis, widening inequalities, and the ever rising numbers of immigrants in societies on the edge with a growing sense of insecurity, have all taken their toll. Europe has disappointed many of those who had invested their hopes in it and others who had more passively accepted the European project as part of modernity. The permissive consensus of the past has thus been transformed into an important political cleavage in its own right in many countries. The origins of this transformation date back to around the time of the Maastricht Treaty on EMU, although things have been moving much faster in recent years. European integration has become increasingly identified with globalization, while the division between winners and losers has gone deeper in times of growing uncertainty and volatility—particularly when the economic pie has ceased to grow. It is, of course, not just a problem that concerns the common European project. It is much bigger and relates to the way in which globalization has been managed (or not managed), the way in which financial markets have been regulated (or not regulated), and the way in which adjustment costs have been distributed between and within countries after the bursting of the big bubble.

According to Eurobarometer surveys, public support for the EU reached a record low in 2013, when positive replies referring to the image that citizens had of the EU were almost as numerous as negative ones. The decline in public support was particularly pronounced in

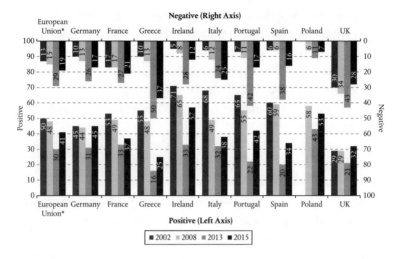

**Graph 6.1** Public Support for the EU (2002, 2008, 2013 and 2015)

*Source*: European Commission, Standard Eurobarometer surveys (SE 57-Spring 2002, SE 69-Spring 2008, SE 79-Spring 2013, SE 83-Spring 2015).

Percentage (%) of respondents answering "Very positive" and "Fairly positive" or "Very negative" and "Fairly negative" to the question: "In general, does the European Union conjure up for you a very positive, fairly positive, neutral, fairly negative or very negative image?"

* European weighted average: EU15 for 2002, EU27 for 2008 and EU28 for 2015

countries worst hit by the crisis, precisely those countries that used to register very high positive figures in the past. Southern Europe turned Eurosceptic, as the UK has always been, although for different reasons. It is not so much an issue of identity in the south. Core Europe began to have serious doubts as well, as shown by figures for Germany and France, while Poland, a relatively new member still growing fast outside the eurozone, appeared to be less affected by rising Euroscepticism (Graph 6.1).

Permissive consensus thus took another big turn for the worse. The partial recovery experienced since then has gone hand in hand with the slow recovery of European economies, thus confirming once again that love for Europe goes largely through the pocket of European citizens—but remains in short supply today. Popular trust in political institutions and elites also declined in a big way across Europe during the crisis; in the south, it plummeted. In 2014, fewer than one in five citizens in southern European countries said they had trust in their own governments. The large majority in these countries treated domestic political elites as both inefficient and corrupt. Not surprisingly, they tended to trust European institutions more than national ones. In this respect, France was closer to the south than to the north. And the situation was hardly any better in most of the former communist countries to the east where democratic roots have not yet gone deep enough and popular trust in political institutions and elites has been low.

However, high levels of public support for the euro have persisted in all countries through the difficult years. This also applies to countries that crossed the economic desert through painful adjustment programmes (Graph 6.2). Here comes the puzzle: how can weak public support for European integration be reconciled with strong

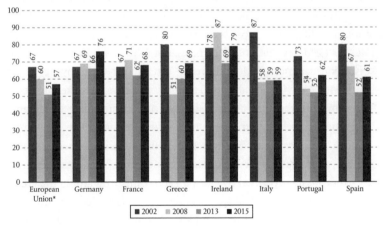

**Graph 6.2** Public Support for the euro (2002, 2008, 2013 and 2015)

*Source*: European Commission, Standard Eurobarometer surveys (SE 57-Spring 2002, SE 69-Spring 2008, SE 79-Spring 2013, SE 83-Spring 2015).

Percentage (%) of respondents answering to the question: "Are you for or against a European economic and monetary union with one single currency, the euro?"

*European Union weighted average: EU15 for 2002, EU27 for 2008 and EU28 for 2015.

support for the euro? After all, the euro has been at the centre of the crisis. Have many Europeans turned masochist or schizophrenic under stress? I suspect the explanation is much more simple and mundane. It is not so much love for the euro that lies behind these positive figures but fear, fear of the consequences of a break-up that makes euro-holders cling to the euro no matter what. In other words, the fear of hanging separately, if Europeans do not succeed in hanging together, seems to have so far kept everybody on board.

The economic consequences of a break-up of the euro are extremely difficult, if not impossible, to predict. Attempts to quantify them make little sense, although that has never stopped economists from trying. Trade and financial interdependence in the eurozone (and Europe at large) is very high and the return to national currencies could be an extremely costly and messy affair. It would not be in any way comparable with the breakdown of regional exchange rate arrangements in the past. Several commentators have spoken of a gigantic financial shock wave or a meltdown if the euro were to break up, to be followed by big losses in trade and output, large numbers of bankruptcies, and a huge amount of litigation across borders following large shifts in exchange rates between new national currencies, not to mention the political and social consequences.[22] Nobody really can predict with any degree of confidence. But virtually all would tend to agree that the stakes are huge. The demise of the euro could also lead to the unravelling of regional integration, thus bringing Europe back several decades.

More specifically, Germany would suffer the consequences of a rapidly appreciating Deutschmark for its export-led growth. The fears repeatedly expressed by German economists regarding the credit risks their country has taken, together with other creditor countries through bailout programmes and also through the European System of Central Banks (ESCB), could easily materialize in the event of a break-up: a nightmare come true. On the other hand, if you live in southern Europe and have little trust in your politicians, how can you trust them with the daunting task of an exit from the eurozone? For the Greeks in particular, who have come closer than anybody else to the exit, leaving the euro would constitute a return to the Balkans—a frightening thought for most Greeks, hence the rising levels of domestic support for the euro as the prospect of Grexit came closer (Graph 6.2). This is precisely what kept Greece's radical coalition government on board in the difficult summer of 2015, when the rest of the eurozone, with the notable exceptions of France and Italy, seemed to have reached the conclusion that Grexit might be the least bad option and contagion effects could be manageable.

It looks like the equilibrium of terror. Many Europeans, in both creditor and debtor countries, as well as in countries outside the eurozone, have all (for their own different reasons) been clearly unhappy about the way that the long euro crisis has been managed. The economic and political costs have been debated at great length and several commentators have referred to the eurozone as an unhappy marriage or an unhappy union. But still, many of them continue to stress the likely high costs of a divorce.[23] This view seems to be shared by the large majority of Europeans who are unhappy with their union but more scared of the consequences of an eventual break-up, yet apparently also unable to agree about ways of radically improving the terms of their cohabitation. Europe is thus in a bind.

## The end of an era?

The fate of the European project will not be decided in Europe's capital Brussels, but among its member states. The domestic political landscape in member states has changed a great deal in recent years. One of the key features is the decline in popular support for the old mainstream parties and the rise of new political challengers from the right and left of the political spectrum, challengers who usually identify themselves as anti-systemic or anti-establishment. It is the latest phase in a longer-term trend going back to the 1980s and characterized by rapidly declining party membership, higher rates of abstention in elections, especially among the young,[24] and more political apathy in general. Apathy is now turning into protest and political radicalization for a growing minority of the population. At the same time, nationalism has been on the rise and so has Euroscepticism in its different varieties.

New political forces that challenge the status quo are often branded as populist, which risks becoming a label attached to anybody and anything we do not like or simply do not find politically correct. It would be more constructive to look instead for the causes and try to deal with them. In many countries, corruption is surely not a figment of the imagination of populists nor is the close ideological convergence of mainstream parties and the growing depoliticization of important issues over a long period of time. Democracy without much choice is no democracy. A large part of the problem lies with the one-way thinking that prevailed in Europe and elsewhere in the Western world, what the French call *la pensée unique*, or the 'Golden Straightjacket' proudly announced by Tom Friedman[25] several years back as a corollary to globalization and the alleged primacy of economics. But the economics then went wrong, and politics is now beginning to take revenge in its usual, rather messy fashion. To put it bluntly, too much consensus for years among the mainstream parties on economic neo-liberalism, immigration, and European integration boomeranged after the bursting of the bubble and the Great Recession that followed, creating a space for fanatics and others.

There are particular traits that distinguish populist parties. One of them is the notion of society being divided basically into two groups: the (pure) people and the (corrupt and/or conspiring) elite.[26] There is not much room for pluralism in populist parties. They rely on charismatic leaders who are usually adept in the use of social media and who specialize in simple solutions to complex problems. In so doing, they also offer an alternative to citizens, especially the losers, even if it is often an imaginary one. There are mostly right-wing populists in the north of Europe and left-wing populists in the south. For the populist Right, the EU is run by foreigners trespassing on national sovereignty and flooding the country with immigrants. For the populist Left, the EU is an agent of neo-liberalism run by

Germany for the benefit of capitalists and bankers in particular. None of the two propositions is completely false, yet the analysis is very partial and, even worse, the solutions offered are over-simplistic. This is the essence of populism.

Right-wing populists want no Europe and a return to the nation state behind protective barriers. They do not make the effort to spell out the costs of cutting oneself off and they reminisce about a nation state that is simply no longer there. But they address themselves mostly to people who feel (wrongly?) that they have little to lose. Their rhetoric has infiltrated the political discourse of traditional pro-European parties. One of the best examples is the Netherlands, one of the founding members of the EEC, where the rhetoric of anti-European and anti-immigration parties has been in part already adopted by the old establishment parties. Left-wing populists are not necessarily anti-European. They propose instead a different kind of Europe which is best left vague. Theirs is a different tradition, anti-capitalist and more class-oriented, although many of them have now succeeded in reconciling the internationalist tradition of the old Left with a new variety of nationalism. In an era of market-driven global-ization, this may not be entirely surprising.

Populists refer to another world which often exists only in their imagination. They certainly dislike the one they live in right now and they find many people who are receptive to their message, particularly among the young. Feelings of injustice and disempowerment are strong and widespread in Europe today. The old system is not deliver-ing the goods as seen by many citizens, although when faced with a choice, the majority in most countries still prefer the devil they know to the unknown. In this respect, the contrast between Germany and Greece is quite revealing. Until very recently, mainstream parties in Germany were holding up remarkably well and there was also cross-party consensus on Europe, even with periodic concessions made to German populism of the kind exemplified in Germany's premier tabloid newspaper, the *Bild-Zeitung*.[27] The reason was simple: in Germany, the system was still delivering the goods. It remains to be seen what kind of political collateral damage the refugee crisis will leave behind. By contrast, the old political system in Greece has literally imploded. It was weak in the first place, inefficient and corrupt, and the crisis finished it off.

Populism in the countries of central and eastern Europe is more widespread. Unlike western and southern Europe, it is not directed against old mainstream parties simply because they do not exist; they have not had enough time to establish themselves since the fall of communism.[28] Populism is directed against the incumbents. 'Get the rascals out so we can take their place, because we are less corrupt than them': this is often the message heard in countries where there is little trust in political elites, generally deemed to be corrupt, combined with strong volatility in electoral behaviour and widespread disenchantment with democratic politics. Countries in central and eastern Europe have produced a variety of populist leaders who have already made it to the top with a kind of rhetoric that often sounds antediluvian to the ears of western European liberals, and with practices that should be of real concern to anybody who adheres to a pluralist democratic system.

Mr Orban, the prime minister of Hungary, is not alone. He now has good friends and admirers in power in Poland (and not only there), where a long period of high growth did not stop people from voting out the party that had been in charge. Corruption and growing inequalities surely played a role. But there may also be something much deeper: large sections of the population, especially in the countryside, feel left out, scared of rapid change, and with a sense of powerlessness. Patriotism and religion can then provide the life jacket they desperately need.

Secessionism is a different case altogether, even though populists have been only too keen to jump on this particular bandwagon. While we were all meant to become more European with time and closer interaction with each other, many of us also began to feel more Scottish, Catalan, Flemish, or whatever, and sought a distinct collective identity with institutions and the power to back it up. Multiple identities are possible, we are told, but the European one is by far the weakest. In a strange way, European integration may indirectly encourage autonomist movements in Europe and thus add to centrifugal forces inside member countries. Scottish independence, for example, would make very little sense outside a European organized framework of interdependence—and most Scots apparently realize it, unlike the English. The European political scene has become extremely complex. In some national capitals, central authority has been increasingly squeezed from above and below and those in the middle feel extremely uncomfortable.

Is it the end of an era? There are good reasons to believe it might be, for reasons that go well beyond European integration, although obviously nobody can be sure about precise timings when caught in an important turning point of history—which is perhaps what we are living through today. The Italian political thinker Antonio Gramsci wrote: 'The crisis consists precisely in the fact that the old is dying and the new cannot be born; in this interregnum a great variety of morbid symptoms appear'.[29] Today in Europe, there are many signs of the old dying, but only fuzzy impressions and guesses as to what the new might look like. Most politicians from mainstream parties still find it hard to think that this may be the end of an era; they find it even harder to think out of the box. Meanwhile, the monsters have arrived: wild demagogues, rabid nationalists, and all kinds of extremists. It may be the time when, in the words of the great Irish poet W. B. Yeats,[30]

> The best lack all conviction, while the worst
> Are full of passionate intensity.

# 7

# Difficult Choices

To the unkind observer, the EU today may look like an overextended empire with a weak centre, ageing population and semicomatose economy, growing internal fragmentation and a world of trouble on its porous borders. Nobody can be sure whether the next crisis will prove to be a final tipping point. Will it be the uncontrollable flood of refugees, a British divorce, another episode in the long Grexit saga, a coordinated challenge against the austerity orthodoxy from the south, a new political crisis in Italy or even France, secessionist movements within countries, a populist revolt from the east raising the flag of nationalism, panic-driven markets in yet another financial crisis, a new Russian provocation, or any of the 'unknown unknowns' in times of great flux and uncertainty? The list of potential threats or accidents can be very long indeed.

There have been many crises before, and professional Europeans—rather complacently—often like to repeat the famous words of the acknowledged father of the common project, Jean Monnet, who warned us early on that Europe would be forged in crises. It has happened several times before, and it can happen again. But don't be so sure. This time, it does look different and much more threatening: multiple, overlapping crises that strike at the very core of European integration, sapping the capacity of the system to withstand new shocks. Europe's postmodern empire is under attack from within and without, and there is only so much more that it can take. Loyal forces are gradually being demoralized.

Europe does not only have to deal with the euro crisis and the fundamental contradiction of a currency without a state—a problem of its own making, critics would hasten to add, but still an extremely difficult one to resolve (and with no real precedent to learn from). It also has to deal with a big wave of immigration and the security threat emanating from a neighbourhood in a state of implosion. And there is only so much that Europe can do to restore stability in the neighbourhood or to insulate itself from the effects of the instability surrounding it, although admittedly it had not paid enough attention until recently to this problem, at least not in any consistent manner. On the other hand, globalization and the technological revolution are having negative effects on the internal cohesion of Europe's constituent parts, effects that go much beyond European integration but which nevertheless strengthen the internal forces of fragmentation. As the balance between democracy and markets has been constantly shifting in the direction of the latter, there have been growing signs of discontent in our societies. Europe's fragile political system, together with national systems, has been on the receiving end of this discontent. This all makes for a heady mix.

The British historian Timothy Garton Ash has written about Europe being caught during the economic crisis in a dysfunctional triangle of national politics, European policies, and global markets.[1] It is an apt description, but we should try to flesh out the lines connecting these three elements. An ever expanding European model in terms of both members and functions has led to overstretch, especially since common institutions and democratic legitimacy have lagged behind. To a large extent, European integration has become the victim of its own success—an undeniable success given the remarkable progress registered in six or so decades. If you believe it is all a conspiracy of a small minority of federalists, then I would suggest that you will believe anything. Experience shows there are strong forces pushing Europe in the direction of more integration, although there is, of course, no iron law and no guarantee against reversals, or indeed a more generalized disintegration. The chances of disintegration are much stronger today than ever before. If it were ever to happen, the more serious among the Eurosceptics would probably regret what they had wished for, but by then it would be too late.

The euro is the most extreme but also the most important example of overstretch: it is taking its toll in terms of reduced effectiveness and legitimacy for the European project as a whole. During the recent crisis, growth ground to a halt in most countries, in some it went into reverse gear, unemployment rose further and so did inequalities, while domestic social contracts came under renewed pressure and some are already breaking up. The (mis)management of the euro crisis has caused much damage in terms of lost growth and employment. But there are, of course, other reasons as well for Europe's poor economic performance. The slowdown in productivity growth, for example, goes further back. Others speak of an expensive and unreformed Europe. Theories abound, but the experience of the last two decades and more, going further back than the euro, is not encouraging for Europe in comparison to other parts of the world. On the other hand, predictions of 'secular stagnation' and the 'new mediocre' in economic performance only add to the worries.[2]

'It's not just the economy, stupid!', one might add, reversing the electoral slogan employed with much effect many years ago by (then) US presidential candidate Bill Clinton. Identity politics is back with a vengeance in our societies. Immigrants become the obvious target. In some countries, identity politics also provides the fuel for secessionist movements. Globalization, as well as European integration, has not been the all-powerful melting pot that many well-wishers had hoped for and a growing number of people are distinctly unhappy with its effects.

Anti-establishment political forces are on the rise virtually everywhere in Europe, in the United States as well: it is a general phenomenon. Most are not able (as yet?) to articulate a coherent alternative to the prevailing order—and some may never do because they are just a bunch of demagogues. But such forces are, nevertheless, for good or for bad, an expression of protest against policies promoted for a long time by a broad coalition of political elites. These policies have become increasingly divisive and large numbers of citizens are deserting the old mainstream parties or looking for non-mainstream leaders to replace the old guard: the election of Mr Corbyn to the leadership of the British Labour Party could set a precedent here.

We have had too much consensus and too much complacency for too long and the results have not been brilliant, to put it mildly: a very uneven distribution of economic gains in our societies that goes back three decades and more, the biggest financial crisis since 1929, and the Great Recession that followed in Europe.[3] Now we are witnessing a populist backlash leading to a process of realignment of political forces: economics and politics are closely tied together. European integration may not be the primary cause of popular discontent. But it has largely failed in the eyes of many Europeans to provide a credible model of *managing* globalization rather than simply going along with it; it has failed to be part of the solution and not just part of the problem. Hence, nationalism becomes a vehicle for protest against change that is seen as being imported from outside. Alas, nationalism has many ugly faces.

## Leaders, free-riders, misfits, and laggards

Europe is divided along different, overlapping lines. The division between creditor and debtor countries was very pronounced at the peak of the euro crisis. It was also often presented as a division along the north–south axis, with the exception of Ireland, which was treated as an 'honorary member' of the south. The division often took the form of a power struggle in which the strongest countries, namely the creditors, were able to impose not only their will but also a very asymmetrical distribution of the burden of adjustment on the debtors. This division is much less stark today, largely due to ECB interventions, although there is no guarantee it will be a lasting lull. For the time being, Greece is on its own, a country in distress.

But if one looks closer, the real division may relate more to the different capacity of individual countries to adjust in the never-ending, almost zero-sum game of competitiveness played out in a fast globalizing world. In this respect, Ireland's placement in the weak group of southern debtors may prove to be only temporary, while much of southern Europe looks like facing an existential threat, even more so within a monetary union operating under German rules. Does southern Europe risk turning into a Mezzogiorno writ large? It would be even worse, since southern Europe would have absolutely no hope of being the beneficiary of large transfers from the north of Europe, as the Mezzogiorno is from the rest of Italy.

In a division of countries within Europe based on their willingness and/or ability to adjust, the role of Italy would be crucial. A big country and a founding member of the European project, Italy has not been a successful or happy member of the eurozone since the very beginning. Its economy has been languishing, for too long unable to find its place in an ever more competitive global economic environment and in a regional monetary system in which devaluations are no longer available as the instrument of last resort to restore lost competitiveness. Italy has been slow in following the international textbook rules on structural reform, while its political system has often been the epitome of gridlock. Most of the opposition in the Italian political system has now turned against the euro, and it has also turned increasingly Eurosceptic.

This is completely new in a country where support for European integration had been traditionally very strong across the political spectrum (the former Italian Communist Party, one of the biggest in Western Europe, had in fact been the first one to break the taboo among communists by publicly supporting the European project). Italy becoming Eurosceptic says a great deal about how much the country has changed, but perhaps also about how much European integration itself has changed. And both should be a good reason for Italians and Europeans in general to worry.

If it is difficult to imagine an integrating Europe without a secure place for Italy, it is simply out of the question to even try to imagine an integrating Europe without France as a key part of the core. After all, the European project had started as a French project and largely remained so for a long time. The economic crisis has shifted the balance of power inside Europe in a big way—and certainly not in France's favour. But the problem goes further back in time. The feeling of gradually losing ownership of the European project for the French has much to do with the increasingly more liberal orientation of integration in economic terms and with successive rounds of enlargement, especially to the north and to the east. The common project became more and more unrecognizable in the eyes of French elites and the public. Growing unhappiness was registered in the referendums on the Maastricht Treaty and the constitutional treaty, referendums that presidents Mitterrand and Chirac had called in 1992 and 2005 respectively, thinking (wrongly) that they would be an easy ride. The second one effectively killed the constitutional treaty and led to a major political crisis in the EU.

During the big euro crisis, France sometimes behaved as if it were a junior partner to Germany, which was indeed a shocking experience for the French. Governments in Paris had a strong interest in defending their own banks with a big exposure to the embattled periphery of Europe, an interest they shared with their German partner, while also being very worried that the panic in financial markets could eventually hit France. In trying to reconcile those two concerns, they often ended up as mediators between north and south, between creditors and debtors, with a variable degree of success. They did not succeed in making a serious dent in the austerity orthodoxy of the eurozone, but President Hollande succeeded, for example, with the support of Italy, in keeping Greece as a member in the summer of 2015.

France has been slow to reform, especially with regard to its big state and its generous welfare system.[4] The high rate of unemployment in the country is a sign of economic failure. An unhappy France—unhappy with itself and with the rules of the game—a France that turns more inward and more Eurosceptic, especially with the rise of the nationalist Right under the leadership of Ms le Pen (even if she does not actually attain power), would be a further big blow for European integration in crisis. If Ms Le Pen were to be elected president, this could be the death knell for the European project. France is a key player and everybody knows it, including the Germans.

In fact, there are only a few countries in the twenty-eight-member EU of today where the political elites, while defending their perceived national interests, nevertheless occasionally still afford themselves the luxury of thinking about a wider collective European public good, above all the survival of the European project itself. That much-needed European reflex, drawn from a strong sense of shared ownership of European integration and all that it represents, is rather weak in most EU countries today. One might have thought it would be a matter of size, with small countries usually being expected to defend the narrow national interest while letting the big ones lead the pack. However, this is not necessarily the case. When the chips are down, the defence of the European public good is mostly in the hands of political elites in the old founding members, with France and Germany constituting the core of old Europe. In this respect, things have not changed that much over the years.

On a good day and with the right people in power, they may also count on a few more countries, such as Spain, Sweden, Poland, Austria, or Finland, but the group of those who tend to think not only nationally but also at a wider European level is really limited. In its long and turbulent relationship with the European project, the UK has by and large not belonged to this group. It all probably boils down to a question of identity. Whatever the rights and wrongs of this situation, under present conditions, the best one can hope for is to keep the UK in the EU, even if only with a semi-detached status, hoping that at some point in the future it will become clear to the British that sailing away from the continent is not really an option.

But looking beyond the UK, there is no shortage of free-riders and also an increasing number of misfits and laggards especially since the economic crisis struck. To make matters worse, when leadership was indeed exercised during the recent crisis or crises, it was poor, ad hoc, and hostage to national interest narrowly defined. Seen from outside, it was sometimes difficult to decide whether Europe was badly governed or simply becoming ungovernable.

The more recent members want to catch up economically with the more developed countries on the European continent and they have gone through a succession of painful adjustments in order to do so. They therefore show little sympathy or understanding for the predicament of countries often richer than themselves facing difficult reforms. They like, of course, being on the receiving end of EU Structural Funds and the Common Agricultural Policy (Poland is now by far the biggest recipient of funds through the European budget), and many of their most dynamic and mobile citizens greatly appreciate the freedom to look for jobs in London, Munich, or elsewhere.

But the new members are not keen on transfers of power to European institutions and certainly not at all keen to follow the multiculturalist route by letting in non-European refugees or immigrants. They are zealous of their regained national sovereignty and generally suspicious of any new integration initiatives emanating from a European centre that psychologically remains far away. Furthermore, they sometimes give the impression that their idea of European solidarity is only one-way. Most of their citizens do not bother to vote in European elections: abstention rates were shockingly high in 2014. They do not much trust their own political elites, which probably has a lot to do with the way the transition to market economies happened and also with widespread corruption. And they often go for the populist/nationalist variety of politician: there are plenty of them around and illiberal practices are spreading, which is a serious cause for concern. Populists/nationalists are thriving particularly in the Visegrád countries, comprising the Czech Republic, Hungary, Poland, and Slovakia (and named after the historic Hungarian town where they first convened). As for the small Baltic countries, they are uncomfortably close to Russia. For them, Washington is a more relevant reference point than Brussels, Berlin, or Paris. Thus, for a variety of reasons, there is considerable divergence between east and west, between 'new' and 'old'. The British initially thought they had natural allies in the east, and so did the Germans, with their strong economic presence in the region and enough people among the local political elites to take their side in the creditor/debtor division. They both found that they had to revise their opinions in due course.

Divisions in Europe do not only run along national lines. Domestic cleavages within countries have become much deeper in recent years because of the increasingly unequal distribution of gains and losses from the operation of global free markets and financial markets in particular, also because of growing anxiety (and anger) among large sections of the population[5]—increasingly the middle classes—that they will be next in the firing line. And, last but not least, because of immigration. The result is fragmentation within national political systems that may lead to ungovernability. Thinking mostly in terms of divisions *between* countries misses a big part of the political picture in Europe today. Internal divisions are in turn reflected in European council meetings: national representatives are much more constrained and they also feel the need to constantly play to the gallery back home. An important division *within* countries (although this applies in some cases more than in others) is the one between generations. Young Europeans on average have a rough deal: they inherit large debts from the older generations and have poor job prospects. It is worth noting that in the countries worst affected by the economic crisis, the interests of pensioners have been in general better protected than those of the young unemployed. Perhaps one explanation is that there are more old people in our ageing societies and they also vote in larger numbers than the young.

## Growth on the way to Tipperary

Recovery from the Great Recession, which was essentially a lost decade for large parts of Europe coupled with wide divergence between and within countries, has been slow, fragile, and uneven. At the time of writing, the external economic environment was highly unstable while Europe was still courting the risk of deflation, with high rates of unemployment in many countries, especially among the young, thus raising the spectre of a lost generation on top of a lost decade. Public debts shot up during the crisis as governments tried to bail out banks and cope with the aftershocks of the debt crisis on the real economy. And if all that were not enough, private debt was also very high and some of the European banks still looked vulnerable. The economic state of Europe was thus reminiscent of the old joke about the man who loses his way in the Irish countryside and asks a local for the way to Tipperary. And the reply he gets is that 'If I were you, I wouldn't start from here'. Yet, it is from here that Europe has to start and it will be a difficult journey to Tipperary, especially bearing in mind the politics of discontent and fragmentation that normally accompany a poor economic situation.

Alas, economic growth has been painfully slow in coming. On the other hand, policy attitudes still differ a great deal. For advocates of the prevailing, largely German-inspired, economic orthodoxy, European countries need to persist with structural reform and fiscal consolidation, and they will be repaid in the end for their efforts. 'Look at Germany and follow its example' is the often implicit advice offered to all kinds of misfits and laggards in Europe. And to make sure there is not much deviation from orthodox behaviour, the same advocates call for a stricter application of common rules and for an EU Commissioner who should have the right to veto national budgets in eurozone countries.[6]

This would make the European straitjacket even tighter, retort critics of the prevailing orthodoxy. They argue that the export-led growth that Germany has been able to get away with for so long ('beggar-thy-neighbour policies', to use less polite language) cannot logically be applied to the eurozone as a whole: every country cannot have a trade surplus with every other country. But then again, who knows, the eurozone (and Europe) might be able to pull this trick by free-riding on the Americans. Other commentators refer to the so-called OHIO ('Own House In Order') doctrine[7] that treats EMU as a collection of individual national economies, and thus ignores the overall macroeconomic reality of the eurozone. But their criticism of the negative effects of a pro-cyclical European macroeconomic policy stance in times of slow growth, close-to-zero inflation, and high unemployment is countered by their opponents with the argument that deficits are bad and should be banned. In sum, the official European debate on economic policy still sounds like a dialogue of the deaf, although one in which some of the interlocutors have much more power than others.

In an inter-institutional European study[8] which tried to identify key global trends to 2030 and the challenges for Europe, the authors concluded, among other things, that the ongoing economic and technological revolution would offer huge opportunities in terms of productivity, welfare gains, and individual empowerment. They warned, however, of societal disruptions related to a further rise in unemployment, increasing inequalities, and the impoverishment of the middle classes in developed countries and Europe in particular. They looked forward to more empowered and better connected individuals, who would also be less wedded to lifetime jobs, but in more individualized societies in which traditional forms of representation through trade unions or political parties would be further weakened. They also predicted that globalization would be increasingly driven by new actors with different values from those of the erstwhile dominant West. They expected the median age in Europe to rise to 45 years by 2030, compared to 40 years in North America and 33 for the world as a whole, and, last but not least, they predicted slow growth. An ageing and declining population, continued slow growth, and a widening wedge between winners and losers from globalization and technological change, not to mention the growing challenge of global warming, will make the journey to Tipperary a very difficult one indeed: not to be recommended for delicate or inexperienced travellers (and politicians).

Irrespective of the reasons, domestic or international, a much longer period of slow and uneven growth in Europe, coupled with persisting high unemployment in several countries, would test to the limit the capacity of the European system to hold together and of the eurozone to avoid individual country exits or a generalized break-up. And if the latter were to happen, all hell would be let loose with massive bankruptcies among governments, banks, companies, and households. The fear of the costs of divorce has kept the eurozone—and Europe—together during the difficult period following the bursting of the international financial bubble. But how long can fear keep Europeans together? It is anybody's bet, but surely an extremely dangerous bet (or bluff) for all parties concerned, including those outside. The European bloc or just the eurozone with its 340 million people, more than €10 trillion of combined GDP, and one of the biggest shares in international trade is certainly not a small or closed economy.

It is difficult to imagine a sustainable monetary union in the long run without some degree of fiscal union, at the very minimum with a modest budget that contains automatic stabilizers and transfers, some joint issuing of debt, and the mutualization of risk in relation to the banking system. It is also difficult to imagine such an economic and monetary edifice without a solid and legitimate political base on which to rest.[9] Many people from different schools of thought would agree on this general long-term requirement/objective. But the emphasis must be on the long term here. For now, the lack of mutual trust and of a generally accepted strategy among member states as to how to get from here to there may well act as a drag on progress for a very long time to come. In the meantime, the risk of a dysfunctional monetary union with major negative repercussions on the economics and politics of its constituent parts (and beyond) would be very high. This is where we are today.

Europe will need to address the problem of low investment and the productivity gap. There are still big holes in the internal market, including notably the energy sector. It will need to take better advantage of the digital revolution while trying to strike a balance between privacy and security. It has a poor record in transforming knowledge into innovation, which means it will have to think again about how to link its high-quality education and research with the real economy. These are all factors that can contribute to higher growth. But Europe will also need to combine a reform package, especially for countries that are lagging behind, with coordinated measures to stimulate demand and especially to boost investment. Borrowing at close-to-zero interest rates to finance investment in infrastructure, innovation, training, and education, may not be such a mad idea after all. It could be combined with a more relaxed fiscal stance in Germany and more aggressive quantitative easing by the ECB.

Such a compromise would help to reconcile supply-side economics with a modest dose of Keynes on the macro-side. It would help to lift 'animal spirits' in depressed markets and get the message across to European citizens that there is life beyond austerity. It would hardly be a revolution. It has many advocates, including apparently Mr Draghi, the president of the ECB, although he would never admit it in so many words. Some pieces of the jigsaw are, however, still missing: further market integration creates losers, reforms are politically difficult in some countries, while the Germans are not willing to budge on their macroeconomic policy priorities. All this turns into a vicious circle.

Banks and financial markets remain the elephant in the room. Given the nature and the size of the shock back in 2007–8, the spate of regulatory reform that has followed may not be sufficient or radical enough to prevent another big financial crisis. Continuing large macroeconomic imbalances at world level combined with global banks and liberalized markets, but with no global regulator and lender of last resort, could be the recipe for the next disaster to come.[10] Europe is more vulnerable than other parts of the world given the size (and fragility?) of its banks.

## Reform, cohesion, and taxation

Is Europe in need of reform? Thus formulated, the question can only have one answer: yes. In a rapidly changing and ever more competitive world, you need to adjust in order to survive. This need to adjust can be the result of economics, technology, demographics, or other factors. For instance, take this striking statistic: between 1965 and 2005, life expectancy in Europe increased by nine years and the retirement age by six months.[11] So it should come as no surprise that many pension systems looked increasingly unsustainable. Overinflated public sectors, heavy bureaucratic procedures, and legal environments hostile to business are also examples of the kind of problems that structural reform would need to tackle across Europe. Some countries seem to have most, if not all, of these problems in abundance.

However, behind the generic term of 'structural reform' generally advocated by international organizations and European institutions alike, there usually lies a particular model of political economy and of society by implication. The emphasis continues to be on liberalization and deregulation, of labour markets in particular, usually also on the scaling down (rationalization?) of welfare systems. The goal, of course, is competitiveness. But how does one reconcile the sacred goal of competitiveness with social cohesion? Hardly anybody has succeeded so far. Is the Scandinavian model of 'flexicurity', combining flexibility in labour markets with security for the workforce through generous welfare systems, the answer for Europe in an attempt to preserve some of the main traits of the admittedly expensive (and much abused) European social model? Yet, even the Scandinavians have been experiencing great difficulties in recent years in trying to reconcile the interests of protected 'insiders' and the unemployed 'outsiders' with respect to labour market reform, not to mention reconciling the interests of local workers with the growing number of immigrants.[12]

Is there a trade-off between efficiency and equality, between competitiveness and social cohesion? And if this is true of the more developed economies, then what about those countries that have not yet succeeded in climbing fast enough up the ladder of the international division of labour, still specializing mostly in price-sensitive goods, which compete increasingly with exports from developing countries and hence are forced to operate under a tight constraint on domestic wages? Can they afford the 'flexicurity' model? Most unlikely, would be the honest answer. As a consequence, will they simply have to accept flexible labour markets, lean welfare states, and the growing inequalities that go with them as the inevitable price to pay for competitiveness in a rapidly globalizing world? In this respect, 'new' Europe may be indeed showing the way.

According to the American economist Adam Posen, the new global economy means a return to the Old Normal, as he calls it, of the late nineteenth century, with distinctly Victorian traits.[13] Such a development would have major political and social repercussions. We are already witnessing them on an everyday basis across Europe, more so in the weaker countries or those less able to adjust, as well as across the Atlantic. Social democratic parties in particular have paid a heavy price, seeing much of their erstwhile political constituency (representing many of the losers from economic and technological change) migrate to other parties and often to the extremes of the political spectrum, in fact more to the right than to the left.

There is no credible alternative, argue the self-proclaimed economic realists, repeating the words of Mrs Thatcher while also defending the alleged primacy of economics over politics. Politics will simply have to adjust to the logic of global competition and technological change, they insist. The stronger countries may still be able to afford relatively generous redistributive policies, together with policies to raise the educational standards of their citizens, but they should not overdo it. As for the rest, it will be back to variations of social Darwinism and the survival of the fittest. Can the European project survive under such conditions, with Europe in the role of the economic liberalizer and the guardian of the straitjacket, while national governments are left to pick up the pieces at home and deal with the increasing number of those who fall by the wayside, yet with fewer and less effective instruments at their disposal? Such a division of labour between Europe and the member states would not be easily sustainable but neither would unfettered global markets.

There is, of course, no simple answer to this dilemma. Welfare and redistributive policies will remain mostly in the national domain as long as political loyalties are predominantly national and the European political system continues to be decentralized, i.e. for a long time. But in conditions of growing disparities not only between countries but also within countries, and with European integration becoming a divisive issue in national politics precisely because it is having unequal effects, Europe needs a social and caring dimension in order to be able to address itself effectively to sections of society that increasingly believe there is little or nothing for them in the European project. It would be a similar logic to the one used earlier on with the Structural Funds, when European political leaders still dared to go for the European grand bargain that created a win-win situation for all. Today, the offer would have to be modest, well targeted, and with conditions attached in order to satisfy concerns about moral hazard. European solidarity and rationalization at national level, within a broad framework of jointly agreed objectives and with European instruments in the role of facilitator, should provide the basis for a fruitful new division of labour[14]—as long as it is not at the expense of the weakest members of society.

A European unemployment insurance scheme complementary to national action could also be part of the overall new bargain, as well as an integral part of a (modest and targeted) system of automatic stabilizers within the euro budget. Alas, such proposals are still non-starters. Proposals for the setting up of a European unemployment insurance scheme have been made by the French and the Italian ministers of finance.[15] Such proposals usually meet with dismissive comments or just a deafening silence from Berlin. The side of 'austerians' is not prepared as yet to open a discussion on a eurozone budget, not to mention automatic stabilizers and transfers. First and foremost, they want to make sure that the current rules are respected and reforms enacted—and they also want to make sure they will continue to be the ultimate judge.

One area where the Union has already begun to make significant progress relates to the big issue of tax evasion or tax avoidance, the distinction often being only in the eye of the beholder. This particularly applies to large multinational firms which for a long time have been exploiting existing loopholes and the competition among national authorities which offer favourable tax deals to attract investment to their country. It has been a privileged area for free-riding inside the European internal market (and beyond) that those directly concerned have tried to justify with appeals to national sovereignty (and subsidiarity) on taxation matters while also trying to preserve their right of veto on such issues. Good principles are often used in the wrong causes.

In recent years, we have discovered (often through leaks to the media) that some governments have turned so-called 'sweetheart' tax deals with multinationals into an industry, with Luxembourg and Ireland being the most productive. This is unfair competition not only vis-à-vis partners in the EU and countries outside, but also vis-à-vis less privileged companies that had to pay normal taxes. The European Commission has been both courageous and inventive in trying to get companies to pay the amounts of tax they had evaded (or avoided) in the past by treating such amounts as illegal state aid. Those working on EU law have learned to operate often at the frontier of what may be legally possible. But in going after large multinationals for tax evasion, or for breaking competition rules, the Commission has also provoked the ire of both Washington and Moscow. This is the price you pay when you decide to juggle with Google, Apple, or Amazon—not to mention Gazprom.

A financial transactions tax has been on the European agenda for several years: a tax that should go to EU coffers to be levied at a rate of 0.1 per cent on all transactions on financial instruments (0.01 per cent for derivative contracts) between parties, at least one of which is located in the EU. It would be a way of raising revenue, of taxing an industry that has been a free-rider for a long time, and also a means of throwing sand in the wheels of international finance, in the words of its originator, the American economist James Tobin, whose intention was to help reduce the speed with which capital moves around the system, and hence decrease the volatility of financial markets. Not a wildly radical proposal, if we only stop and think of the huge damage caused by the big financial crisis. Yet countries with a large financial sector, and a powerful financial lobby, are dead against such a tax. Their argument of last resort is that in a globalized sector, such as the financial one, it would make no sense to proceed with such a tax unless it was universally applied—and they have always tried to make sure it would not be.

Similar arguments had been employed for years to make the case for doing nothing against tax evasion by private individuals, because of the existence of all kinds of tax havens around the world and the alleged impossibility of gaining access to data. But in recent years, we have discovered it was indeed possible. If both Americans and Europeans have the requisite will on such issues, then it should not prove impossible to find a way. The financial transactions tax in the EU has been stalling; only a minority of members has agreed in principle to proceed and implementation thus looks difficult. But taxation is precisely the area where the EU *can* make a big difference by adopting minimum common rules (and rates) aimed at unfair competition and free-riding. In today's political environment, it would also be a potent political message that there is much more to the European project than free markets. In fact, without such a message, the project will not have a great future. It was always about reconciling democracy and markets, was it not? And this can only be achieved today at European, no longer at national, level.

## Democracy in a monetary union

Europe does not have a government, and it is unlikely to acquire one for some time—at least in the form that most of us would recognize. Instead, it has a multitude of national governments accountable to their respective citizens and a complex system of common institutions, rules, and norms to manage the extended web of interdependence that has developed over several decades. Commentators often refer to 'European governance', a term ambiguous enough to allow room for different interpretations (hence, perhaps, its growing popularity).

With the continuous expansion of the European project, tensions were bound to arise regarding the division of powers between European and national levels, and also regarding democratic accountability in this hybrid system. More powers have been steadily transferred to the European Parliament as a democratic check in a system where the Council, representing the collection of national interests through democratically elected governments, has been increasingly asserting its authority over the 'supranational' institution, namely the European Commission. On the other hand, the creation of the common currency has led European integration into totally new territory. With the benefit of hindsight, it is now clear that hardly anybody was prepared for the journey. With regard to the euro, political institutions and democratic legitimacy were conveniently forgotten or ignored. Perhaps, if a proper public debate had taken place before the introduction of the euro, instead of just relying on elite consensus and a conspiracy of silence, Europe might have been better prepared for the difficult tests that lay ahead. One of the few good things to come out of the recent economic crisis has been an increasingly lively European public debate: a European public sphere is slowly taking shape.

When the big crisis struck, the democratic deficit of EMU reached gigantic proportions.[16] The Council took over completely, while both the Commission and the European Parliament were sidelined. Perhaps adding insult to injury, at least for those with a modicum of democratic sensibility, the ECB was repeatedly called upon to act as the saviour of last resort for the euro system, and in so doing it had to take decisions that were highly political. It is perhaps inevitable that in emergencies the executive gets stronger: quick decisions are of the essence. However, decisions were not so quick in the case of the euro crisis, nor were they particularly wise, as the unkind observer might be tempted to add. This particular emergency has been going on for years.

In fact, the problem was often not so much one of lack of democratic accountability generally defined. It was rather that specific decisions were shovelled down the throat of unwilling governments and countries in the eurozone on a take-it-or-leave-it basis by those who took advantage of their position as creditor countries. And national parliaments of creditor countries appeared to have much more of a say over adjustment programmes destined for the debtor countries than the parliaments of countries on the receiving end. It was often ugly and reminiscent of periods of European history that are best forgotten. Sure, we have known all along that some are more equal than others in the European animal farm (and quite understandably so), but the European model was meant to protect the weak from an excessive and arbitrary exercise of power by the stronger ones—alas, no longer. This came as a big shock to many.

Further institutional and political integration will be needed in order to ensure the viability of the common currency. In fact, it has been happening throughout the crisis in the form of much closer surveillance of national economic policies operating under the threat of sanctions, with the Commission now in the role of stern policeman overseeing the enforcement of new rules, plus a banking union and new safety mechanisms that will gradually (very gradually) mutualize risk. The transfer has therefore been going on, but it is not enough and not in the right way.

More or different than this is not, however, politically possible, realists will add, referring to public debates in member countries or public opinion surveys in support of their argument. There is simply no appetite for major transfers of power to the European level, we are told. Yet, appetite is a relative thing: mine always depends on what is on the menu, unless I am completely starving. Indeed, if it is more of the same that we have been fed for the last few years inside the eurozone, then I for one fear turning anorexic.

When the argument against a major transfer of powers in the name of political realism is used by politicians and opinion makers, it sounds like a circular argument: it is politically impossible because we have made it so. If you have been arguing for years that it is all the fault of cheating Greeks or nasty Germans, if you have been trying to pass all responsibility for unpopular decisions on to Brussels while trying to appropriate for yourself as a national politician all the popular ones, then what are the chances that citizens will be happy to endorse the transfer of more powers to European institutions? And what is the chance that they will be happy to countenance further constraints on a national veto that has been portrayed as the best means to protect them against all kinds of villainous machinations from Brussels? At the end of the day, who is there to defend Europe?

Sure, democratic legitimacy will continue to flow mainly through member states. But democracy at European level will need to be strengthened in different ways, especially for the group of countries that have already ceded a big part of their economic sovereignty as members of the currency area. It will certainly have to involve more directly the European Parliament (and national parliaments?) in the governance of the euro. Proposals for a new euro treaty[17] often include the setting up of a separate parliament for the countries sharing the common currency, either along the lines of the existing European Parliament with more powers and fewer members or a parliament that brings together directly elected MEPs with representatives of national parliaments. Such a parliament should provide the democratic control for a small European executive with clearly defined powers: discretion combined with rules.

No doubt these are radical steps which are, however, necessary to make governance of the euro not only more effective but also more legitimate. Will member countries be ready for such a move, and when? Can you have democracy, even within narrowly defined areas of policymaking, without a *demos*? And can a *demos* be created from above? Massimo d'Azeglio, one of the leading figures of Italian unification in the nineteenth century, is reputed to have said: 'We have made Italy, now we must make Italians.' Europe is no doubt engaged in a revolutionary political experiment, the most advanced of its kind anywhere in the world, to find new forms of jointly managing interdependence and the sharing of sovereignty. You can call it exploratory governance, a project in the making, or anything else you like, but the question of democracy needs to be addressed. And we will often have to think out of the box.[18]

There are many imponderables. The eurozone of nineteen members is a highly heterogeneous group of countries. Will there be room for misfits and laggards, and will the fear that an individual country's exit could create a domino effect by signifying that the euro marriage is no longer an irrevocable act help to keep everybody on board? It is a difficult question to answer. On the other hand, if the euro survives, backed by institutional and political reforms, a further big gap is bound to open between members and non-members. Historical experience suggests that, in such a case, very few countries in Europe could afford to stay out for long. But there are many big ifs on the way.

## Treaty revisions, people's power, and sacred cows

Any proposal for further treaty revision intended to render European (and euro) governance more effective and also more legitimate immediately comes up against a wall of disbelief and horror. Given the experience with the constitutional treaty, followed by the Lisbon Treaty of 2009, who in his or her right mind would want to go through such an experience again? This is even more true today, when popular trust for political elites has hit rock bottom in many (perhaps most) European countries and public support for European integration is close to its lowest level historically. How to explain the complexities of European integration in times when mass politics turns into populism and simple messages? And how to defend Europe when people turn back to national and local identities as a protective shield against a rapidly changing, indeed often menacing, external environment? Politics in today's world is surely not for the faint-hearted, and defence of the European project requires courage to go against the trend. It also requires knowledge that is usually in short supply. Thus, better to go for the easy stuff you know that also goes down well with many of your fellow citizens: it is an easy and convenient conclusion to draw for many people engaged in public affairs.

Referendums are the new fashion in European integration: 'people's power', ranging all the way from the sublime to the ridiculous. In July 2015, the new radical government in Greece held a referendum and urged the Greek people to reject the package on offer by the country's creditors, which they did with a large majority, only to proceed some days later to sign under pressure an even tougher package. Later on, Denmark held a referendum on whether it should take part in the justice and home affairs policies of the EU, and the answer was no. The Netherlands holds a referendum in April 2016 on the new trade deal with Ukraine: do Dutch citizens really have strong views on this issue? In June comes the UK referendum which is, of course, a much more serious affair: the outcome will have major repercussions for the UK and the EU as a whole. And there will also be a referendum in Hungary called by the government to obtain a popular endorsement for its decision to keep immigrants and refugees out of the country.

Thus, in a totally unexpected way, European integration has ushered direct democracy into European politics. On defining, and highly divisive, issues that are (just about) amenable to a yes or no, in or out answer, referendums may actually offer a way out of a political impasse. The Scottish referendum of 2014 is, however, not the most reassuring example in this respect, because it does not seem to have succeeded in taking the issue of Scottish independence out of the political agenda for very long. But referendums are here to stay, for good or bad. Combined with the rule of unanimity on major European decisions, treaty revisions included, recourse to national referendums is bound to lead to total gridlock. Therefore, something will have to give, if Europe is not to become completely ungovernable. The answer can only be more majority decisions coupled with more differentiation, whenever possible, in order to cater for the needs of the minority.

Further treaty revisions will be unavoidable as a way of adjusting Europe's treaties to changing needs. But no country should have the right to stop others from going ahead, which means that in a future referendum (and/or national parliamentary ratification of a treaty revision), the question to ask should be whether people want to take part in, say, the new form of euro governance or quit the euro. A qualified majority of countries and citizens should be required for the new treaty to come into force and those in a minority should either submit to majority decision or stay out. The Fiscal Compact has set a useful precedent in this respect, which will need to be explored further. No right of veto also means much less danger of everything being brought down to the lowest common denominator during the negotiations.

The one-size-fits-all model simply cannot work, and it has not been working for years—the euro and Schengen are the best examples—given the political and economic diversity in an ever enlarging EU. Provision should also be made for countries that are not willing or able to take part in more advanced forms of integration: the UK is the country that has been accumulating most opt-outs and exceptions. More internal differentiation and flexibility should therefore become an integral part of the fundamental law of the EU in recognition of existing diversity, while at the same time making sure that rights match obligations. Easier said than done? True, but we should keep on trying and try harder. A more flexible approach to integration should make further enlargements easier in the future. The EU door cannot remain closed for too long.

More internal flexibility and differentiation will also need to be accompanied by the return of some powers back to member states. Integration simply for its own sake is not a good thing, and the zealots in Brussels may have indeed gone too far in some areas, creating in the process a little bureaucratic monster. The European Commission has been reassessing its role in an attempt to do less and to do it better: it should have the courage to cut the Gordian knot when necessary. Much more difficult, though, will be any attempt to touch the sacred cows of European integration. The free movement of labour and welfare benefits associated with it is surely the first one that comes to mind. It worked well in times of growth when the European convergence machine was operating and the differences in standards of living were not that big between member countries, but no longer. If present conditions persist, such sacred cows may have to become much leaner if Europe is to be spared the ritual of sacrifice.

If economic stagnation persists, the sanctity of sovereign debt—for several countries and not just Greece—will come under question. It will be too heavy a burden for them, and the younger generations in particular, to carry. Throughout the crisis, Europe collectively has tried to wish this problem away, but it may not succeed in the end: another sacred cow in danger.

Democracy is the sacred cow that should, however, remain inviolate. How much of a say can Europe collectively have on what happens within its member states? The answer is a great deal, but mostly before they join. The EU has made extensive use of such powers in the past by setting preconditions relating to the application of the rule of law and the functioning of liberal democracy in the case of several candidate countries. But once they have a seat around the table, it gets much more complicated. National political leaders are wary of treading on the toes of their colleagues in the Council, or within the large European political families to which most of them belong.

The problem first arose when an extreme right-wing party joined a coalition government in Austria some years back. Later on, it became much more serious when the government of Mr Orban in Hungary introduced measures to curb the freedom of the media and also seized control of the constitutional court. His example seems now to be followed by the government of the Law and Justice party in Poland. How far should the EU go in defending minimum standards of liberal democracy inside its member states? Far enough should be the answer, and it has some powerful instruments at its disposal to achieve this, including access to European funds and the threat of political quarantine. If Europe does not defend democracy within its own ranks, then what is Europe *for*? There are worrying signs in several countries. Democracy may be under threat and Europe should be the collective defender of this most precious of public goods. But it will need to tread with extra care: it is a political minefield.

# Ready for adult life?

Economic weakness and internal divisions combined with the return of geopolitics and an imploding neighbourhood have sapped European confidence about being able to project an alternative model of behaviour in international affairs. There is little talk nowadays about Europe's model of 'soft' power or 'normative' influence. Arguably, there was much wishful thinking about that model in the first place but, let us be fair, Europe has not had the best of luck in recent years. Having your young currency being tested by the biggest international financial crisis for several decades was bad luck, even allowing for your own failings, and having much of your neighbourhood collapsing around you is one crisis too many, all in the context of the strong centrifugal forces unleashed in this latest phase of global capitalism.

In theory, the external environment could be the strongest unifying force for Europe. How can individual European countries deal with a revisionist Russia, or begin to think about ways to stabilize their neighbourhood and help it develop? How can they aspire to a leading role in policies to combat climate change, or to promote multilateral rules and practices in the management of global economic interdependence, following their own much more ambitious example at regional level? And how can they hope to exert some moderating influence on periodic excesses of US power, stemming from a strongly held belief among many Americans that they are on a world mission?[19] Even countries that are big by European standards no longer have the size and the weight to exert much influence on their own in a rapidly changing world where the centre of power slowly but surely shifts away from the Atlantic area. Most Europeans know that much, but reaching some form of unity vis-à-vis the rest of the world does not come easy.

In documents drafted in Brussels,[20] one often comes across references to the 'G3', consisting of the United States, China, and Europe, which is expected to dominate world economic affairs: a tripolar world in economic terms. Although this sounds perhaps more like an aspiration of Brussels bureaucrats rather than a prediction based on hard evidence, nevertheless the experience of multilateral trade negotiations clearly suggests that European unity premised on a common trade policy and a joint negotiating stance does in fact invariably translate into a leading role for Europe. Can one imagine what negotiations on the Transatlantic Trade and Investment Partnership (the famous or notorious TTIP) would be like, or whether they would have ever started, if European countries were negotiating separately with the United States? However, while European unity can be proven to work when it comes to trade negotiations, transferring the experience from trade to other areas of policy has been difficult, to say the least. There are notable successes and several failures: the record is mixed.

Europe has been a pioneer in the creation of the World Trade Organization (now stalled for some years), the International Criminal Court, and the fight against climate change. In all those cases, policies pursued have been consistent with the values that Europe purports to stand for. But keeping the pack together and having internal policies that match joint European pronouncements in international negotiations has proved to be a tough job, as one might expect. Climate change policy is the example that immediately comes to mind.[21] The economic stakes are high and reconciling the interests of EU member countries is extremely difficult: internal agreements often do not work or are simply not implemented. Yet, Europe should keep on trying; what is the alternative? The Paris Climate Change Conference of November 2015 was a success. France was in the driving seat and Europe's influence was significant. By contrast, although sharing a common currency, eurozone countries have so far failed (or refused) to have a joint representation at the IMF. Presumably, some countries attach great importance to exerting influence or control by having their own representative on the executive board of this organization. But it makes a mockery of the monetary union in the eyes of non-Europeans.

Successive enlargements of the EU have always been treated as the most effective form of EU foreign policy—and this is most probably true. But taking on ever more responsibilities and problems, allowing in new countries with much weaker economies, administrative structures, and (dare we also say?) weak democratic traditions, while the European centre remains weak, is simply not a valid proposition: at some point, the system risks grinding to a halt. The EU is not that far from such a position of stasis today. And yet, for example, stability in the part of the Balkans that is still left out very much depends on the extension of Pax Europaea to that corner of the continent. Arguably, the solution lies with a stronger centre and a much more differentiated model of regional integration which would make further enlargements easier.

Turkey served for some time as a rare example of a Muslim country with a democracy and robust economic growth. And it presented a big challenge to Europe by asking to become part of the European project: a huge compliment as well as an almighty challenge. Turkey is big, still rather poor, and very different. How broad can the European church become and how much diversity can a weak European centre handle? They are not at all easy questions to answer. The Europeans decided, mostly by default, not to rise to the challenge. In the meantime, Turkish democracy has moved on to a slippery path and authoritarian attitudes have become increasingly prevalent. Now, Turkey controls the gates through which millions of refugees and economic immigrants are trying to enter Europe. Europeans have been trying to strike a deal with the gatekeeper, but the price they are being asked to pay may be very high not only in terms of money but also in having to compromise on their principles concerning democracy and the rule of law.

The EU shares a neighbourhood with Russia and is dependent on imports of energy from it. Some countries import all their gas from Russia and hence feel extremely vulnerable. Others perceive a broader relationship of mutual interdependence. Is Russia an enemy or a potential strategic partner? Foreign policy has a self-fulfilling dimension, but also requires a cold-blooded assessment of facts on the ground. European attitudes towards Russia have evolved over time, but they also vary significantly from country to country, depending largely on history and geography. Therefore, forging unity out of diverse interests and perceptions, especially when they are of an existential nature as in the case of countries too close for comfort to Russia, is bound to be a long and painful process. One needs to build trust and give assurances to those who are vulnerable. A European energy union would do a lot to help forge such unity while also strengthening in a big way the negotiating power of Europeans, but we are not there yet. The continuous disputes about which pipelines to build and which countries they should go through are just one more illustration of the difficulties in reconciling national interests and also of the lack of trust among European partners.

When it comes to security and high politics, Europe as a collective entity is still a novice and operates mostly on an intergovernmental basis.[22] Mr Putin wants to talk to the Germans or the French, possibly to the British, and preferably to the Americans. He may also talk to others in a clear divide-and-rule strategy. But there is hardly anybody in Brussels that he is particularly interested to talk to. From their side, the Europeans realize that they risk being picked off one at a time, if they go in different directions. Relations with Russia are very important for Europe, for both economic and security reasons, and they involve difficult trade-offs. Developments in Ukraine have served as a stern reminder: it is not easy to reconcile European values about self-determination, democracy, and human rights with the dictates of realpolitik, but one should at least try to avoid major mistakes.

Europe collectively cannot easily handle relations with Russia,[23] or with any other big power. By default, it delegates to its member states, the bigger ones in particular. The only European countries with global ambitions and a defence capability on a totally different scale from the rest, notably France and the UK, continue to be ambivalent and often inconsistent in their approach to a common European foreign policy.[24] They would be assured a leading role if they chose to play the game. Should the British, for example, begin to rethink their attitude in this respect? Meanwhile, Germany will continue to be a key country in relations with Russia, given its geographical position and its size.

Finding a modus vivendi with Russia is difficult enough, but insulating the EU from the turmoil that prevails in much of Europe's neighbourhood seems to be a close-to-impossible proposition. From Ukraine, Georgia, and Moldova to the east, down to Syria (and perhaps Turkey?), Israel and Palestine, Egypt and Algeria to the south, and with Iraq, Iran, and Afghanistan further to the east, there is a wide arc of instability, encompassing regional conflicts, civil wars, regional strongmen, and/or failing states. The instability in the neighbourhood translates itself into a direct security threat for Europe, mainly through terrorism, and in an ever increasing number of refugees and immigrants who try to flee from war and poverty at home.

The wider Middle East used to attract European and American interest largely because of energy supplies and the Arab–Israeli conflict. But their successive interventions in the past could hardly be said to have helped much to stabilize the region or help it to develop. Colonial and postcolonial masters have not left a good legacy behind them. And Europe's Mediterranean policy has been a failure. Now that the fires of hell have been unleashed, the capacity of Western powers to influence events on the ground is limited. In trying to make the best of them, they will unavoidably have to engage with all kinds of unpleasant interlocutors and make difficult compromises: such is the art of diplomacy.

Faced with an unprecedented wave of refugees and immigrants, Europe has no way of effectively closing its borders, short of resorting to methods that would take us back to dark periods of history. Some people are apparently tempted instead to close off Greece (and tomorrow Italy, or other countries?) and turn it into a large refugee camp. Not in my own backyard: is this potentially the future of European solidarity? If some countries feel very strongly about not taking their fair share of refugees, they could perhaps instead contribute more to the European border force. Europe will also need to reach agreements with transit countries and draw a clearer line between political refugees and economic immigrants. On the other hand, creating the conditions for stability and development in the region looks like an uncertain and long-term proposition; it will also be costly. Would it not be a great irony of history if refugees from the Middle East contributed to the undoing of the European project? There is, however, a more general question to ask. For many years, European integration was insulated from the world of hard power and geopolitics through the provision of the US security umbrella. Is Europe still not ready for adult life?

## What if?

A sober analysis of the experience of recent years and the challenges facing Europe today can easily lead to the conclusion that European integration has indeed reached the end of the road. It could be a big bang—or more probably a long crawl. The latter would not necessarily mean the end of the EU. After all, institutions often last much longer than their capacity to perform useful functions. But it could mean an increasingly weak and gridlocked centre pulled in different directions by internal centrifugal forces and vulnerable to all kinds of external shocks. This would surely have broader implications for the rest of the world, including the wider process of globalization. The end of the European postmodern empire that had aspired to provide a new model for managing interdependence between states and peoples based on consensus and democracy could be long and agonizing, although surely not as long as the end of the old Roman Empire that dragged on for centuries. Everything happens so much more quickly nowadays.

A weak and divided Europe, in decline and increasingly irrelevant, may continue to offer, if it is lucky, a relatively good life to many of its citizens, although with much less inclusive societies than in the old days and hence more social tensions and political instability, poor prospects for many of its young people, with internal borders once again and the more vulnerable parts of this empire possibly falling by the wayside. Many of the key elements for such a scenario are already there: a dysfunctional monetary union and languishing economies, internal fragmentation and weak common institutions, coupled with a whole range of strong external pressures that tend to divide rather than unite Europeans.

But it could get much worse than this. Populism is on the rise and illiberal ideologies are gaining strength in societies where large sections of the population are on the losing side of the long economic and technological transformation. Social safety nets are less effective, and nationalism is being offered as a kind of placebo for all kinds of social or economic ills. History suggests that Europe is capable of both the best and the worst. Democracy is not a given, nor is peace. And the rest of the world may not even allow Europe the luxury to decline gracefully.

Oxford-based political scientist Jan Zielonka thinks the EU is doomed.[25] He is not the only one: the number of genuine Europeans who have become increasingly apprehensive about the future of the European project has been rising in recent years. As an alternative, Zielonka envisions a Europe of complex networks and circles, a 'neo-medieval' Europe as he calls it. The problem, though, is that today's world is anything but neo-medieval: global power politics played by continental powers and global markets that bear little resemblance to those perfect competition models we still read about in economics textbooks. In today's world, you need institutions and organized political power to be able to deal with this kind of reality. A neo-medieval Europe simply could not do it.

Muddling through and damage limitation are the instinctive European reactions. And they have admittedly produced some results. Given the kind of shocks to which Europe has been subjected in recent years, from the economic crisis to the refugee crisis, it is no small achievement at all that it has kept more or less in one piece and has (so far) avoided major accidents. The instinct of collective survival is indeed strong and so is the fear of the possible costs of disintegration among political elites and the public at large, although the dissenting voices of those who think of life after the EU have been growing in numbers and intensity.

Europe is faced with multiple challenges and difficult choices: how to regenerate growth and how to reconcile it with more inclusive societies and with the objective of sustainable development; how to improve the prospects for the younger generations in Europe's ageing societies; how to make European and euro governance more effective but also more legitimate; how to reconcile the rise of nationalism with the ever growing needs for shared sovereignty arising from a highly interdependent world; how to cater for wide diversity within its ranks; how to defend common interests and values in an unstable and rapidly changing world in which it is (or rather, could be) one of the big players; and last but not least, how to help stabilize and assist the development of its neighbours whose ills easily spill over its borders. And if you think the list is not long enough, you might perhaps want to add the need to put the financial genie back into the bottle, which is not, however, a problem just for Europeans to deal with.

Meeting these challenges (or even beginning to deal with some of them) would be a very tall order indeed. Hard realists will tell you that meeting them is simply beyond the capacity of our political elites to handle under present conditions, hence their natural inclination to muddle through. Muddling through buys time at best and brings about change gradually, if at all. It is perhaps unavoidable when dealing with emergencies, but once emergencies are transformed into major structural problems the incremental approach (or muddling through) can no longer deliver. To put it differently and bluntly, Europe's problems today are more akin to malignant tumours than the flu. And you do not cure tumours with aspirin or vitamins.

Europe needs a game changer, one of those big initiatives that sometimes in history succeeds in radically transforming the scene and creating the conditions for win-win solutions. Continuing on the course it has been following for some years now is like waiting for the next accident to happen, after each of which it emerges weaker than before. It can't go on like this. The initiative that could serve as a game changer can only come from the strong, not the weak.

What if Germany were to come forward with such an initiative,[26] adopting an enlightened long-term approach to its own national interest which is intimately linked with the survival of the European project? It would have to do so in close cooperation with France and a few countries of the old core. But in order for this to happen, Germany must first recognize that the present situation is not sustainable for long. Its main partners should take it upon themselves to make this abundantly clear. They would be doing a great service to everyone, not least to the Germans themselves.

It is a big historical responsibility that falls on German shoulders. Can Germany compromise on some of its main policy priorities for the sake of the common European good? And how much will Germans be willing to underwrite the European project? Perhaps more so when they realize how much is at stake for them. Of course, the buck does not just stop with the Germans. How much will other countries be ready to undertake painful reforms, and not just of the deregulatory variety? And will the French be willing or able to reclaim their role as co-leaders? These are essential parts of the puzzle; once they are there, the other pieces could gradually fall into place. Even the British could decide eventually, seeing that the rest are determined to rescue (and reform) the European project, to play a more active role. It would certainly not be easy, although it has happened before in earlier stages of European integration. Admittedly, it used to be much simpler then in terms of both members and functions—and citizens by and large used to trust their political elites. Now it is much more complex and difficult. And it will be a choice between differentiated integration or no integration at all.

You can call it a grand bargain, a new pact, or perhaps more accurately a new historical compromise between countries, between the main political families and between generations in Europe. And it would require a new treaty that needs to pass the democracy test, but only on condition that unanimity no longer applies. The initiative could be taken after the presidential election in France and the federal election in Germany in 2017, assuming that the European car has made it that far more or less in one piece and with all passengers on board. Such an initiative would constitute a major turning point in the history of European integration. Yet, I am fully aware that the odds are against it.

The real question today is not so much about 'more Europe' or 'less Europe'. There will be more Europe in some policy areas, less in others, and of course differentiated membership options on offer. The real question is about what kind of Europe we want to build. The European project has become in many ways dysfunctional. We should try to work on it and improve it, instead of throwing it away. We simply cannot afford to let it fail. Just think of the alternative.

It will not be the United States of Europe anytime in the foreseeable future. And it will not be a European superpower throwing its weight around in a multipolar world. What it can be, however, is a Europe with a healthy economy and a common currency that has made real progress in resolving the contradiction of a currency without a state, a Europe that cares for the old and prepares a future for the young, a Europe that allows room for differentiation, a Europe with open borders, democratic institutions, and inclusive societies, a Europe that takes greater responsibility for its own security, confident in its diversity and proud not only of its past, perhaps also a Europe that is an example for others. This is what European integration, I believe, should be all about. I trust the game is not yet lost.

# NOTES

All the websites cited in the Notes were accessed in January 2016.

## Chapter 1

1. Mark Mazower, *The Dark Continent* (London: Allen & Lane, 1998).
2. François Duchêne was the first one to introduce the concept of 'civilian power' for Europe as an alternative form of big power behaviour on the international scene. See François Duchêne, 'Europe's Role in World Peace', in R. Mayne (ed.), *Europe Tomorrow: Sixteen Europeans Look Ahead* (London: Fontana, 1972), 32–47. It was still a time when many Europeans believed that Europe could set an example for the rest of the world. On the concept of normative power as applied to European integration, see Ian Manners, 'Normative Power Europe: A Contradiction in Terms?', *Journal of Common Market Studies*, 40/2 (2002), 235–58, http://onlinelibrary.wiley.com/doi/10.1111/1468-5965. 00353/pdf. Soft power was first introduced as a concept by Joseph Nye, *Bound to Lead: The Changing Nature of American Power* (New York: Basic Books, 1990). At the other end of the spectrum, Robert Kagan wrote rather disparagingly several decades later, at the time of the Iraq War, about Europeans coming from Venus and the Americans from Mars, suggesting that Europeans were simply trying to make a virtue out of their weakness in international affairs. See Robert Kagan, *Of Paradise and Power: America and Europe in the New World Order* (New York: A. Knopf, 2003). Although this may often be true—and it is equally true that Brussels Europe has often tried to make too much out of its purported soft power—one wonders whether the author might be willing to reconsider, with the benefit of hindsight, the virtues of the Martian approach.
3. Fritz Scharpf, *Governing in Europe: Effective and Democratic?* (Oxford: Oxford University Press, 1999).
4. See Dani Rodrik, *The Globalization Paradox: Why Global Markets, States and Democracy Can't Coexist* (Oxford: Oxford University Press, 2011).
5. A famous quote from Shakespeare's *Julius Caesar*, I. ii. 141–2.
6. See the celebrated book of Francis Fukuyama, *The End of History and the Last Man* (London: Penguin, 1992).

7. One of the leading prophets is Kishore Mahbubani, *The New Asian Hemisphere: The Irresistible Shift of Global Power to the East* (New York: Public Affairs, 2008).
8. Martin Wolf, *The Shifts and the Shocks: What We've Learned—and Have Still to Learn—from the Financial Crisis* (London: Allen & Lane, 2014).
9. Richard Vinen, 'The Pope is Wrong—Ageing Europe's Ideas Have Life in Them Yet', *Financial Times*, 28 November 2014, http://www.ft.com/intl/cms/s/0/7b702c2a-7661-11e4-9761-00144feabdc0.html#axzz41Y10THJc.
10. Pope Francis in his address to the European Parliament on 25 November 2014. http://m.vatican.va/content/francescomobile/en/speeches/2014/november/documents/papa-francesco_20141125_strasburgo-parlamento-europeo.html
11. Loukas Tsoukalis, 'The JCMS Annual Review Lecture: The Shattering of Illusions—and What Next?', *The JCMS Annual Review of the European Union in 2010*, suppl. issue of *Journal of Common Market Studies*, 49 (2011), 19–44, http://onlinelibrary.wiley.com/doi/10.1111/j.1468-5965.2011.02185.x/epdf.

# Chapter 2

1. One of the best early accounts of the creation of the ECSC was written by Ernst Haas, *The Uniting of Europe* (London: Stevens, 1958). See also Alan Milward, *The Reconstruction of Western Europe* (London: Methuen, 1984).
2. There is a vast literature on the birth and early history of EMU. The non-economist may consult, among others, David Marsh, *The Euro: The Battle for the New Global Currency* (New Haven and London: Yale University Press, 2009); Kenneth Dyson and Kevin Featherstone, *The Road to Maastricht* (Oxford: Oxford University Press, 1999). For an earlier history of European monetary integration, see also Loukas Tsoukalis, *The Politics and Economics of European Monetary Integration* (London: Allen & Unwin, 1977).
3. Loukas Tsoukalis, *What Kind of Europe?* (2nd edn., Oxford: Oxford University Press, 2005). See also Barry Eichengreen, *The European Economy Since 1945* (Princeton and Oxford: Princeton University Press, 2007).
4. In Graph 2.1, I have used moving five-year averages in order to smooth out year-to-year fluctuations, since we are interested here in the long-term trend. The two bumps in the line depicting growth, one in the late 1980s and the other in the mid-1990s, are closely correlated with an economic boom at global level. They could also be in part related to the internal market programme and the introduction of the euro respectively, which created a climate of optimism. Alas, they did not last for very long.
5. One of the standard works on the dilemmas related to economic regulation at European level has been written by Giandomenico Majone, *Regulating Europe* (London: Routledge, 1996).
6. One of the main schools of thought, especially in the early stages of European integration, with a strong presence in the academic world and

some, albeit limited, impact among policymakers. For the origins of functionalist thinking, see David Mitrany, 'Functional Approach to World Organization', *International Affairs*, 23 (1948), 350–63, http://www.lsu.edu/faculty/lray2/teaching/7971_1s2009/mitrany1948.pdf. For its application to European integration, see Haas, *The Uniting of Europe*, and for a recent, critical perspective on European integration and functionalist logic, see Giandomenico Majone, *Rethinking the Union of Europe Post-Crisis: Has Integration Gone Too Far?* (Cambridge: Cambridge University Press, 2014).

7. Barry Eichengreen, *Exorbitant Privilege* (Oxford: Oxford University Press, 2011).

8. For one of the most representative works of the academic orthodoxy on efficient markets, see Nobel Laureate Eugene F. Fama, 'Efficient Capital Markets: A Review of Theory and Empirical Work', *Journal of Finance*, 25/2 (1970), 383–417, http://efinance.org.cn/cn/fm/Efficient%20Capital%20Markets%20A%20Review%20of%20Theory%20and%20Empirical%20Work.pdf. For a critical view from a practitioner, see Adair Turner, *Economics After the Crisis: Ends and Means* (Cambridge, MA and London: MIT Press, 2012).

9. Tommaso Padoa-Schioppa, *The Euro and Its Central Bank: Getting United After the Union* (Cambridge, MA: MIT Press, 2004).

10. Mainstream economists usually have little to say about distributional issues, although this has been changing fast in recent years because of widening income and wealth inequalities in the developed world, which are now difficult to ignore. International organizations have provided evidence and expressed concern about the broader implications. The Organisation for Economic Co-operation and Development (OECD) has repeatedly done so, and so has the IMF. See, for example, OECD, *Divided We Stand: Why Inequality Keeps Rising* (Paris: OECD, 2012), http://www.keepeek.com/Digital-Asset-Management/oecd/social-issues-migration-health/the-causes-of-growing-inequalities-in-oecd-countries_9789264119536-en#page1. Some of the best minds among economists have tried to trace the trends and explain the forces behind them. See Thomas Piketty's magnum opus, *Capital in the Twenty-First Century* (Cambridge, MA: Harvard University Press, 2014) and Anthony Atkinson, *Inequality* (Cambridge, MA: Harvard University Press, 2015). Inequality has turned into a hot political issue once again, and it is certainly not confined to Europe. We shall return to this subject in Chapter 6.

11. According to World Bank data adjusted for purchasing power in each country, per capita income was US$6,800 in Ukraine and US$6,000 in Poland in 1990. By 2013, per capita income in Poland had reached US$23,700 and in Ukraine it was only US$8,800.

12. On the basis of World Bank data, per capita income in Bulgaria was US$5,400 in 1990 and US$15,700 in 2013.

13. Ivan Krastev, 'Britain's Gain is Eastern Europe's Brain Drain', *The Guardian*, 24 March 2015, http://www.theguardian.com/commentisfree/2015/mar/24/brit ain-east-europe-brain-drain-bulgaria.

14. See, for example, Kevin Featherstone and Claudio M. Radaeli (eds.), *The Politics of Europeanization* (Oxford: Oxford University Press, 2003).

15. *The Crisis of EU Enlargement* (LSE Ideas, 2013), http://www.lse.ac.uk/IDEAS/ publications/reports/SR018.aspx.

16. For one of the most recent and comprehensive accounts of European trade policy, see Alasdair R. Young and John Peterson, *Parochial Global Europe* (Oxford: Oxford University Press, 2014).

17. Christopher Hill, 'The Capability-Expectations Gap, or Conceptualizing Europe's International Role', *Journal of Common Market Studies*, 31/3 (1993), 305–28, http://onlinelibrary.wiley.com/doi/10.1111/j.1468-5965.1993.tb00466.x/epdf.

18. For the intellectual debates on Europe in different national contexts, see Justine Lacroix and Kalypso Nicolaïdis (eds.), *European Stories* (Oxford: Oxford University Press, 2011).

19. Several politicians and analysts have argued all along that it is both desirable and feasible to gain more direct legitimacy for European institutions through more open political competition at European level. This could be achieved by making European elections more like national elections, with European parties fighting for power on the basis of Europe-wide programmes. See, among others, Simon Hix, *What's Wrong with the European Union & How to Fix It* (Cambridge: Polity, 2008).

20. Richard Eichenberg and Russell Dalton, 'Post-Maastricht Blues: The Transformation of Citizen Support for European Integration, 1973–2004', *Acta Politica*, 42 (2007), 128–52, http://www.palgrave-journals.com/ap/journal/ v42/n2/full/5500182a.html.

21. See Sara B. Hobolt, *Europe in Question: Referendums on European Integration* (Oxford: Oxford University Press, 2009).

22. See, among others, Paul Taggart, 'The Domestic Politics of the 2005 French and Dutch Referendums and Their Challenge for the Study of European Integration', *Journal of Common Market Studies*, 44 (2006), suppl. issue: *The JCMS Annual Review of the European Union in 2005*, 7–25, http://onlinelibrary .wiley.com/doi/10.1111/j.1468-5965.2006.00641.x/epdf.

23. For an interesting collection of articles with a critical stance on neo-liberal ideas and policies in Europe, see Vivien A. Schmidt and Mark Thatcher (eds.), *Resilient Liberalism in Europe's Political Economy* (Cambridge: Cambridge University Press, 2013).

## Chapter 3

1. Robert Mundell, 'A Theory of Optimum Currency Areas', *American Economic Review*, 51 (1961), 657–65—the article that started the whole debate on

optimum currency areas. For a comprehensive study on the subject, see Paul de Grauwe, *Economics of Monetary Union* (10th edn., Oxford: Oxford University Press, 2014).

2. See Martin Feldstein, 'EMU and International Conflict', *Foreign Affairs*, 76/6 (1997), 60–73, https://www.foreignaffairs.com/articles/europe/1997-11-01/emu-and-international-conflict.

3. The terms honeymoon and polygamy have been widely used by people commenting on the early period of the euro. I, therefore, lay no claim to originality.

4. One of the best and most readable histories of the honeymoon period of the euro and the early years of the crisis has been written by Jean Pisani-Ferry, *The Euro Crisis and Its Aftermath* (Oxford: Oxford University Press, 2014). See also Martin Sandbu, *Europe's Orphan* (Princeton and Oxford: Princeton University Press, 2015), chs. 1 and 2, and relevant chapters in Wolf, *The Shifts and the Shocks*.

5. I have borrowed the data on the total exposure of banks by nationality to the countries of southern Europe plus Ireland from Helen Thompson, 'Germany and the Eurozone Crisis: The European Reformation of the German Banking Crisis and the Future of the Euro', *New Political Economy*, 20/6 (2015), 851–70, http://www.tandfonline.com/doi/abs/10.1080/13563467 .2015.1041476?journalCode=cnpe20 (abstract). Similar calculations have been made by Baldwin and Giavazzi who found out that total lending by banks of the European core (including Germany, France, Austria, Belgium, and the Netherlands) to the southern periphery, and Ireland as an honorary member, had reached €1 trillion by the end of 2009, almost five times their total exposure in 1999, when the euro started. Risk was not at issue, apparently, for banks in the honeymoon years of the new common currency. See Richard Baldwin and Francesco Giavazzi, 'Introduction', in Baldwin and Giavazzi (eds.), *The Eurozone Crisis: A Consensus View of the Causes and a Few Possible Remedies* (2015), a VoxEU.org eBook, http://www.voxeu.org/sites/default/files/file/reboot_upload_1.pdf.

6. Among the plethora of books and articles that have been written about the big financial crisis of 2007–8, its origins and aftermath, I would single out Wolf, *The Shifts and the Shocks*; Alan S. Blinder, *After the Music Stopped* (New York: Penguin, 2013); and Joseph E. Stiglitz, *Freefall: Free Markets and the Sinking of the Global Economy* (New York: Norton, 2010).

7. Figures quoted in Wolf, *The Shifts and the Shocks*, and Baldwin and Giavazzi (eds.), *The Eurozone Crisis* respectively.

8. This phrase is usually attributed to Mervyn King, former governor of the Bank of England, sometimes also to Charles Goodhart of the London School of Economics.

9. 'Let Them Eat Credit' is the title of the first chapter of a book written by the former chief economist of the IMF and currently governor of the Central

Bank of India. See Raghuram Rajan, *Fault Lines: How Hidden Fractures Still Threaten the World Economy* (Princeton and Oxford: Princeton University Press, 2010).

10. Susan Strange was the first to write about casino capitalism: Susan Strange, *Casino Capitalism* (Oxford: Blackwell, 1986).

11. For a broad application of the concept of borrowed time in Western democratic capitalism, see Wolfgang Streeck, *Buying Time: The Delayed Crisis of Democratic Capitalism* (London and New York: Verso, 2014). For a comparison of individual European countries hit by the crisis, see Mark Blyth, *Austerity: The History of a Dangerous Idea* (Oxford: Oxford University Press, 2013), 51–93; see also Sandbu, *Europe's Orphan*.

12. See *Quelle France dans dix ans?* (2014), report submitted to the President of the Republic under the direction of Jean Pisani-Ferry, http://www.actu-environnement.com/media/pdf/news-22033-france-10-ans.pdf; Eric Monnet and Claudia Sternberg (eds.), *Euro, les années critiques* (Paris: Presses universitaires de France, 2015). For a very critical approach advocating the dissolution of the euro, see also François Heisbourg, *La Fin du rêve européen* (Paris: Stock, 2013). When several convinced Europeans in the old member countries began to speak in favour of a euro break-up or individual country exits, one knew that the problem could at some point get out of control.

13. Loukas Tsoukalis, 'Rebalancing and Completing the European Monetary Union', in Mark Dawson, Henrik Enderlein, and Christian Joerges (eds.), *Beyond the Crisis: The Governance of Europe's Economic, Political and Legal Transformation* (Oxford: Oxford University Press, 2015), 44–61.

14. Leaving aside some elements of conspiracy theory and journalistic hype, the book by Marc Roche, *La Banque: Comment Goldman Sachs dirige le monde* (Paris: Albin Michel, 2010), provides interesting information as to how Goldman Sachs helped the Greek government to conceal part of its public debt.

15. European Commission, *Successes and Challenges after 10 Years of Economic and Monetary Union*, European Economy 2/2008 (Luxembourg: Office for Offical Publications of the European Communities, 2008), http://ec.europa.eu/economy_finance/publications/publication12682_en.pdf.

# Chapter 4

1. The reader may consult Matthias Matthijs and Mark Blyth (eds.), *The Future of the Euro* (Oxford: Oxford University Press, 2015) for a comprehensive account of the euro crisis from a political economy perspective. Together with Baldwin and Giavazzi (eds.), *The Eurozone Crisis*; Pisani-Ferry, *The Euro Crisis and Its Aftermath*; Wolf, *The Shifts and the Shocks*; and Sandbu, *Europe's Orphan*, it is among the best general sources on how Europeans have tried to deal with this mother of crises. For a more partisan view, see also

Philippe Legrain, *European Spring: Why Our Economies and Politics Are in a Mess—and How to Put Them Right* (no pub., 2014).

2. See, for example, Sandbu, *Europe's Orphan*, ch. 4.

3. Paul de Grauwe, 'The Governance of a Fragile Eurozone', *CEPS Working Document*, 346 (May 2011), http://www.ceps.eu/system/files/book/2011/05/WD%20346%20De%20Grauwe%20on%20Eurozone%20Governance.pdf.

4. Orphanides, a former governor of the Central Bank of Cyprus and also senior adviser to the US Federal Reserve, now professor at MIT, has argued that the original sin, as he calls it, of the euro crisis goes back to the way the Greek crisis was handled in order essentially to protect the interests of the big countries in the eurozone and their banks using the IMF as a cover. See Athanasios Orphanides, 'The Euro Area Crisis Five Years After the Original Sin', *MIT Sloan Research Paper*, 5147–15 (October 2015), http://papers.ssrn.com/sol3/papers.cfm?abstract_id=2676103&download=yes. See also Olivier Blanchard (former chief economist of the IMF), 'Greece: Past Critiques and the Path Forward', *iMFdirect*, 9 July 2015, http://blog-imfdirect.imf.org/2015/07/09/greece-past-critiques-and-the-path-forward/; and the response by Ashoka Mody (also a former IMF official), 'Olivier Blanchard Fails to Recognise Two Major IMF Mistakes on Greece', *Bruegel Blog*, 13 July 2015, http://bruegel.org/2015/07/olivier-blanchard-fails-to-recognise-two-major-imf-mistakes-in-greece/.

5. For an assessment of adjustment programmes and the role of the troika, see, among others, André Sapir et al., *The Troika and Financial Assistance in the Euro Area: Successes and Failures* (2014), Study presented to the Committee on Economic and Monetary Affairs (ECON) of the European Parliament, http://bruegel.org/wp-content/uploads/imported/publications/20140219ATT79633EN_01.pdf.

6. It had happened many times before. For a very good history of debt crises and the conclusions to draw from them, see Carmen Rheinhart and Kenneth Rogoff, *This Time Is Different: Eight Centuries of Financial Folly* (Princeton and Oxford: Princeton University Press, 2009).

7. Atif Mian and Amir Sufi, *House of Debt* (Chicago and London: Chicago University Press, 2014).

8. For a fascinating account of the first years of intra-European negotiations, following the bursting of the bubble, which highlights the decisive role of national politics, see Carlo Bastasin, *Saving Europe: How National Politics Nearly Destroyed the Euro* (Washington, DC: Brookings, 2012).

9. Thompson, 'Germany and the Eurozone Crisis'. See also Sandbu, *Europe's Orphan*; and Pisani-Ferry, *The Euro Crisis and Its Aftermath*.

10. Miranda Xafa, 'Sovereign Debt Crisis Management: Lessons from the 2012 Greek Debt Restructuring', *Centre for International Governance Innovation Papers*, 33 (June 2014), https://www.cigionline.org/sites/default/files/cigi_paper_33.pdf.

11. See Lucrezia Reichlin, Elias Papaioannou, and Richard Portes, 'End "Extend and Pretend" with Greece', *Project Syndicate*, 15 June 2015, http://www.project-syndicate.org/commentary/greece-troika-fiscal-reform-by-lucrezia-reichlin-et-al-2015-06.

12. See also Donal Donovan and Antoin E. Murphy, *The Fall of the Celtic Tiger: Ireland and the Euro Debt Crisis* (Oxford: Oxford University Press, 2013); Karl Whelan, 'Ireland's Economic Crisis: The Good, the Bad and the Ugly', *UCD Centre for Economic Research Working Paper* (July 2013), https://www.ucd.ie/t4cms/WP13_06.pdf.

13. Wolfgang Münchau, 'The Wacky Economics of Germany's Parallel Universe', *Financial Times*, 16 Nov. 2014, http://www.ft.com/intl/cms/s/0/e257ed96-6b2c-11e4-be68-00144feabdco.html#axzz3poqrU9Vx. See also Simon Wren-Lewis, 'Macroeconomic Stabilisation in the Eurozone: Lessons from Failure', *Global Policy*, 4, suppl. 1 (2013), 66–73, http://onlinelibrary .wiley .com/doi/10.1111/1758-5899.12048/epdf.

14. Jürgen Stark, 'The Historical and Cultural Differences that Divide Europe's Union', *Financial Times*, 11 February 2015, http://www.ft.com/intl/cms/s/0/e08ec622-ad28-11e4-a5c1-00144feab7de.html#axzz3s1R3256w.

15. The editors' introduction in Baldwin and Giavazzi (eds.), *The Eurozone Crisis*, a book which brought together leading economists with a wide range of opinions, is quite representative of this (almost) consensus view. Several German economists, however, beg to differ. See, for example, Hans-Werner Sinn, *The Euro Trap: On Bursting Bubbles, Budgets and Beliefs* (Oxford: Oxford University Press, 2014). See also Stark, 'The Historical and Cultural Differences'; and Otmar Issing, 'The German Leadership Question', *Project Syndicate*, 14 April 2014, http://www.project-syndicate.org/commentary/otmar-issing-wants-germany-to-lead-europe-with-good-economic-policy–not-by-bailing-out-governments-and-banks. Issing resigned as chief economist of the ECB in 2012 because of his opposition to purchases of government bonds. He has also been very critical of bailout programmes.

16. On the new economic governance in the eurozone, see also Henrik Enderlein, 'The Euro as a Showcase for Exploratory Governance: Why There Are No Simple Answers', in *The Governance Report 2015* (Oxford: Oxford University Press/Hertie School of Governance, 2015).

17. Jürgen Habermas, the well-known German philosopher and social theorist, criticizes intergovernmental rule in the EU, as a form of executive federalism, exercised through the European Council. See, for example, Jürgen Habermas, 'Europe's Post-Democratic Era', *The Guardian*, 10 November 2011, http://www.theguardian.com/commentisfree/2011/nov/10/jurgen-habermas-europe-post-democratic, and also his book *The Crisis of the European Union: A Response*, trans. Ciaran Cronin (Cambridge: Polity, 2012).

18. Wolf, *The Shifts and the Shocks*, 338.

19. This is one of the most often cited quotes from this wily and seasoned politician, although I have been unable to trace where and when he actually said it. Perhaps he never did but everybody seems convinced of it.

20. See also Dani Rodrik, 'The Mirage of Structural Reform', *Project Syndicate*, 8 October 2015, https://www.project-syndicate.org/commentary/greece-structural-reform-mirage-by-dani-rodrik-2015-10.

21. IMF, *World Economic Outlook: Uneven Growth—Short- and Long-Term Factors* (Washington, DC: IMF, 2015), 104–7, http://www.imf.org/external/pubs/ft/weo/2015/01/pdf/text.pdf.

22. Ben Crum, 'Saving the Euro at the Cost of Democracy?', *Journal of Common Market Studies*, 51/4 (2013), 614–30, http://onlinelibrary.wiley.com/doi/10.1111/jcms.12019/epdf.

23. Euro Area Summit Statement, Brussels, 29 June 2012, http://www.consilium.europa.eu/uedocs/cms_Data/docs/pressdata/en/ec/131359.pdf.

24. Emmanuel Mourlon-Druol, 'Banking Union in Historical Perspective: The Initiative of the European Commission in the 1960s–1970s', *Journal of Common Market Studies* (forthcoming), http://onlinelibrary.wiley.com/doi/10.1111/jcms.12348/pdf.

25. Speech made by Mario Draghi at the Global Investment Conference in London on 26 July 2012, https://www.ecb.europa.eu/press/key/date/2012/html/sp120726.en.html.

26. Nothing short of distributing free money to European citizens, or dropping money from helicopters in the words of Milton Friedman, will enable Europe to escape today from deflation and economic stagnation: this argument is now being used by several economists. See, for example, the analysis by Willem H. Buiter, chief economist of Citibank London, in 'The Simple Analytics of Helicopter Money: Why It Works—Always', *Economics-E-Journal*, 8 (21 August 2014), 1–38, http://www.economics-ejournal.org/economics/journalarticles/2014-28; and Adair Turner, *Between Debt and the Devil: Money, Credit, and Fixing Global Finance* (Princeton and Oxford: Princeton University Press, 2015).

27. See also Bastasin, *Saving Europe*, ch. 19, with the characteristic title 'Berlusconi's Moral Hazard and the German Waterboarding Strategy'.

28. Pisani-Ferry, *The Euro Crisis and Its Aftermath*, 165.

29. Hans-Werner Sinn and Timo Wollmershaeuser, 'Target Loans, Current Account Balances and Capital Flows: The ECB's Rescue Facility', *National Bureau of Economic Research*, Working Paper 17626 (November 2011), http://www.nber.org/papers/w17626. See also the response by Paul de Grauwe and Yuemei Ji, 'TARGET2 as a Scapegoat for German Errors', *VoxEU*, 2 November 2012, http://www.voxeu.org/article/target2-scapegoat-german-errors. In this article, the authors point out that the creditor/debtor positions in Target 2 are simply the other side of the coin of current account imbalances between the two sides.

30. Ashoka Mody, 'Living (Dangerously) Without a Fiscal Union', *Bruegel*, 24 March 2015, http://bruegel.org/2015/03/living-dangerously-without-a-fiscal-union/.

31. Nicolas Véron, 'Europe's Radical Banking Union', *Bruegel*, 5 May 2015, http://bruegel.org/2015/05/europes-radical-banking-union/.

32. Data provided by the Federal Ministry for Economic Affairs and Energy of Germany.

33. Olivier Blanchard, Mark Griffiths, and Bertrand Gruss, 'Boom, Bust, Recovery: Forensics of the Latvia Crisis', *Brookings Papers on Economic Activity* (Fall 2013), http://www.brookings.edu/~/media/projects/bpea/fall-2013/2013b_blanchard_latvia_crisis.pdf. See also Wolf, *The Shifts and the Shocks*, 299–301.

34. For a wide range of views from leading analysts, see the collection of articles in Matthijs and Blyth (eds.), *The Future of the Euro*; and Baldwin and Giavazzi (eds.), *The Eurozone Crisis*.

35. Peter Hall, 'Renewal in the Post-Crisis Landscape: The Limits of Technocratic Social Democracy', in O. Cramme, P. Diamond, and M. McTernan (eds.), *Progressive Politics After the Crash* (London: I. B. Tauris, 2013), 26.

36. IMF, *World Economic Outlook, October 2012: Coping with High Debt and Sluggish Growth* (Washington, DC: IMF, 2012), 41–3, https://www.imf.org/external/pubs/ft/weo/2012/02/pdf/text.pdf; and the article by Karl Whelan, 'Olli's Follies: Is Debate About Fiscal Multipliers Unhelpful?', *Forbes*, 17 February 2013, http://www.forbes.com/sites/karlwhelan/2013/02/17/ollis-follies-is-debate-about-fiscal-multipliers-unhelpful/.

37. The debate on symmetry of adjustment in European monetary integration has a long history. See, among others, Loukas Tsoukalis, *The New European Economy: The Politics and Economics of Integration* (2nd edn., Oxford: Oxford University Press, 1993), ch. 7.

38. Barry Eichengreen and Charles Wyplosz, 'How the Euro Crisis Was Successfully Resolved', *VoxEU*, 12 February 2016, http://www.voxeu.org/article/how-euro-crisis-was-successfully-resolved.

## Chapter 5

1. In the 'Melian Dialogue', part of the *History of the Peloponnesian War* written in the fifth century BC.

2. In 2014, the foreign minister, Mr Steinmeier, asked experts from Germany and abroad what was wrong with German foreign policy and what needed to be changed in a unconventional self-examination exercise. The results can be found at http://www.valletta.diplo.de/contentblob/4474378/Daten/5256302/publication.pdf.

3. Timothy Garton Ash believes that more reality-based controversy within Germany would be good for the country and for Europe as a whole, arguing that too much consensus has smothered domestic politics in

Germany. See Timothy Garton Ash, 'Why a Germany of Robust Debate Would Be Better for Europe', *The Guardian*, 27 July 2015, http://www .theguardian.com/commentisfree/2015/jul/27/germany-domestic-politics-europe.

4. *The Economist* referred to Mrs Merkel as 'The Indispensable European' on the cover of its 7 November 2015 issue. See http://www.economist.com/news/ leaders/21677643-angela-merkel-faces-her-most-serious-political-challenge-yet-europe-needs-her-more.

5. This is the term used by Radosław Sikorski, former foreign minister of Poland, who also added that he feared German power less than German inactivity and called on Germany to lead the eurozone out of the crisis, in a speech he gave in Berlin on 28 November 2011, http://www.mfa.gov.pl/ resource/33ce6061-ec12-4da1-a145-01e2995c6302:JCR.

6. So much has been written in recent years on the nature of Germany's leadership role during the crisis and the conclusions range from reluctant leader to coercive hegemon. For representative views, see Simon Bulmer and William Paterson, 'Germany as the EU's Reluctant Hegemon? Of Economic Strength and Political Constraints', *Journal of European Public Policy*, 20/10 (2013), http://www.tandfonline.com/doi/abs/10.1080/13501763.2013 .822824; Abraham Newman, 'The Reluctant Leader: Germany's Euro Experience and the Long Shadow of Reunification', in Matthijs and Blyth (eds.), *The Future of the Euro*, 117–35; and Ulrich Beck, *German Europe* (Cambridge: Polity, 2013).

7. Tsoukalis, 'Rebalancing and Completing the European Monetary Union'.

8. See also Peter Hall, 'The Economics and Politics of the Euro Crisis', *German Politics*, 21/4 (2012), 355–71, http://www.tandfonline.com/doi/pdf/10.1080/ 09644008.2012.739614. Hall argues that there are different political economies and different models of capitalism in Europe and in the eurozone in particular. They are unlikely to be homogenized into one, the Germanic model, because of the crisis. This is also the view of Streeck, *Buying Time*.

9. There is a big literature on 'ordo-liberalism' and interest has grown because of the crisis and the role played by Germany. See, for example, Mathias Siems and Gerhard Schnyder, 'Ordoliberal Lessons for Economic Stability: Different Kinds of Regulation, Not More Regulation', *Governance*, 27/3 (2014), 377–96, http://onlinelibrary.wiley.com/doi/10.1111/gove.12046/abstract; Sebastian Dullien and Ulrike Guérot, 'The Long Shadow of Ordoliberalism: Germany's Approach to the Euro Crisis', *European Council on Foreign Relations Policy Brief* (Feb. 2012), http://www.ecfr.eu/page/-/ECFR49_GERMANY_BRIEF. pdf; and David Schäfer, 'A Banking Union of Ideas: The Impact of Ordoliberalism and the Vicious Circle on the EU Banking Union', *Journal of Common Market Studies* (forthcoming), http://onlinelibrary.wiley.com/doi/10.1111/jcms .12351/epdf.

10. Paul Krugman, Joseph Stiglitz, and Martin Wolf among many others have written repeatedly and very critically of German policies in academic pieces and newspaper articles.

11. Wolfgang Schäuble, 'Ignore the Doomsayers: Europe Is Being Fixed', *Financial Times*, 16 September 2013, http://www.ft.com/intl/cms/s/0/e88c842a-1c67-11e3-a8a3-00144feab7de.html#axzz3s1R3256w.

12. Vivien A. Schmidt, 'The Forgotten Problem of Democratic Legitimacy: "Governing by the Rules" and "Ruling by the Numbers"', in Matthijs and Blyth (eds.), *The Future of the Euro*, 90–114.

13. Quoted in Edward Luce, 'A Fly on the Wall at a Fund on the Move', *Financial Times*, 27 July 2014, http://www.ft.com/intl/cms/s/2/d17de260-11b7-11e4-8279-00144feabdco.html.

14. For a very good overall treatment of the subject, see also Barbara Lippert, 'Deutche Europapolitik zwischen Tradition und Irritation', *SWP Arbeitspapier*, 7 October 2015, http://www.swp-berlin.org/fileadmin/contents/products/arbeitspapiere/Deutsche_Europapolitik.pdf.

15. For a good general introduction, see Stathis N. Kalyvas, *Modern Greece: What Everyone Needs to Know* (Oxford: Oxford University Press, 2015).

16. Greece in crisis has attracted a great deal of attention from policymakers, academics, and journalists alike. It has also provided the battleground for competing analyses and economic strategies for the European crisis as a whole. The result is a vast amount of literature, inevitably of uneven quality. Among the best are Blanchard, 'Greece: Past Critiques and the Path Forward' and the response by Mody, 'Olivier Blanchard Fails to Recognise Two Major IMF Mistakes on Greece'. See also Thorsten Beck, 'Groundhog Day in Greece', *VoxEU*, 2 February 2015, http://www.voxeu.org/article/groundhog-day-greece; and Paolo Manasse, 'What Went Wrong in Greece and How to Fix It: Lessons for Europe from the Greek Crisis', *VoxEU*, 12 June 2015, http://www.voxeu.org/article/what-went-wrong-greece-and-how-fix-it. From a Greek perspective, see, among others, Nicos Christodoulakis, *Greek Endgame: From Austerity to Growth or Grexit?* (London: Rowman and Littlefield, 2015); and Eleni Panagiotarea, *Greece in the Euro: Economic Delinquency Or System Failure?* (Colchester: ECPR, 2013).

17. For a lively account containing real life stories of Greece in crisis, see Yannis Palaiologos, *The 13th Labour of Hercules* (London: Portobello, 2014). The author summarizes his explanation of an ever-deepening crisis in Greece as follows: 'a state shorn of its guardians, laid waste by plunderers great and small in the good times, had lost too much legitimacy to be able to impose the heavy burden of adjustment when it could no longer be put off' (p. xvi).

18. For a study of populism in Greece, see Takis S. Pappas, *Populism and Crisis Politics in Greece* (New York: Palgrave, 2014).

19. Yanis Varoufakis gained great reputation (and notoriety) during his rather short spell as Greek finance minister during the first half of 2015, while

causing much damage to his country. He is a very good writer and eloquent speaker. His latest book draws from his experience as finance minister: Yanis Varoufakis, *And the Weak Suffer What they Must: Europe's Crisis and America's Economic Future* (New York: Nation, 2016).

20. The quotation is from an article penned by Churchill in the *Saturday Evening Post* on 15 February 1930.

21. Hugo Young tells very eloquently 'the story of fifty years in which Britain struggled to reconcile the past she could not forget with the future she could not avoid'. It is the story of Britain's troubled relationship with Europe. See Hugo Young, *The Blessed Plot: Britain and Europe from Churchill to Blair* (London: Macmillan, 1998). See also Roger Liddle, *The Europe Dilemma: Britain and the Drama of EU Integration* (London: Tauris/Policy Network, 2014), from the viewpoint of an engaged European in the British Labour Party.

22. 'Poisoned chalice' is the term used by Vernon Bogdanor in his Gresham lecture on 'The Growth of Euroscepticism' delivered on 20 May 2014, http://www.gresham.ac.uk/lectures-and-events/the-growth-of-euroscepticism.

23. Discussing identity issues is like walking on a very slippery road. Garton Ash writes about Britain's multiple identities of which the European identity forms a part: Timothy Garton Ash, 'Is Britain European?', *International Affairs*, 77/1 (2001), 1–14, https://europeanization.files.wordpress.com/2011/03/is-britain-european.pdf. And Roger Liddle laments New Labour's failure 'to transform how the British feel in their guts about Europe' (Liddle, *The Europe Dilemma*, p. xxiii). The question of identity keeps cropping up in the British debate on relations with Europe, more than in any other country, for obvious reasons of history and geography.

24. In the words of Robert Cooper, one of the finest products of the Foreign Office and a convinced European: 'It is no good owning a Rolls-Royce if you do not know where you are going…[or] if your plan is to drive it over the cliff.' Robert Cooper, 'Sheep's Eyes and Witchetty Grubs—A Test for British Diplomacy', *Financial Times*, 4 March 2015, http://www.ft.com/intl/cms/s/0/a4e80cba-c262-11e4-ad89-00144feab7de.html#axzz41Y10THJc.

25. Robert Ford and Matthew Goodwin, *Revolt on the Right: Explaining Support for the Radical Right in Britain* (London: Routledge, 2014).

26. The Migration Observatory at the University of Oxford provides a wealth of data on British public opinion on migration. See http://www.migrationobservatory.ox.ac.uk/briefings/uk-public-opinion-toward-immigration-overall-attitudes-and-level-concern.

27. In a speech he gave at the annual conference of Policy Network in the City of London on 28 February 2013, http://europa.eu/rapid/press-release_PRES-13-86_en.htm. See also Anand Menon, 'Littler England: The United Kingdom's Retreat from Global Leadership', *Foreign Affairs*, 94/6 (2015), https://www.foreignaffairs.com/articles/western-europe/littler-england.

28. Helen Wallace, 'Does Britain Need the European Union? Does the European Union Need Britain?', *Journal of the British Academy*, 3 (2015), 185–95, http://www.britac.ac.uk/events/2015/Does_the_European_Union_Need_Britain.cfm. The author explains very eloquently the contradictions between the different kinds of Britain.

29. For a good example of a visionary British European, see David Marquand, *The End of the West: The Once and Future Europe* (Princeton and Oxford: Princeton University Press, 2012).

30. https://www.gov.uk/government/speeches/eu-speech-at-bloomberg.

31. See Michael Emerson (ed.), *Britain's Future in Europe: Reform, Renegotiation, Repatriation Or Secession?* (London: Rowman & Littlefield, 2015).

32. For lessons from the 1975 referendum experience, see also Emmanuel Mourlon-Druol, 'The UK's EU Vote: The 1975 Precedent and Today's Negotiations', *Bruegel Policy Contribution* (June 2015), http://bruegel.org/2015/06/the-uks-eu-vote-the-1975-precedent-and-todays-negotiations/.

33. Dáithí O'Ceallaigh and Paul Gillespie (eds.), *Britain and Europe: The Endgame—An Irish Perspective* (Dublin: Institute of International and European Affairs, 2015), http://www.iiea.com/ftp/Publications/Britain-and-Europe-The-Endgame_DigitalVersion.pdf. The Irish are, of course, particularly concerned and directly affected by what happens, including those on the northern side of the border between the UK and the Republic of Ireland.

34. For British public opinion, European integration has been traditionally an issue of low salience in the words of public pollsters. But linked to immigration, for example, it goes up the scale and then risks being hijacked by demagogues. The great benefit of the referendum is that it will generate a wide debate about the kind of relationship that British people want to have with the rest of Europe that hopefully goes beyond mere stereotypes or caricatures. For a quality and non-partisan reference point, the reader may consult, among many others, the research site *The UK in a Changing Europe*, http://ukandeu.ac.uk/about-us/.

## Chapter 6

1. The European Union Institute for Security Studies, *European Security Strategy: A Secure Europe in a Better World* (Brussels, 2003), 1, http://www.iss.europa.eu/uploads/media/solanae.pdf

2. If not the oldest in historical terms, Europe is now the oldest region in terms of the average age of its inhabitants and will be even more so in the future.

3. Sylvie Goulard, *Europe: Amour ou chambre à part* (Paris: Flammarion, 2013), 121–2.

4. Andrew Gamble, *Crisis Without End? The Unravelling of Western Prosperity* (Basingstoke: Macmillan, 2014).

5. The term was first coined by John Williamson in 1989 to describe the standard reform package for use in developing countries, including fiscal discipline, trade liberalization, privatization, and deregulation. In its subsequent much broader use, it was identified with neo-liberal policies and market fundamentalism.

6. Rodrik, *The Globalization Paradox*.

7. This is cogently argued in Larry Siedentop, *Democracy in Europe* (London: Allen & Lane, 2000). Siedentop does not see much hope in the establishment of a democratic system at European level, which is precisely what Jürgen Habermas, one of the leading European philosophers, has been calling for for many years. See, for example, Habermas, *The Crisis of the European Union*, trans. Cronin. On the other hand, as a staunch defender of the theory of liberal intergovernmentalism, Moravscik argued that democratic legitimacy stemmed from member states. See his classic work, Andrew Moravscik, *The Choice for Europe: Social Purpose and State Power from Messina to Maastricht* (Ithaca, NY: Cornell University Press, 1998), and 'In Defence of the Democratic Deficit: Reassessing Legitimacy in the European Union', *Journal of Common Market Studies*, 40/4 (2002), 603–24, https://www.princeton.edu/~amoravcs/library/deficit.pdf.

8. Who gains and who loses is one of the fundamental questions asked in political economy, although hardly a favourite among contemporary economists. It is a question that was almost taboo for years for those dealing with European integration: see Tsoukalis, *What Kind of Europe?*, 44–66. Nowadays, European integration and globalization constitute an important political cleavage in European societies (Liesbet Hooghe and Gary Marks, 'European Union?', *West European Politics*, 31/1–2 (2008), 108–29, http://www.tandfonline.com/toc/fwep20/31/1-2 (abstract); and various articles in Hanspeter Kriesi et al., *West European Politics in the Age of Globalization* (Cambridge: Cambridge University Press, 2008).

9. Keynes believed that the financial and business environment was characterized by 'radical uncertainty' and was highly critical of the use of probability theory in predicting human behaviour. See, for example, John Kay, 'The Other Multiplier Effect, or Keynes's View of Probability', *Financial Times*, 14 August 2012, http://www.ft.com/intl/cms/s/0/f7660898-e538-11e1-8aco-00144feab49a.html#axzz3wwp55WHA.

10. Quoted in Robert Gilpin, *The Political Economy of International Relations* (Princeton: Princeton University Press, 1987), 355.

11. Atkinson, *Inequality*, 82–109.

12. Piketty, *Capital in the Twenty-First Century*. The main argument is summarized in the few pages of the conclusion for the reader who may not be prepared to go through more than 600 pages of painstaking work, although it is well worth reading.

13. See Atkinson, *Inequality*, 19–20; Raghuram Rajan, *Fault Lines: How Hidden Fractures Still Threaten the World Economy* (Princeton and Oxford: Princeton University Press, 2008), 8.

14. I had a personal involvement in the creation of the Globalization Adjustment Fund, having also written the accompanying paper on the subject presented by the British Presidency of the Council under Prime Minister Blair to the European Parliament on 26 October 2005. See Loukas Tsoukalis, 'Why We Need a European Globalisation Fund', in Patrick Diamond et al., *The Hampton Court Agenda: A Social Model for Europe* (London: Policy Network, 2006), 81–8, http://www.policy-network.net/publications_detail .aspx?ID=144.

15. See Nathaniel Copsey, *Rethinking the European Union* (London: Palgrave, 2015), 112–20.

16. For a comprehensive account of multicultural experiences in different European countries, see A. Triandafyllidou, T. Modood, and N. Meer (eds.), *European Multiculturalisms* (Edinburgh: Edinburgh University Press, 2011).

17. Otherwise known as ISIS (Islamic State of Iraq and Al-Sham), or Daesh from the Arabic acronym. This organization has proved to be even more ruthless in the pursuit of its aims than Al-Qaeda in what seems to be an escalating competition in brutal violence between terrorist groups. See, for example, Roula Khalaf, 'The Deadly Contest between Isis and al-Qaeda', *Financial Times*, 2 December 2015, http://www.ft.com/intl/cms/s/2/297def12-9819-11e5-95c7-d47aa298f769.html#axzz3wwp55WHA.

18. François Heisbourg, 'The Strategic Implications of the Syrian Refugee Crisis', *Survival*, 57/6 (2015), 7–20, https://www.iiss.org/-/media//silos/survival/ 2015/survival-57-6/57-6-02-heisbourg/57-6-02-heisbourg.pdf.

19. See also Nick Witney et al., 'Rebooting EU Foreign Policy', *European Council on Foreign Relations Policy Brief*, September 2014, http://www.ecfr.eu/page/-/ ECFR114_EU_BRIEF_SinglePages_(1).pdf; Christopher Hill, *The National Interest in Question* (Oxford: Oxford University Press, 2013), 214–22.

20. Hedley Bull, one of the leading thinkers on international relations, wrote back in 1982 that '"Europe" is not an actor in international affairs, and does not seem likely to become one' ('Civilian Power Europe: A Contradiction in Terms?', *Journal of Common Market Studies*, 21/2 (1982), 149–70, http:// onlinelibrary.wiley.com/doi/10.1111/j.1468-5965.1982.tb00866.x/pdf (abstract)). He may have been right after all.

21. Two different perspectives on the Ukraine crisis and the role of Europe and the West can be found in John J. Mearsheimer, 'Why the Ukraine Crisis Is the West's Fault: The Liberal Delusions', *Foreign Affairs*, 93/5 (2014), https:// www.foreignaffairs.com/articles/russia-fsu/2014-08-18/why-ukraine-crisis-west-s-fault (abstract); and Andrew Wilson, 'Three Reasons Why the West Should Not Forget about Ukraine', *European Council on Foreign Relations*

*Commentary*, 11 December 2015, http://www.ecfr.eu/article/commentary_ three_reasons_why_the_west_should_not_forget_about_5048.

22. For a general overview and a good summary of various studies on the likely costs of an eventual break-up of the euro, or just of Grexit, see William R. Cline, *Managing the Euro Area Debt Crisis* (Washington, DC: Peterson Institute for International Economics, 2014), 87–118.

23. My *Unhappy State of the Union* came out at about the same time as another book with a very similar title, which was perhaps indicative of the mood prevailing at the time: John Peet and Anton La Guardia, *Unhappy Union: How the Euro Crisis—and Europe—Can Be Fixed* (London: The Economist, 2014), reviewed by Ferdinando Giugliano at http://www.ft.com/intl/cms/s/2/ 82a2f728-020f-11e4-ab5b-00144feab7de.html. Wolf, *The Shifts and the Shocks*, ch. 9 also writes about a bad marriage in the eurozone.

24. According to a post-election survey, only 28 per cent of the 18–24 age group of EU citizens voted in the May 2014 elections to the European Parliament compared to 51 per cent of the 55+ age group. Apparently, young Europeans did not think there was much at stake for them in these elections.

25. Thomas L. Friedman, *The Lexus and the Olive Tree* (London: Harper Collins, 1999).

26. Cas Mudde, 'The Populist Zeitgeist', *Government and Opposition*, 39/4 (2004), 543, http://onlinelibrary.wiley.com/doi/10.1111/j.1477-7053.2004.00135.x/ abstract (abstract).

27. During the euro crisis, *Bild Zeitung* excelled in politically incorrect comments about Germany's partners, Greece in particular, and played an influential role in shaping public opinion.

28. Hanspeter Kriesi, 'The Populist Challenge', *West European Politics*, 37/2 (2014), 361–78, http://www.tandfonline.com/doi/abs/10.1080/01402382.2014 .887879#.VpPEJ_mLSM8 (abstract); Jan-Werner Mueller, 'Eastern Europe goes South', *Foreign Affairs*, 93/2 (2014), https://www.foreignaffairs.com/articles/ eastern-europe-caucasus/2014-02-12/eastern-europe-goes-south (abstract).

29. This is one of the most famous quotes from the *Prison Notebooks* of Antonio Gramsci, a Marxist thinker imprisoned during the Fascist period in Italy.

30. W. B. Yeats, 'The Second Coming' (1919), ll. 7–8.

# Chapter 7

1. Timothy Garton Ash, 'The Crisis of Europe: How Europe Came Together and Why It's Falling Apart', *Foreign Affairs*, 91/5 (2012), https://www .foreignaffairs.com/articles/europe/2012-08-16/crisis-europe.

2. The term 'secular stagnation' has been used by Lawrence Summers, a famous US economist, former Secretary of the Treasury and president of Harvard University, to refer to slow growth and low inflation in times of

zero or even negative real interest rates in developed economies. He explained secular stagnation in terms of high rates of savings and low aggregate demand, in turn related to increases in inequality (the rich save much more than the poor), low expectations linked to slow productivity growth, increased uncertainty and heavier regulation in financial markets, and the reduction in the price and quantity of capital needed to operate a business (Facebook having today a much bigger market value than General Motors). See Lawrence Summers, 'The Global Economy: The Case for Expansion', *Financial Times*, 7 October 2015, http://www.ft.com/cms/s/0/1e912316-6b88-11e5-8171-ba1968cf791a.html#axzz44WPIM4Fb. On the other hand, Christine Lagarde, managing director of the IMF, has appealed to member countries to prevent a protracted period of low growth, which she called the 'new mediocre'. See the speech she gave at the Atlantic Council on 9 April 2015, https://www.imf.org/external/np/speeches/2015/040915.htm. International organizations, European institutions included, forecast relatively low growth (of the order of 1–1.5 per cent per annum) for Europe and the eurozone in particular in the years up to 2020. It takes a very bold forecaster to go beyond.

3. See also Philip Stephens, 'Politicians are Paying Bill for the Crash', *Financial Times*, 17 December 2015, http://www.ft.com/cms/s/0/a1ed508e-a429-11e5-873f-68411a84f346.html#axzz44WPIM4Fb.

4. For a very interesting critical work regarding the slow pace of reforms in France, see Philippe Aghion, Gilbert Cette, and Élie Cohen, *Changer de modèle* (Paris: Odile Jacob, 2014).

5. The US economist Robert Reich speaks of the 'anxious class': Robert Reich, 'The Revolt of the Anxious Class', *Huffington Post*, 15 December 2015, http://www.huffingtonpost.com/robert-reich/the-revolt-of-the-anxious_b_8806988.html.

6. See, for example, Karl Lamers and Wolfgang Schäuble, 'More Integration Is Still the Right Goal for Europe', *Financial Times*, 31 August 2014, http://www.ft.com/cms/s/0/5565f134-2d48-11e4-8105-00144feabdco.html.

7. Jean Pisani-Ferry, 'Rebalancing the Governance of the Euro Area', in Dawson, Enderlein, and Joerges (eds.), *Beyond the Crisis*, 62–82.

8. European Strategy and Global Analysis System (ESPAS), *Global Trends to 2030: Can the EU Meet the Challenges Ahead?* (2015), an Inter-Institutional EU Project, http://europa.eu/espas/pdf/espas-report-2015.pdf.

9. See various chapters in Dawson, Enderlein and Joerges (eds.), *Beyond the Crisis*. See also the more modest proposals, under the constraint of political feasibility, presented by the presidents of European institutions: Herman Van Rompuy, *Towards a Genuine Economic and Monetary Union*, Report by the President of the European Council (2012), http://www.consilium.europa.eu/uedocs/cms_data/docs/pressdata/en/ec/131201.pdf; European Jean-Claude Juncker et al., *The Five Presidents' Report: Completing Economic and Monetary*

*Union* (European Commission, 2015), http://ec.europa.eu/priorities/sites/beta-political/files/5-presidents-report_en.pdf. See also Iain Begg, Annette Borgsten, Kalypso Nicolaïdis, and Francisco Torres, 'EMU and Sustainable Integration', *Journal of European Integration*, 37/7 (2015), 803–16. On the other hand, Mody argues for a decentralized model of European monetary union placing the emphasis on the individual responsibility of member states: Ashoka Mody, 'A Schuman Compact for the Euro Area', *Bruegel Essay and Lecture Series*, 20 November 2013, http://bruegel.org/2013/11/a-schuman-compact-for-the-euro-area/. See also Sandbu, *Europe's Orphan*, ch. 6.

10. For radical ideas for reform from a central banker who does not mince his words, see the book by the former governor of the Bank of England: Mervyn King, *The End of Alchemy: Money, Banking, and the Future of the Global Economy* (London: Little, Brown, 2016).

11. ESPAS, *Global Trends to 2030*, 8.

12. Johannes Lindvall and David Rueda, 'The Insider–Outsider Dilemma', *Policy Network*, 18 July 2013, http://www.policy-network.net/pno_detail.aspx?ID=4441&title=The+insider-outsider+dilemma.

13. Adam Posen, 'The Global Economy Is Now Distinctly Victorian', *Financial Times*, 6 August 2013, http://www.ft.com/intl/cms/s/0/6e4d3ee2-fdd7-11e2-8785-00144feabdc0.html#axzz41Y10THJc.

14. Frank Vandenbroucke with Bart Vanhercke, 'A European Social Union: 10 Tough Nuts to Crack', *Friends of Europe background report*, 7 April 2014, http://www.friendsofeurope.org/quality-europe/10-tough-nuts-to-crack/; Anton Hemerijck, *Changing Welfare States* (Oxford: Oxford University Press, 2013).

15. Pier Carlo Padoan, 'Couldn't Brussels Bail Out the Jobless?', *The Guardian*, 10 June 2015, http://www.theguardian.com/commentisfree/2015/jun/10/russels-bail-out-jobless-european-union-unemployment. Emmanuel Macron, the French finance minister, made similar proposals, if only more radical. See his interview with Ferdinando Guigliano and Sarah Gordon, 'Macron Calls for Radical Reform to Save the Euro', *Financial Times*, 24 September 2015, http://www.ft.com/cms/s/0/6d327720-62c5-11e5-a28b-50226830d644.html#axzz44WPIM4Fb.

16. Fritz W. Scharpf, 'Monetary Union, Fiscal Crisis and the Preemption of Democracy', *Max-Planck Institute for the Study of Societies, Discussion Paper* 11/11 (2011), http://www.mpifg.de/pu/mpifg_dp/dp11-11.pdf.

17. See, among others, proposals made by the Glienicker Group, a bipartisan group of German economists, lawyers, and political scientists (*Die Zeit*, 17 October 2013, http://bruegel.org/wp-content/uploads/imported/publications/Aufbruch_in_die_Euro-Union_laidout.pdf), and the French Eiffel group (*Bruegel*, 14 February 2014, http://bruegel.org/wp-content/uploads/imported/publications/FINAGroupeEiffelFR13022014.pdf). See also *Towards a New Pact for Europe*, New Pact for Europe, Second Report (October 2014), http://www.newpactforeurope.eu/documents/new_pact_for_europe_2nd_report.pdf.

18. See Sylvie Goulard and Mario Monti, *De la démocratie en Europe* (Paris: Flammarion, 2012).
19. Commenting on a Russian and an American film which were candidates for an Oscar in 2015, Nina Khrushcheva, descendant of the former General Secretary of the Communist Party of the Soviet Union, Nikita Khrushchev, contrasted the political abuse, cynicism, and corruption of state power in the contemporary Russian *Leviathan* with America's god of righteousness in the *American Sniper*, reaching the unnerving conclusion that the two countries may be doomed to wage a new Cold War. See Nina L. Khrushcheva, 'Russia and America at the Oscars', *Project Syndicate*, 24 February 2015, https://www.project-syndicate.org/commentary/leviathan-american-sniper-oscars-by-nina-l-khrushcheva-2015-02?barrier=true.
20. See ESPAS, *Global Trends to 2030*.
21. See also Anthony Giddens, *Turbulent and Mighty Continent* (Cambridge: Polity, 2014), ch. 5.
22. See, for example, Zaki Laïdi (ed.), *EU Foreign Policy in a Globalized World* (London: Routledge, 2011).
23. See also the latest Munich Security Report: *Munich Security Report 2016: Boundless Crises, Reckless Spoilers, Helpless Guardians*, https://www.security conference.de/en/news/article/msc-releases-munich-security-report-2016/. For a very interesting approach to EU–Russia relations as affected by the crisis in Ukraine, see Dimitar Bechev, 'Understanding the Contest between the EU and Russia in Their Shared Neighborhood', *Problems of Post-Communism*, 62 (2015), 340–9, http://www.tandfonline.com/doi/abs/10 .1080/10758216.2015 .1067751?journalCode=mppc20 (abstract).
24. Christopher Hill, 'Powers of a Kind: The Anomalous Position of France and the United Kingdom in World Politics', *International Affairs*, 92/2 (2016), 393–414, http://onlinelibrary.wiley.com/doi/10.1111/1468-2346.12556/abstract.
25. Jan Zielonka, *Is the EU Doomed?* (Cambridge: Polity, 2014).
26. Many people have been calling for Germany to take the lead, although they usually disagree with the way in which it has done so up to now. Some take issue with Germany's policies on the euro crisis, others with Mrs Merkel's initial open-door policy in the refugee crisis. See, for example, George Soros with Gregor Peter Schmitz, *The Tragedy of the European Union: Disintegration or Revival?* (New York: Public Affairs, 2014). For a very interesting analysis of why Germany cannot be the agent of change, see Claus Offe, *Europe Entrapped* (Cambridge: Polity, 2015).

# INDEX

Graphs are indicated by an italic *g* following the page number.